I0800316

Magic Ireland

GABRIELLE ALIOTH & MAX SCHMID

Magic Ireland

LEGENDS AND LANDSCAPES

BENTELI

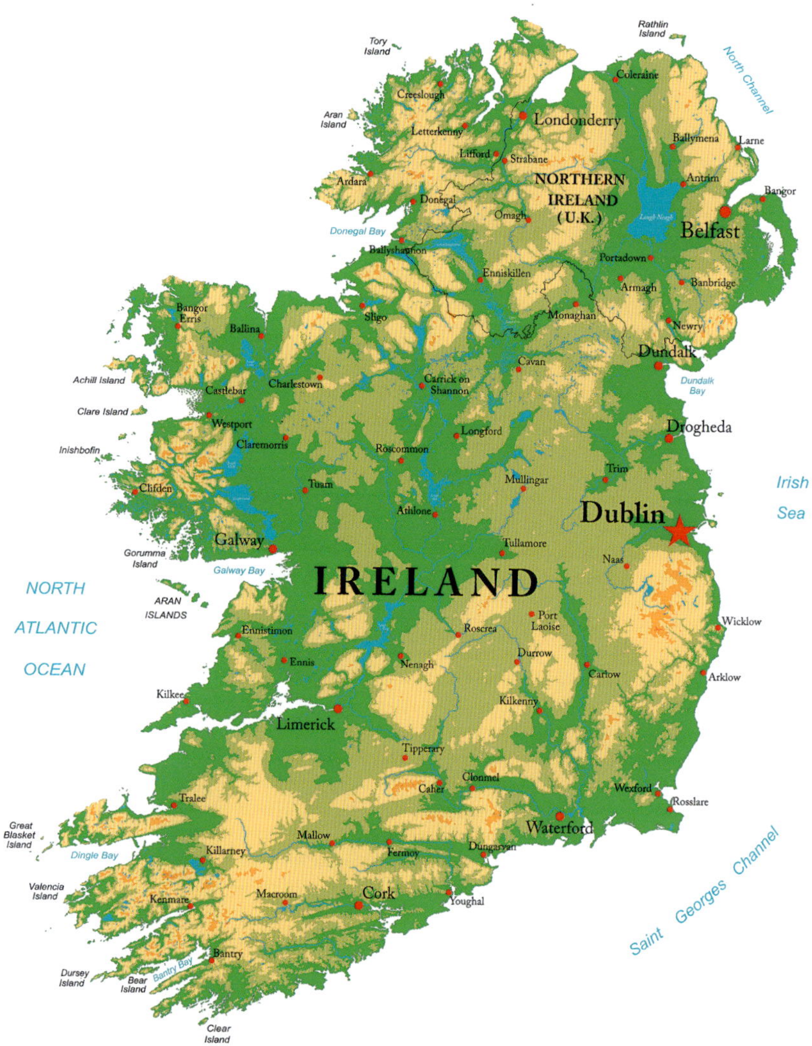
IRELAND
NORTHERN IRELAND (U.K.)
NORTH ATLANTIC OCEAN
Irish Sea
North Channel
Saint Georges Channel
Rathlin Island
Tory Island
Aran Island
Donegal Bay
Achill Island
Clare Island
Inishbofin
Gorumma Island
Galway Bay
ARAN ISLANDS
Great Blasket Island
Dingle Bay
Valencia Island
Dursey Island
Bear Island
Bantry Bay
Clear Island
Dundalk Bay
Coleraine
Creeslough
Londonderry
Letterkenny
Lifford
Strabane
Ballymena
Larne
Antrim
Bangor
Ardara
Donegal
Omagh
Belfast
Ballyshannon
Portadown
Enniskillen
Armagh
Banbridge
Bangor Erris
Ballina
Sligo
Monaghan
Newry
Dundalk
Cavan
Carrick on Shannon
Charlestown
Castlebar
Westport
Longford
Drogheda
Claremorris
Roscommon
Trim
Mullingar
Clifden
Tuam
Athlone
Dublin
Galway
Tullamore
Naas
Port Laoise
Roscrea
Wicklow
Ennistimon
Ennis
Nenagh
Durrow
Carlow
Arklow
Kilkee
Kilkenny
Limerick
Tipperary
Clonmel
Cahir
Wexford
Rosslare
Tralee
Waterford
Mallow
Fermoy
Dungarvan
Killarney
Macroom
Cork
Youghal
Kenmare
Bantry

Content

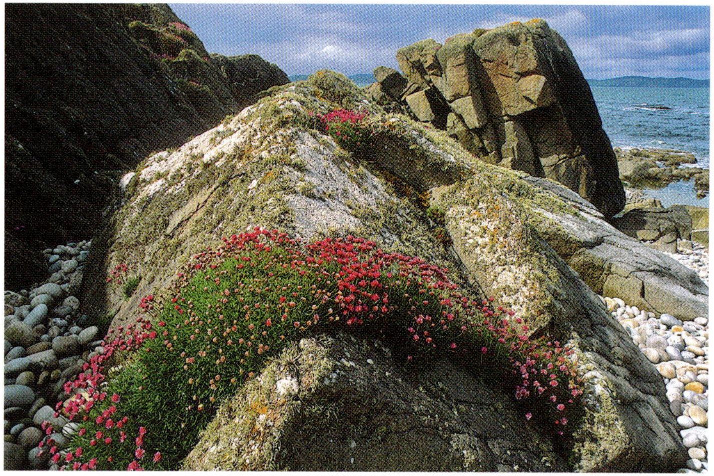

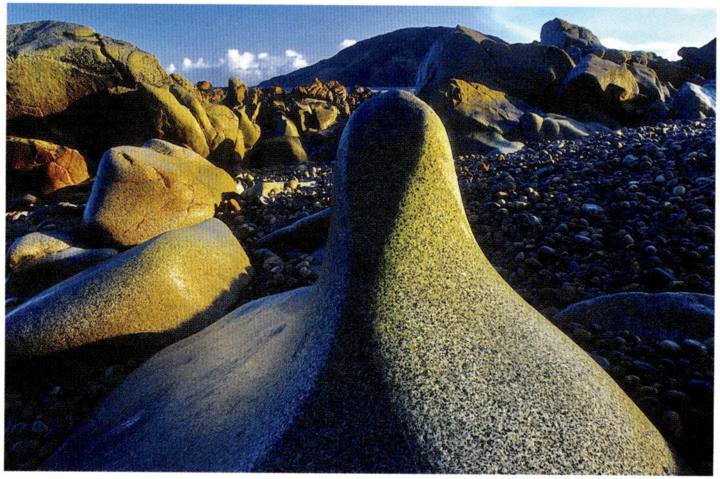

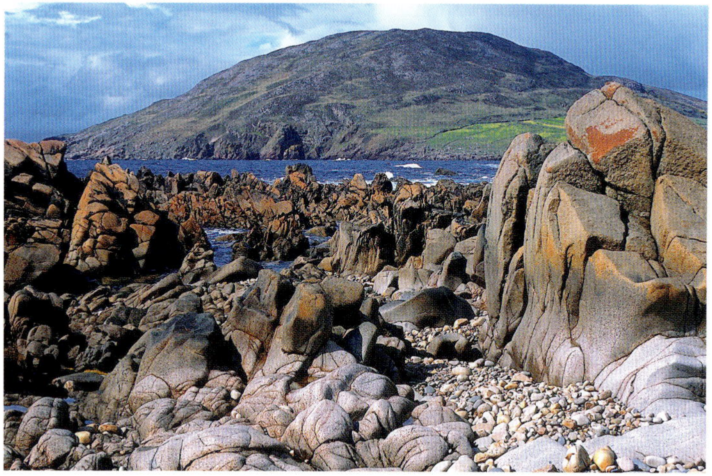

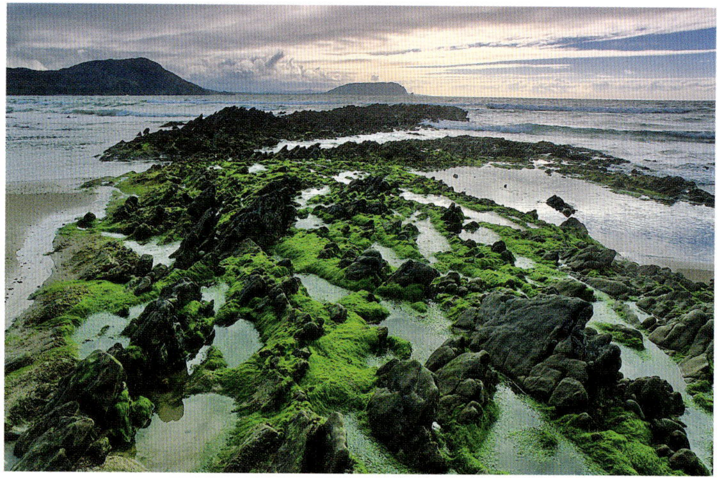

Legendary Ireland

When you inquire about Ireland and what makes it special, inhabitants and visitors alike will point out its landscape and its people. A landscape that reaches from the soft, sandy shores of the East through fields, meadows, hills and woods to the dramatic cliffs of the West, where the Atlantic washes against a coastline dotted with hidden beaches and remote little islands; and people who have maintained their friendly curiosity about life and the living to this day and an ease and joy for talking and telling stories.

This book brings together two legendary features of the Emerald Isle: its magical views, captured in the pictures of the renowned Swiss photographer Max Schmid, and its mythical tales, told by the Swiss writer Gabrielle Alioth, who has been living in Ireland for over forty years, listening to and recording Irish stories.

The oldest signs of human presence in Ireland date back to about 10,000 BC. These people came from the East, as did the ones after them. They followed the rivers inland, settled along their banks, and built the passage graves of Newgrange, Knowth and Dowth in the bend of the river Boyne. There, their myths and legends took root, many of which are connected to the East Coast of Ireland, explaining the placenames that fields and forts hold still today. Hence, while the photographs in this volume cover all of the island of Ireland, North and South, the tales focus more on the East Coast. Together, pictures and stories aim to portray the magic of Ireland in its many facets.

Thunderhill, Ireland, May 2025
Gabrielle Alioth

Preface

Ever since I was a child, I wanted to know where the clouds came from and what it might look like beyond the horizon. Poring over maps, I pieced together a picture of the Earth's surface. Even back then, I was especially intrigued by remote regions and islands on the planet—and I still am today. High on my list of interests were places like the Kerguelen Islands and Iceland, with its volcanoes partly hidden beneath glaciers. I found this absolutely fascinating, and so, after my professional career began, Iceland became my first travel destination. Not Ireland—at least not at first. But due to some geological similarities and the history of Iceland's settlement, there is a connection: there are hints and theories suggesting that the first discoverers of Iceland may have been Irish seafarers. Historically confirmed, however, is that the first settlers came from Norway, although there was also some migration—one way or another—from the Celtic world, that is, from Ireland.

Because of these connections, Ireland had been on my radar early on, but it wasn't until the 1980s that I finally traveled to the Emerald Isle. Green—this color has become deeply ingrained in the collective consciousness when it comes to Ireland. As always, the exceptions prove the rule, and here and there on the island, such exceptions can be found.

In geological timeframes, parts of Ireland's landmass were once located near what is now South Africa. As continental drift progressed, this piece of land moved northward, sank beneath sea level, and rose again. Remnants of tropical forests testify to its former position near the equator. On its further journey north, deserts dominated and green vanished completely, until the land was once again submerged by oceans, only to resurface millions of years later. After many more geological events—such as the dramatic volcanic eruptions at the ancient junction of the Eurasian and North American plates around 50 million years ago—phenomena like the spectacular basalt column formation of the Giant's Causeway came into being.

Many other natural wonders line Ireland's predominantly mountainous coastal regions. Attractions such as the dune landscapes in Donegal, the few remaining primeval forests like those near Strandhill, and others, are a feast for the eyes. A particular highlight is surely the rugged karst landscape of the Burren, where Arctic and Mediterranean plant species coexist, protected in crevices of the rock. A grey yet enchanting scenery, brought to life with vibrant touches of color that quicken the pulse of any photographer. The majestic sea cliffs of Slieve League and the Cliffs of Moher are visual spectacles. The sea inlets of the southwest, as well as other areas, are full of hidden gems. Even the flat, sprawling lowlands in the interior of the island—despite their monotony—harbor moments of quiet beauty.

Equally impressive is the island's deep and mysterious human history, stretching far back into the darkness of time, and marked by enigmatic relics such as the stone fort of Dún Aonghasa on the Aran Islands. Out of the impenetrable mists of ages past, a unique culture has emerged here despite all hardships—one that is reflected particularly vividly in the country's music. Joyful and melancholic at once, it echoes the often challenging path of the Irish nation. Even in the music of U2, this spirit is palpable. An aura of magic resonates through these sounds, just as it does through the world of Irish myth and legend, which so vividly captures the storm-lashed coasts and the mystical landscapes of this island.

May this small patch of Earth's surface, with all its nature and culture, remain preserved!

Winterthur, July 2025
Max Schmid

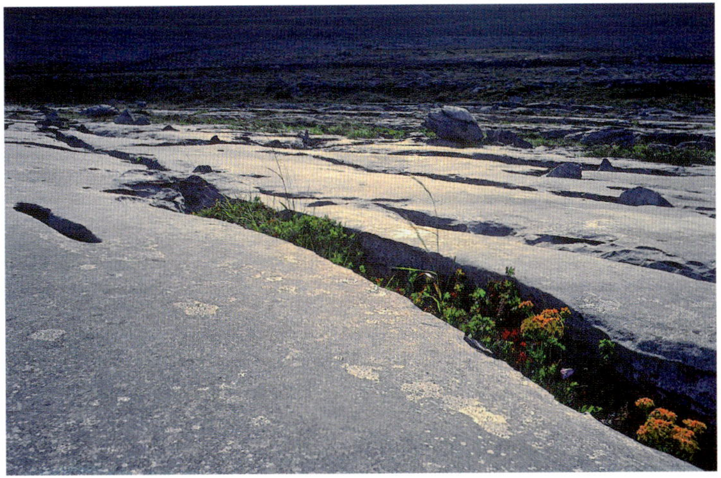
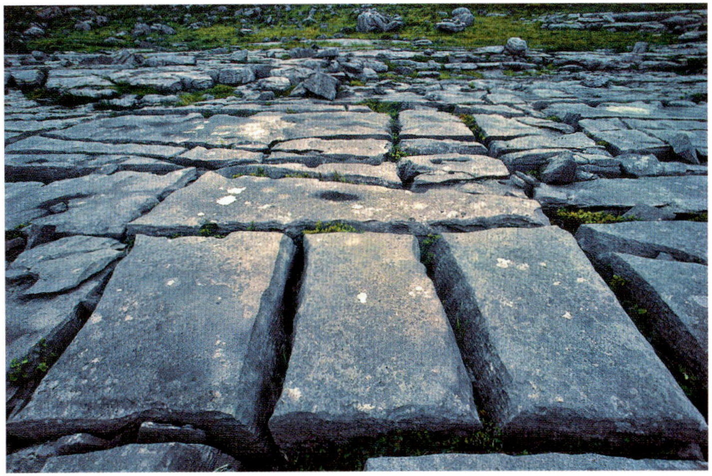
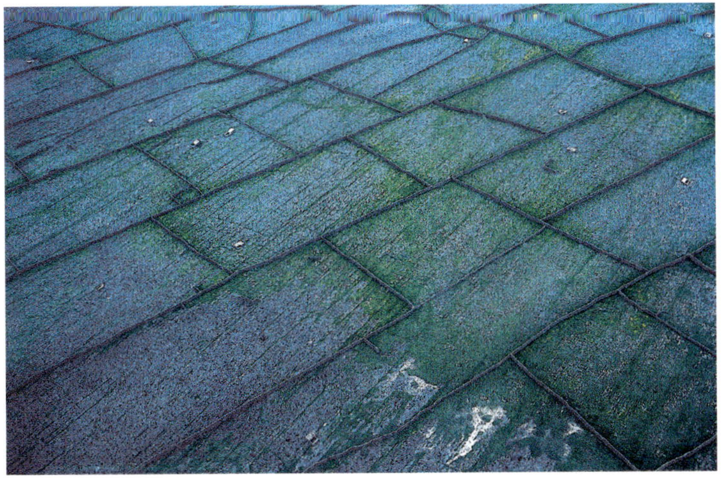
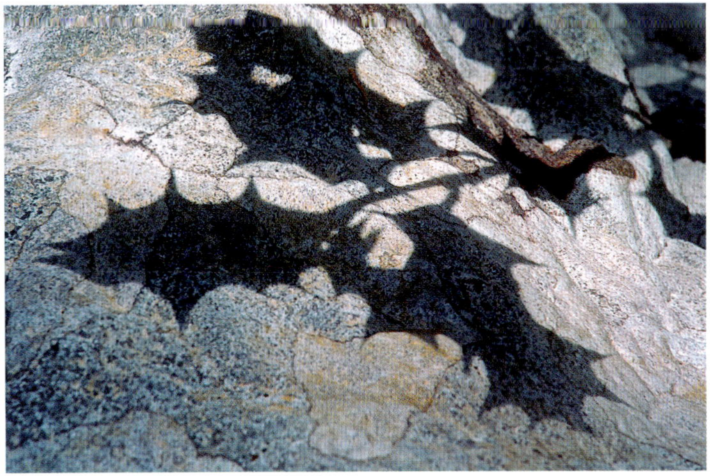

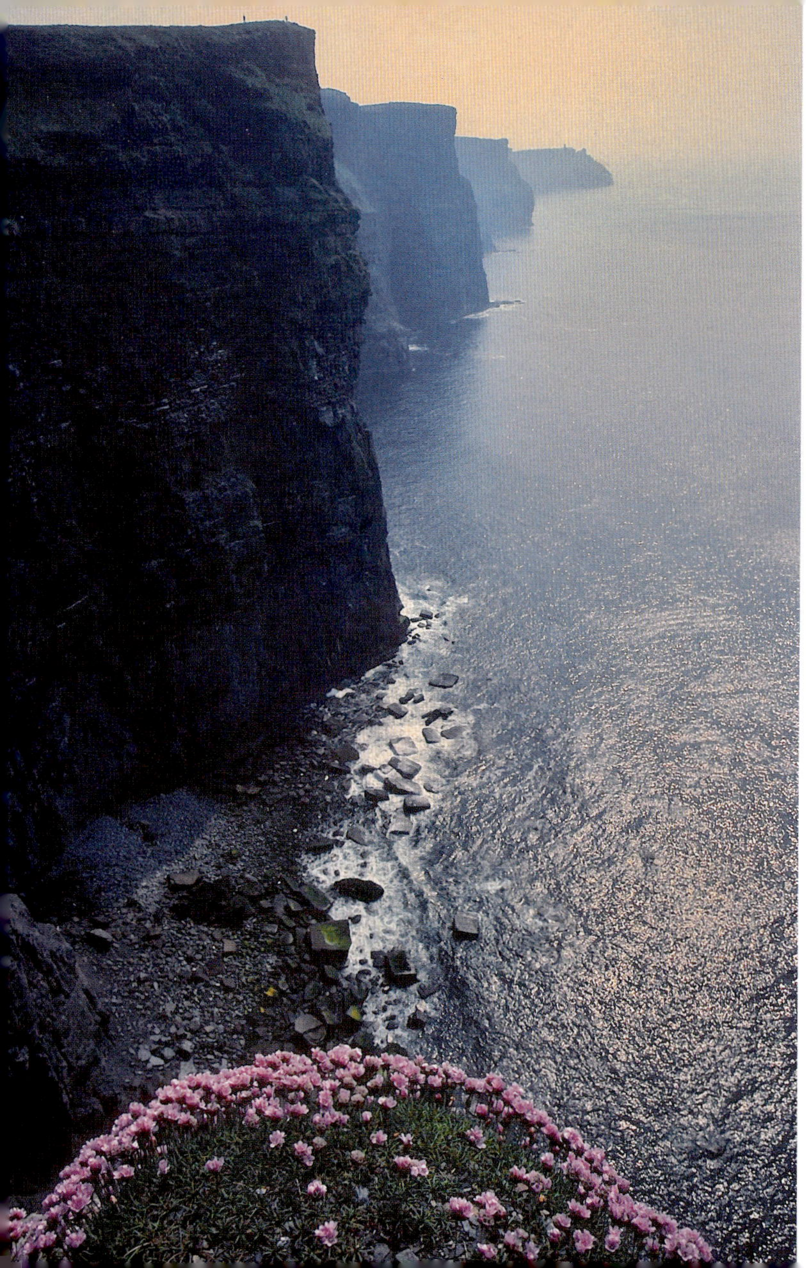

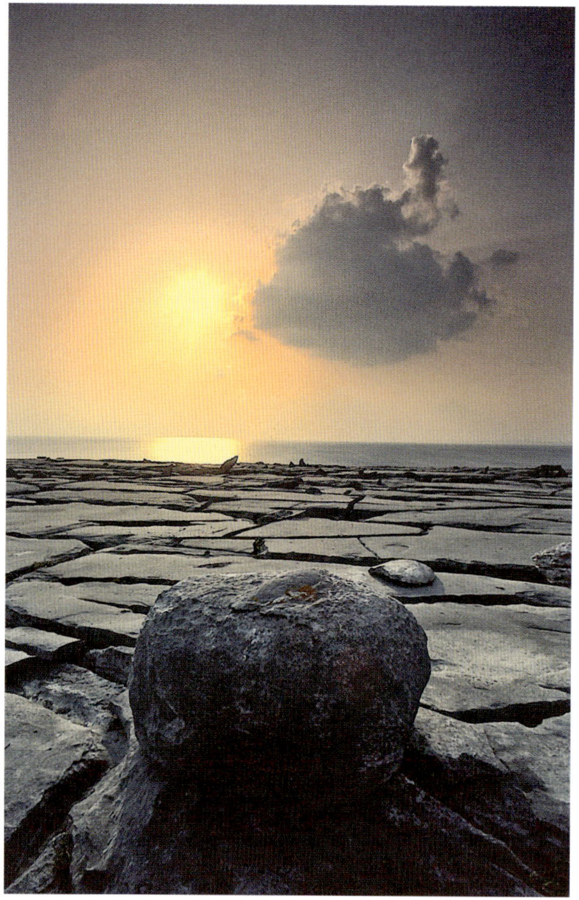

Left: Cliffs of Moher
Right: The Burren

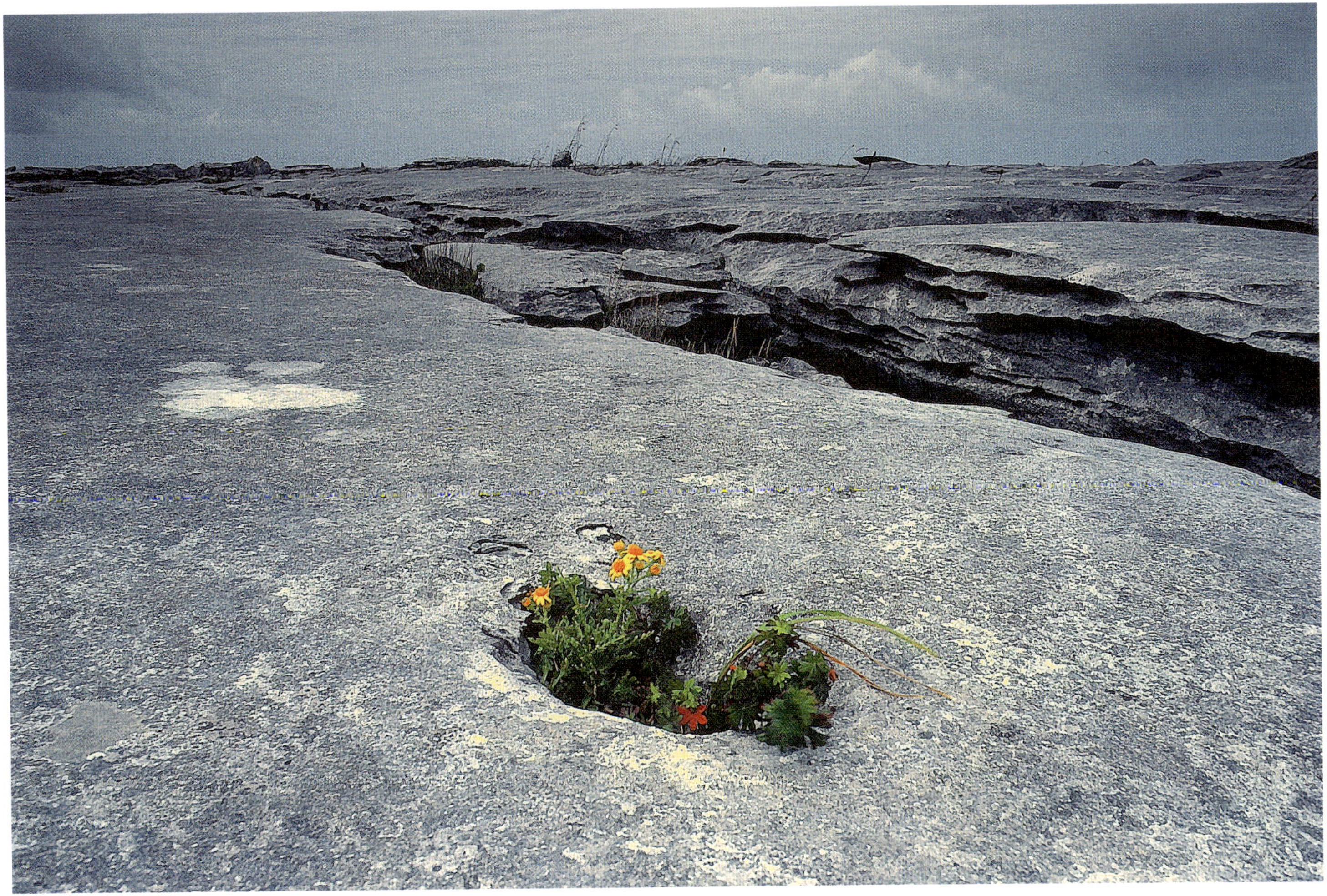

The Burren

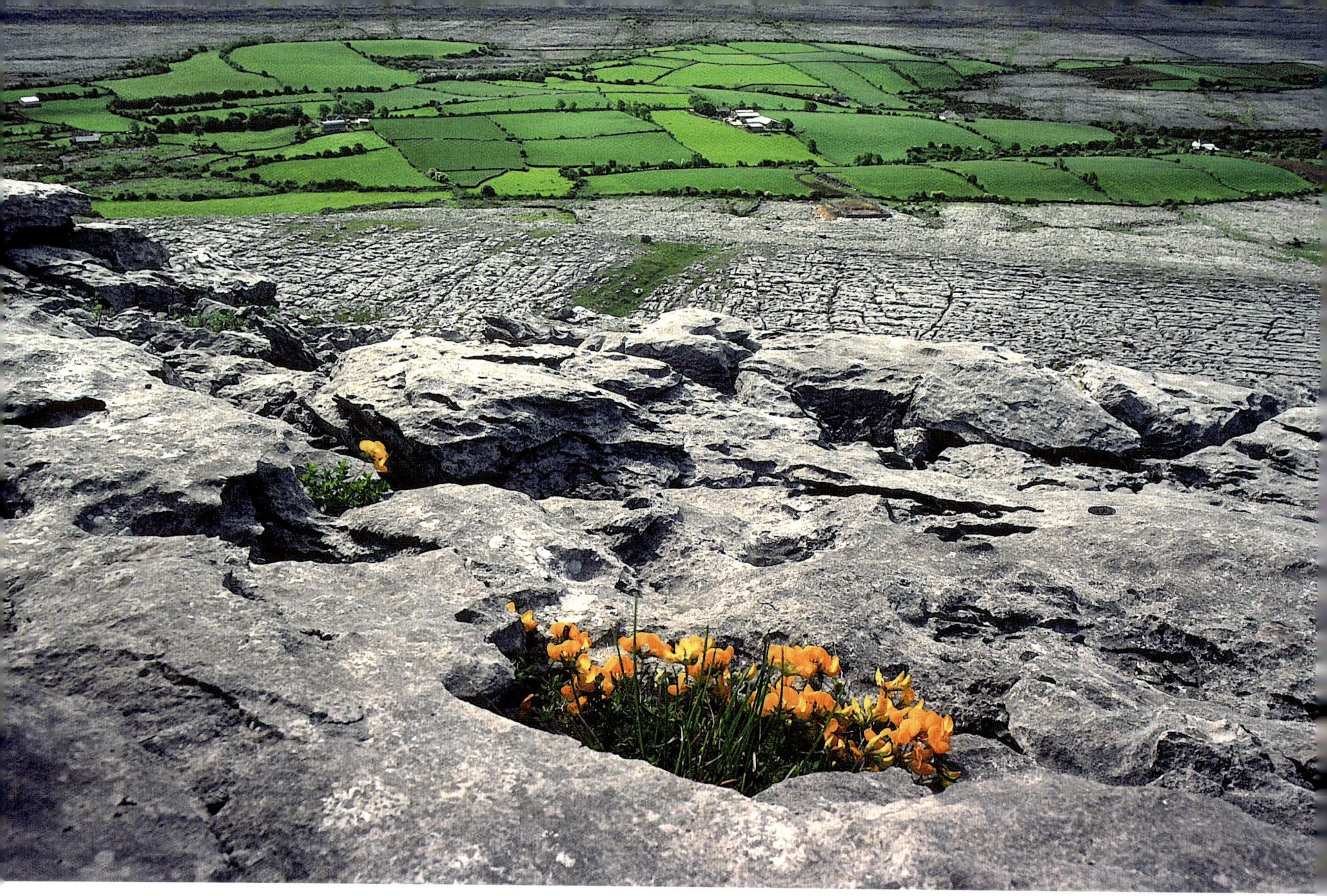

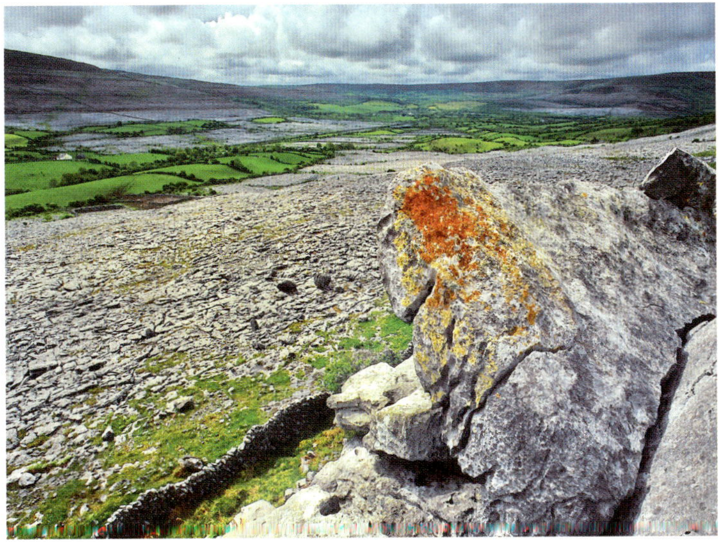

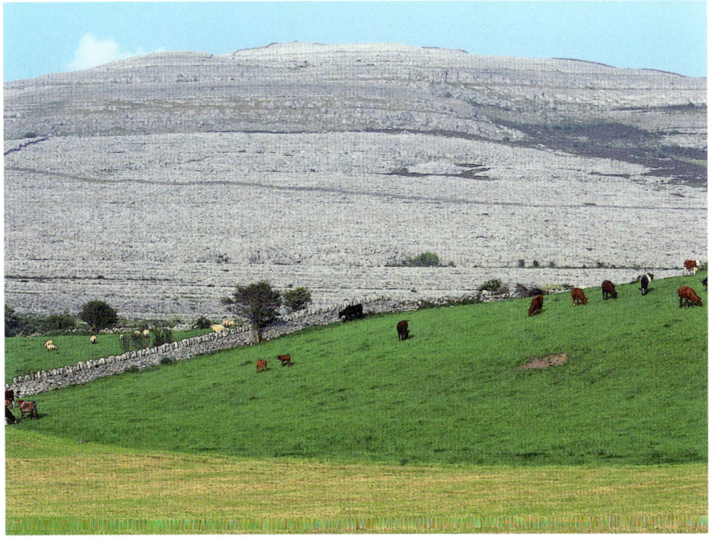

The Burren

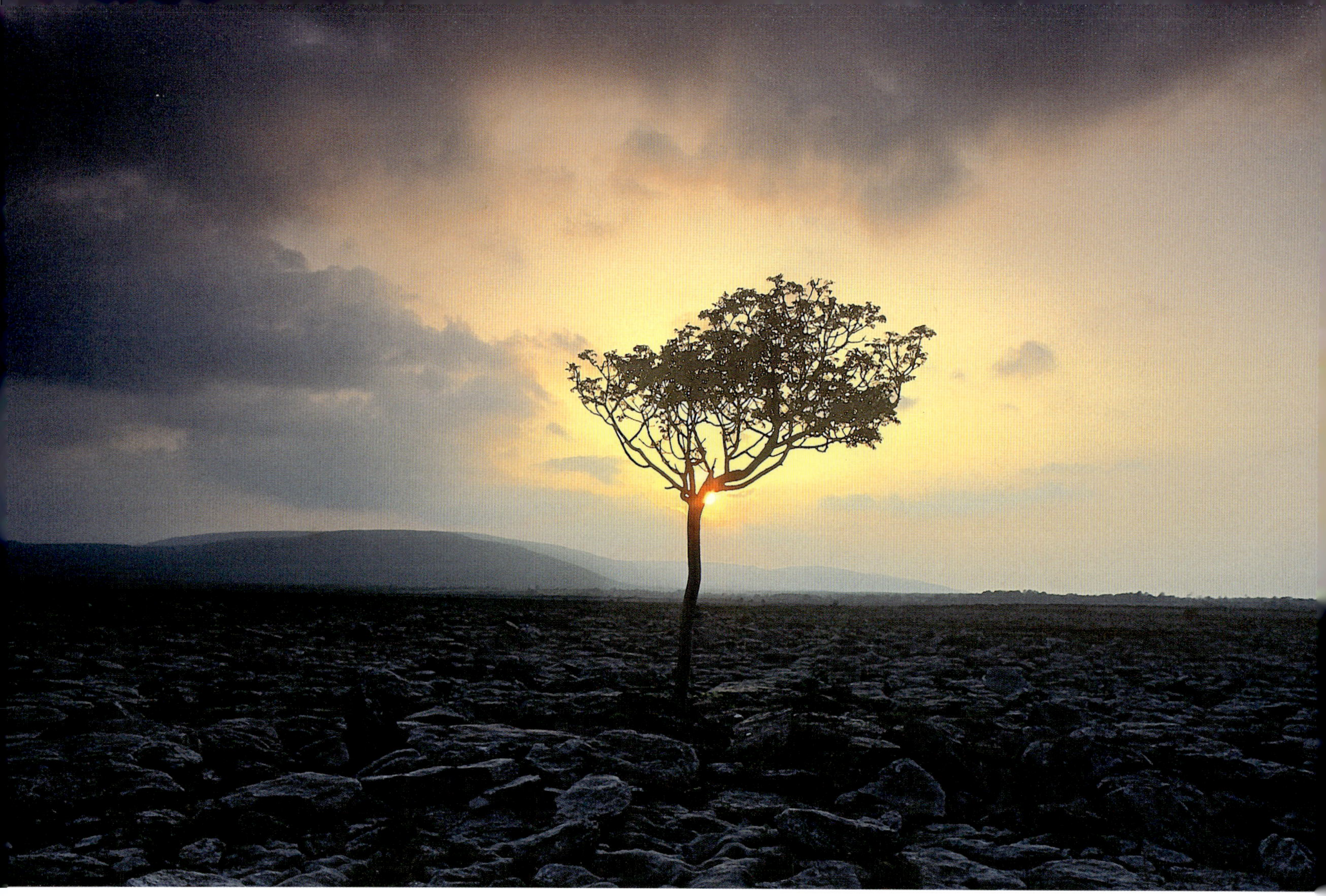

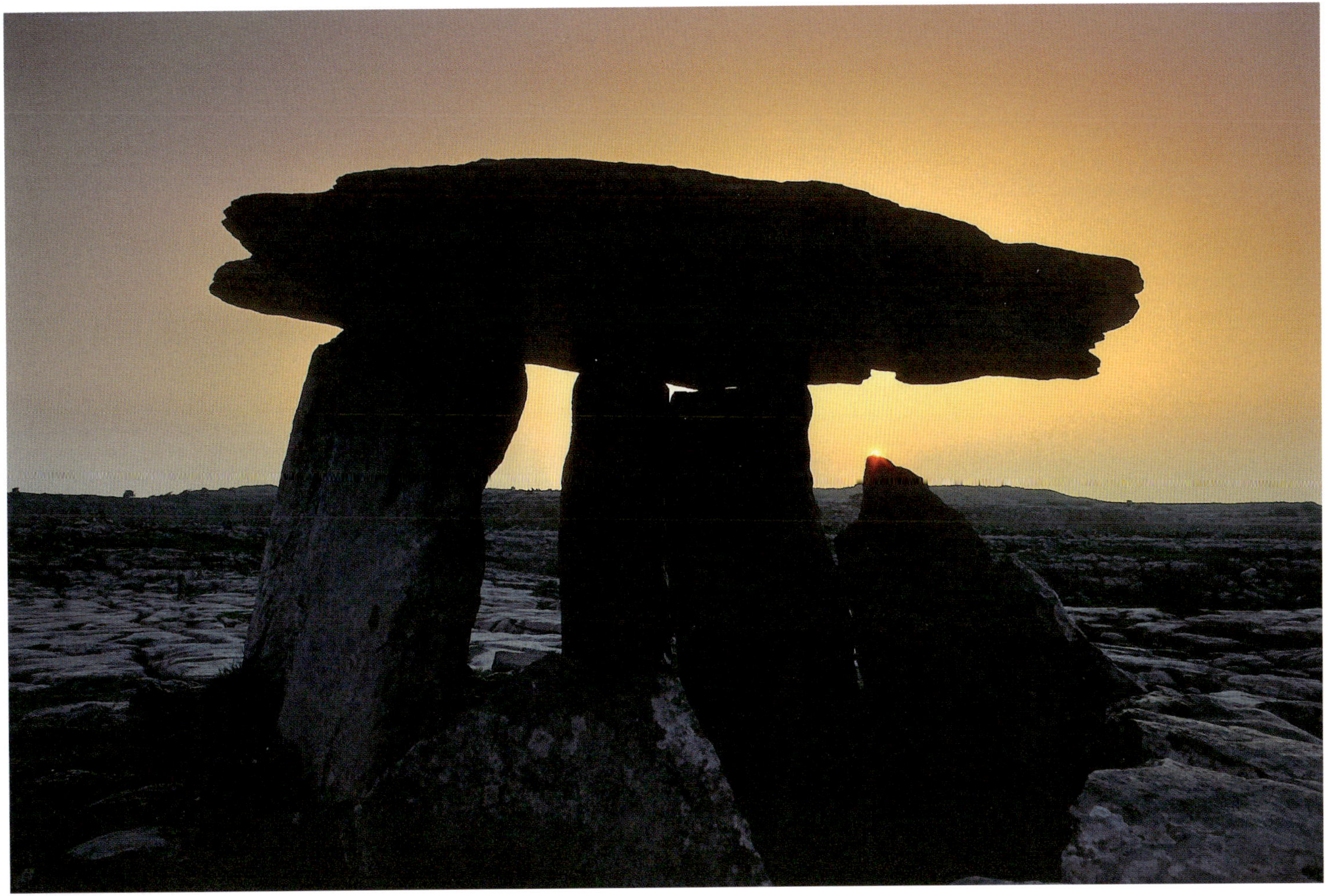

The Burren

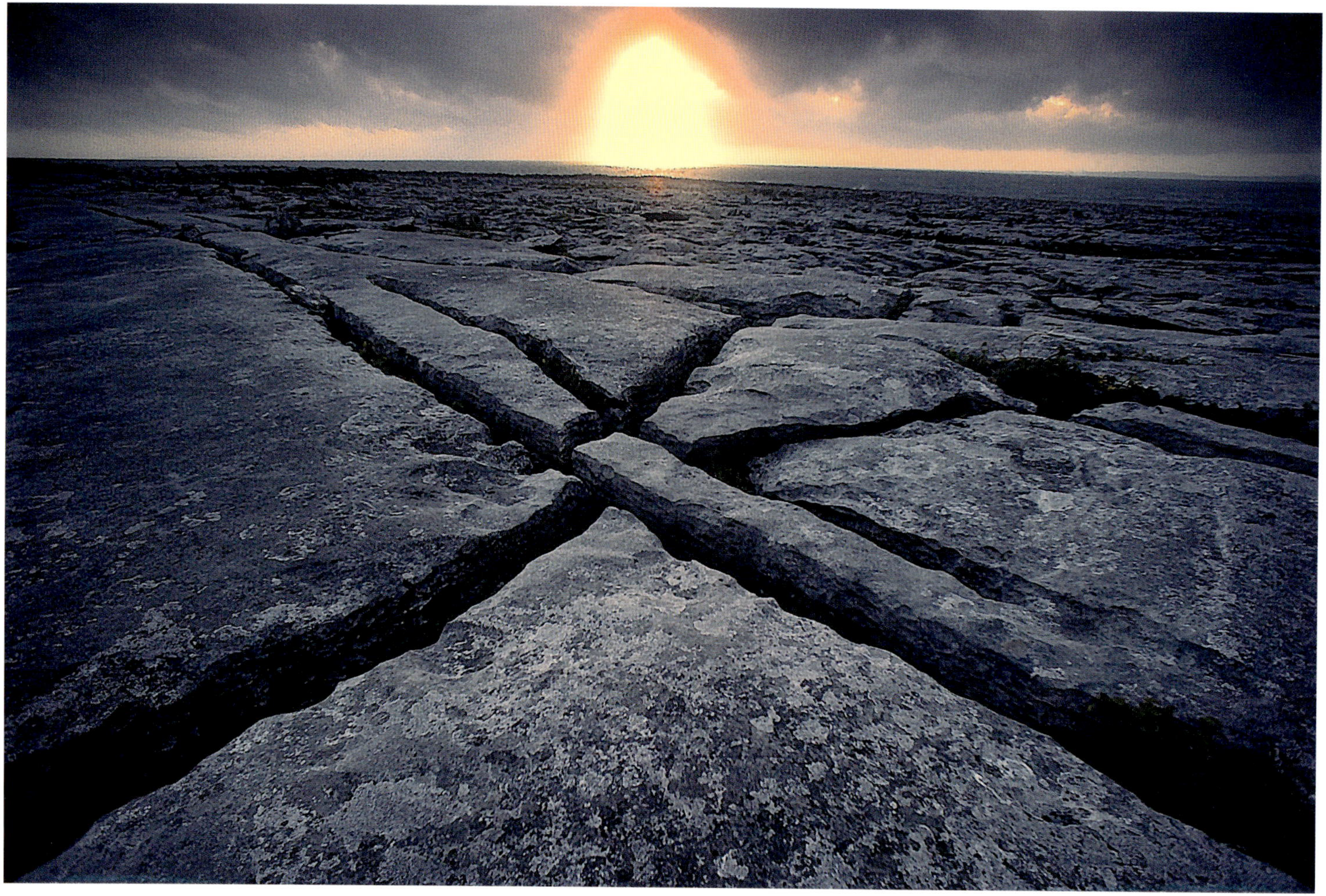

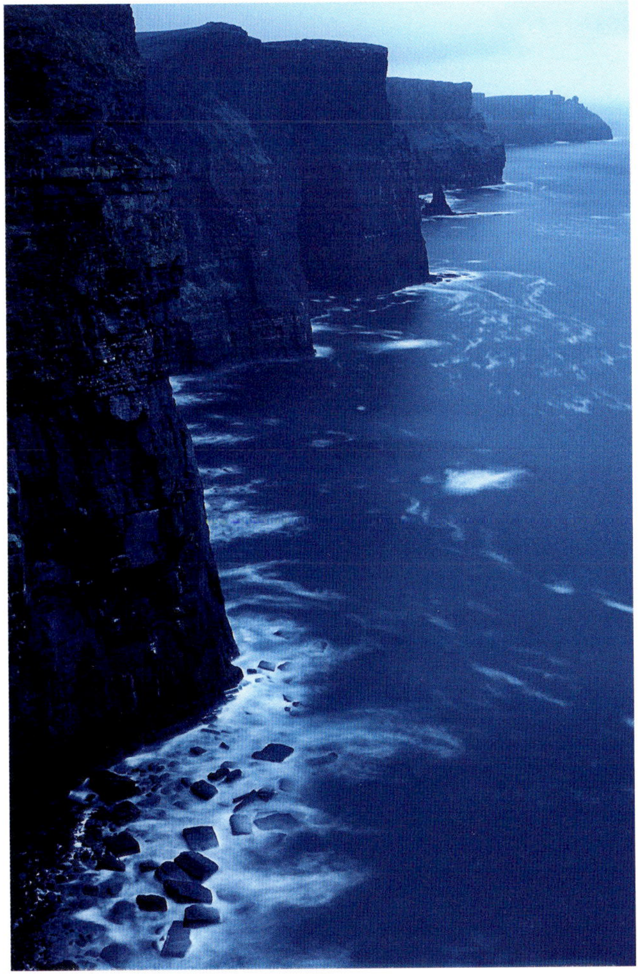

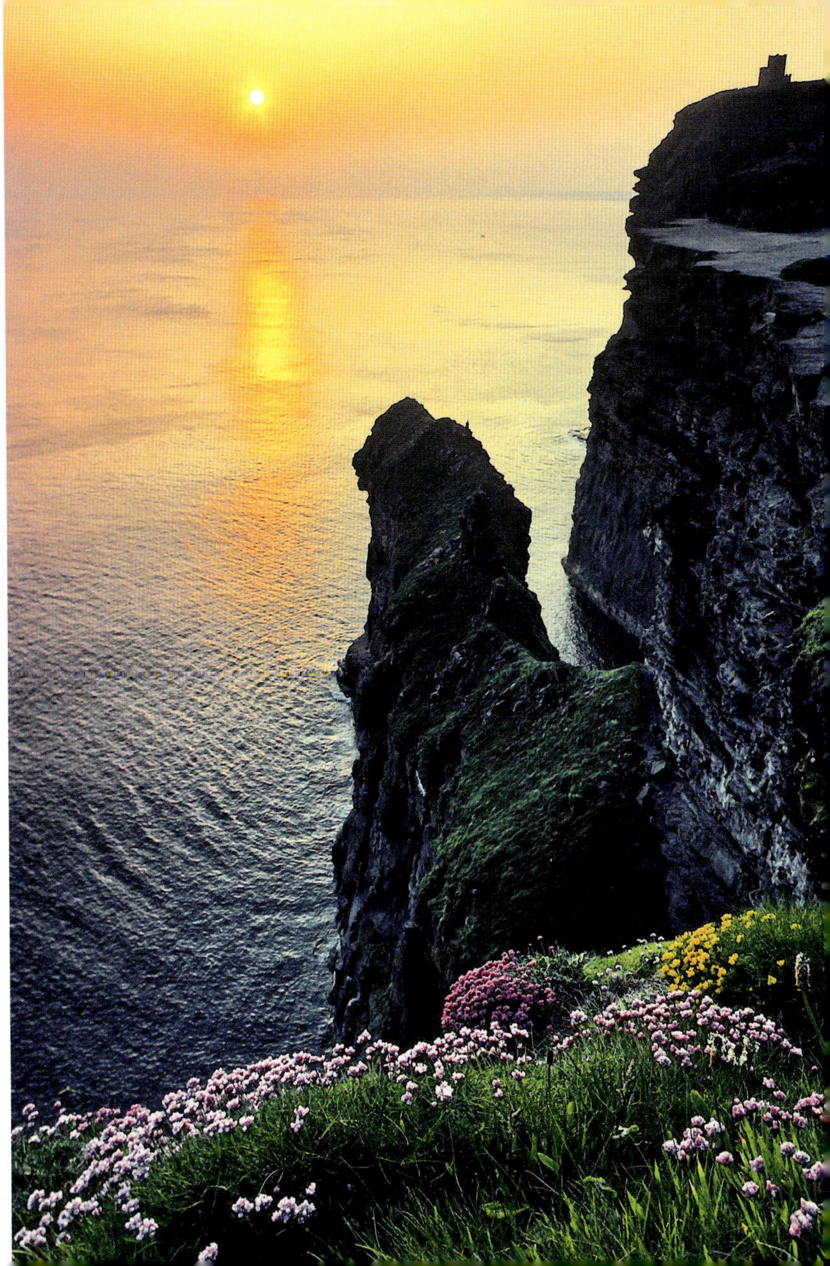

Left page: The Burren
Left and right: Cliffs of Moher

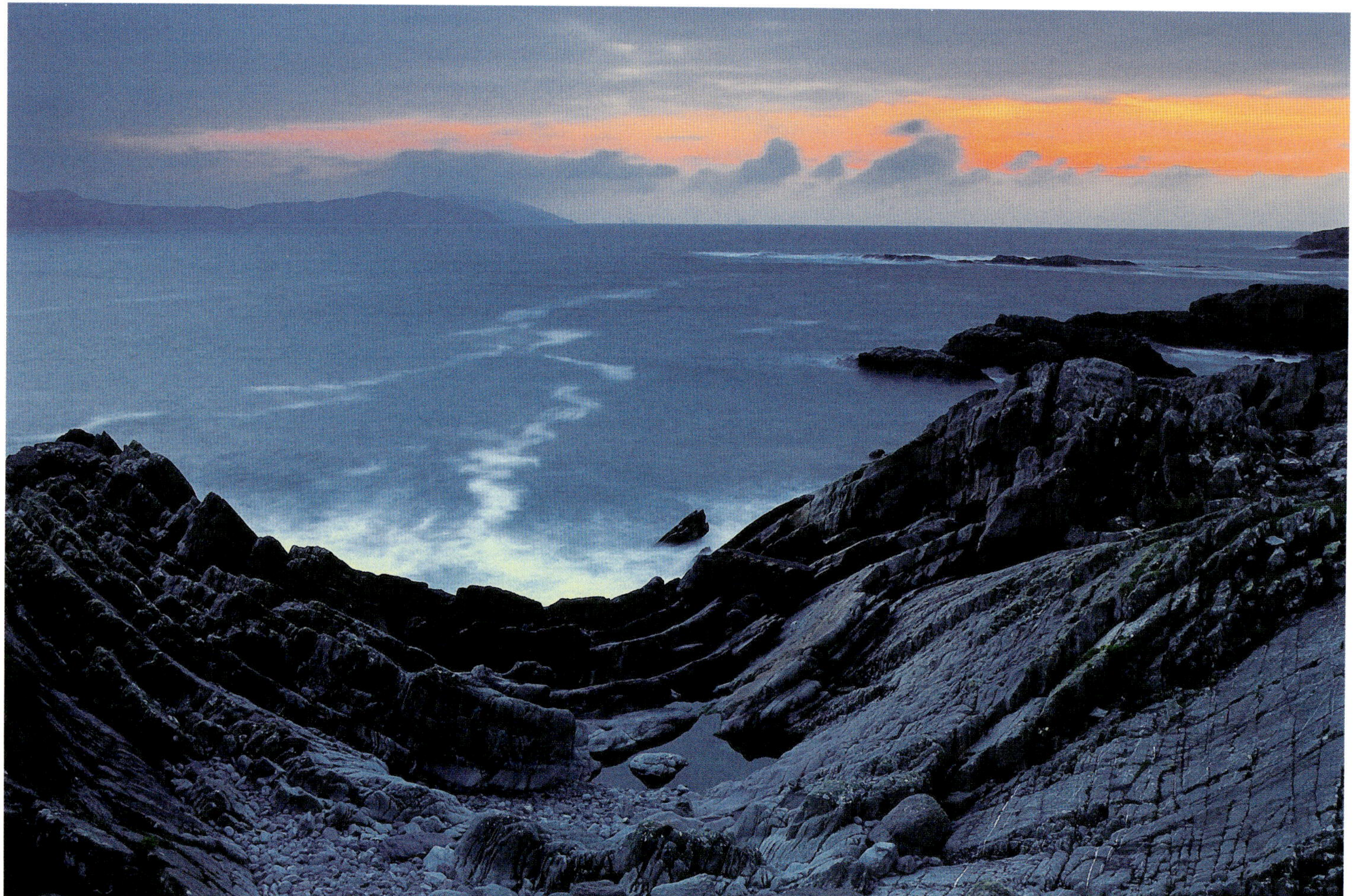

Coulagh Bay

The Taking of Ireland[1]

No matter how long the whirls of time may twist my memories, I will never forget the light that fell on the shore the morning we arrived. Our intentions were spurious. A man, a great-uncle of ours some said, had been killed here and needed to be avenged. But there was also the thirst for adventure, greed, and the heat in the cramped towers our forefathers had built in the hills of Galicia. The light that morning made the sand of the island look so white, its meadows so green that for a moment I forgot to grieve for my love lost at sea.

As was their habit, my brothers sent me out to talk to the three queens who appeared on the shore, because my head was full of words, and white were my knees, as I bowed to no one. The three women were sisters, of course, each trying to outdo the others. Their names sounded like premonitions, and I promised each one of them to call the island after her. The three kings, however, were not so easily persuaded. They demanded that we return to the sea, beyond the ninth wave, and only if we succeeded in landing again would the island be ours. Conceitful and foolish, the sons of Mil, my brothers, saw no harm in humoring them. Only when their druids conjured up a storm that scattered our ships, they saw their blunder and, as it was their habit, they sent me out to calm the waves and the wind.

As I had vowed, I named the white strand after Scéine, my wife lost at sea, and as I set foot on the island once more, I, Amergin, the writer of songs, the poet, claimed it with my words:

I am the wind on the sea;
I am the wave of the sea;
I am the stag of seven battles;
I am the eagle on the rock
I am a flash from the sun;
I am the most beautiful of plants;
I am a strong wild boar;
I am a salmon in the water;
I am a lake in the plain;
I am the word of knowledge;
I am the head of the spear in battle;
I am the god that puts fire in the head.
Who spreads light in the gathering on the hills?
Who can tell the ages of the moon?
Who can tell the place where the sun rests?[2]

[1] Based on the Lebor Gabála Érenn: The Book of the Taking of Ireland, 11th century. The landing of the Milesians took place at “Inbhear Scéine,”, near Waterville, Ballinskelligs Bay, Co. Kerry.

[2] Translated from the Irish by Lady Gregory in: Gods and Fighting Men, 1904.

The Divisions of the Island

These were the first verses ever spoken in Ireland, but of course, it didn't go without battle. My brothers, the Milesians as they called themselves now, were intent on conquering the island in their own way, and for a while they fought the mists and curses raised by the druids of the Tuatha Dé Danann with their spears and swords. The three kings, however, offered a truce, and this time I didn't wait for my brothers to send me out. I proposed to divide the island in two along the crust of the earth, and to my surprise, the three kings accepted. Manannán mac Lir, the son of the sea, led them into the world underground, leaving the one above to us.

This, too, didn't go without battle. Just two of my brothers were left after the storm and the battle, and both of them were intent on ruling alone. So, they fought each other with their insults and swords until I proclaimed a truce and proposed to divide the island in two along the river. To my surprise they accepted. Eber took the south, Erimón the north—at least until he killed his brother and then me. But this is another story.

As long as I lived, I wondered why the Tuatha Dé Danann, the tribe of the goddess, had conceded so easily to surrender the world above ground to us. But of course, we are only passing, leaving no more than traces quickly erased by time. While the Otherworld is forever, the life in the hills, the lakes, below the sea, without age or regrets, and so are the stories that seep through the landscape and shape our desires and fears from generation to generation.

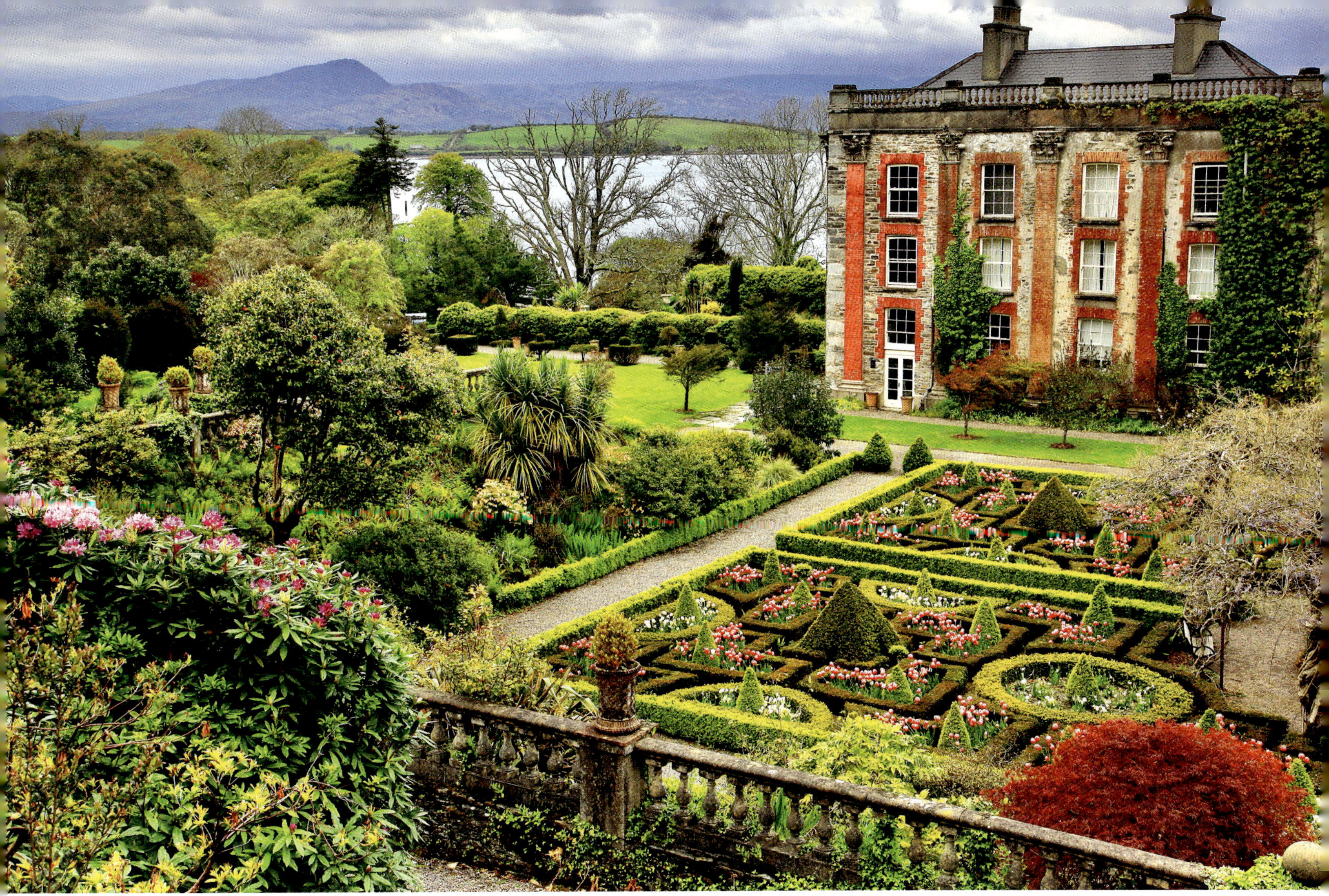

Bantry House

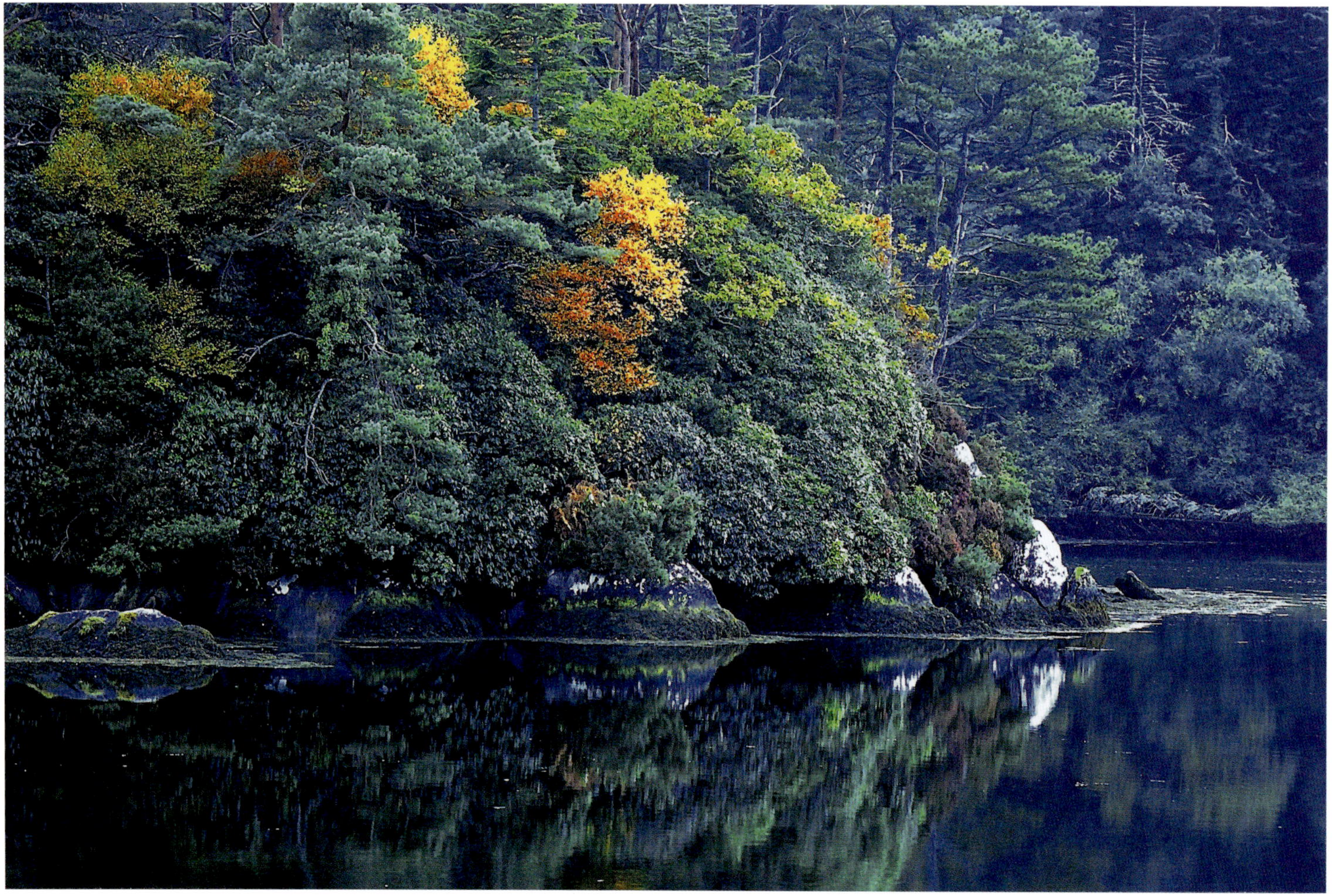

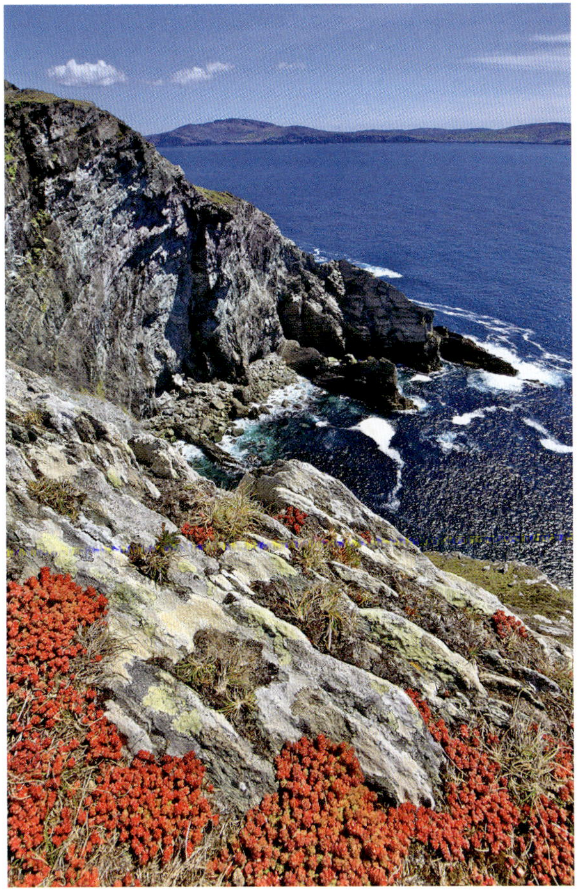

Left page: Kenmare River
Left: Sheep's Head Peninsula
Right: Youghal Coast

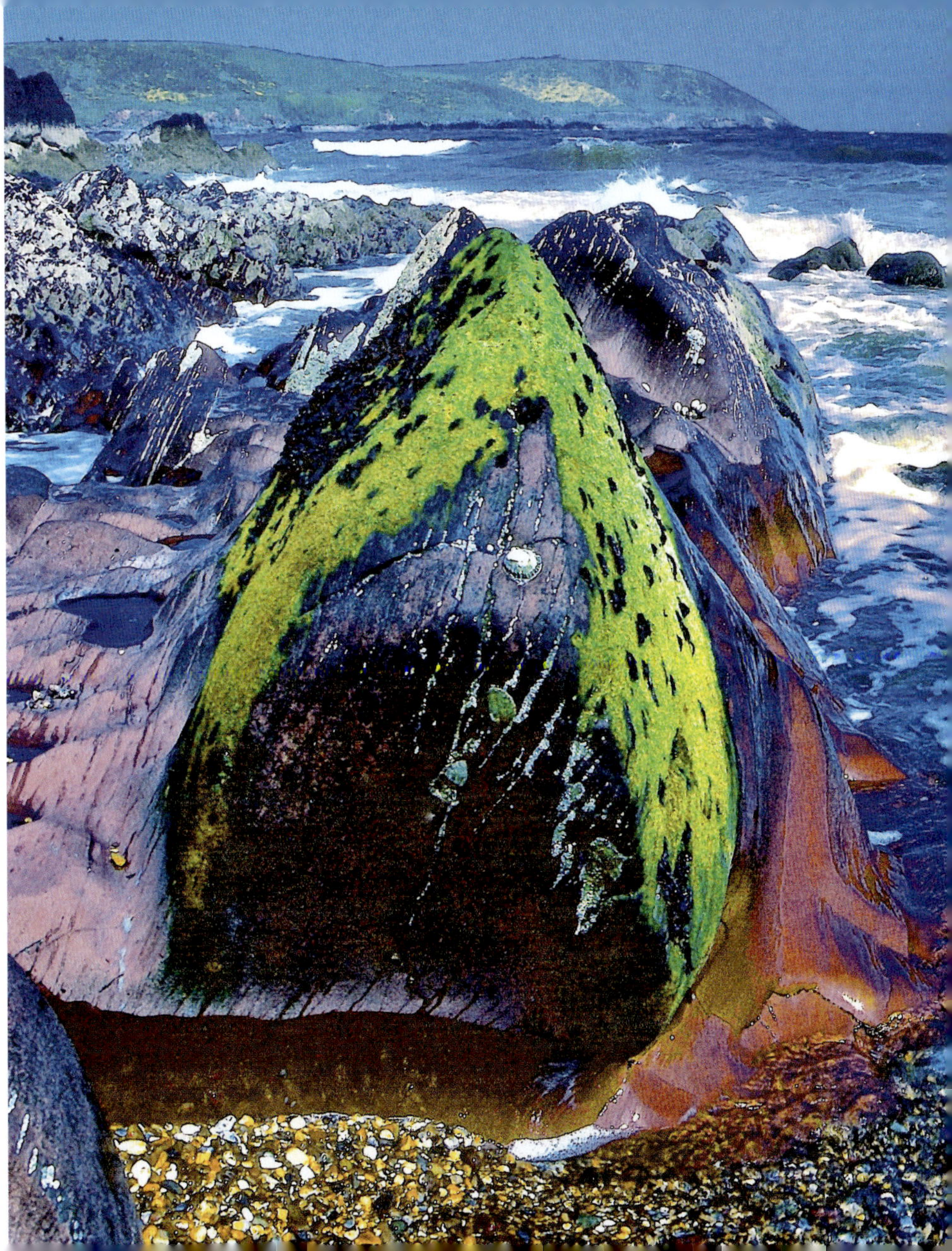

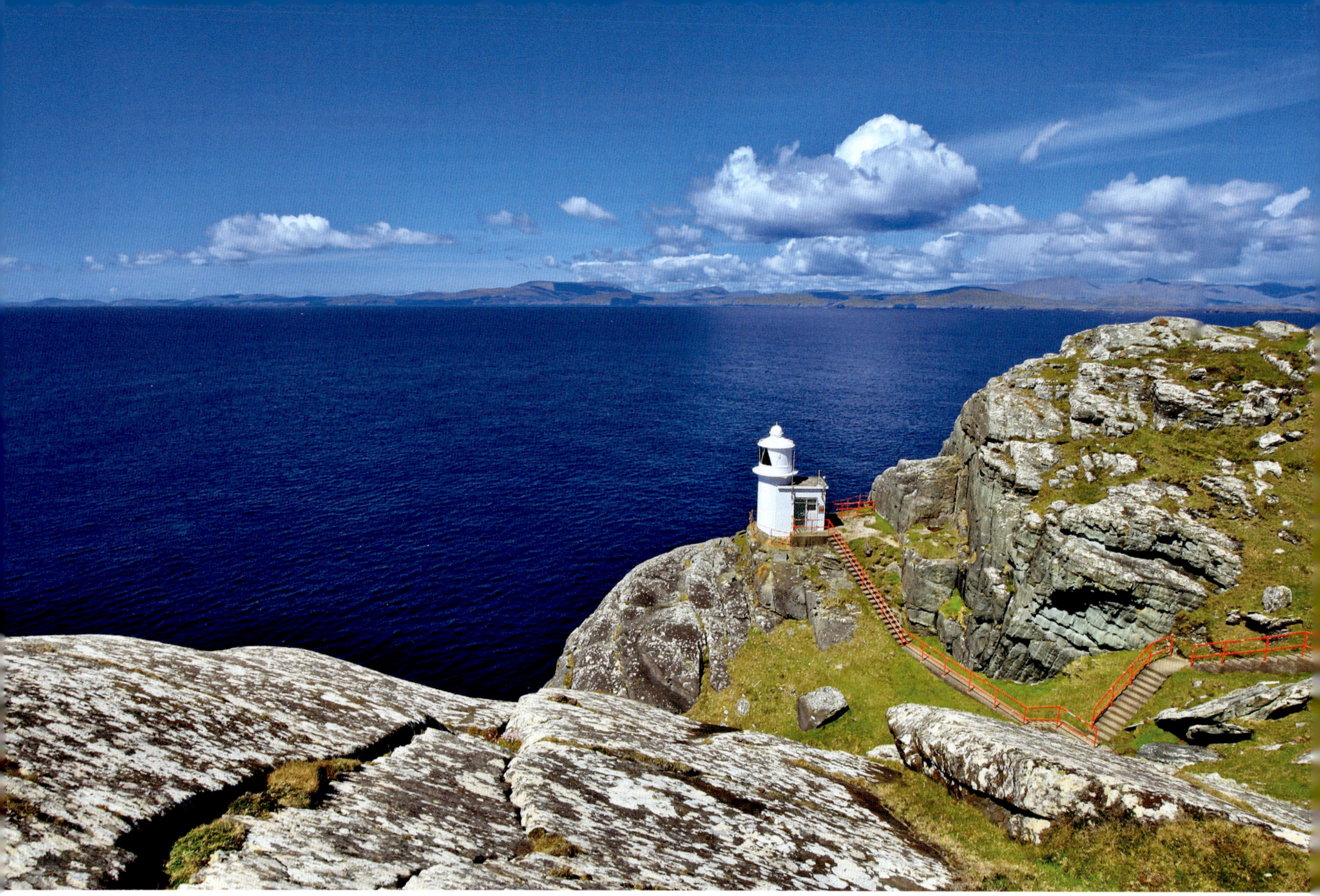

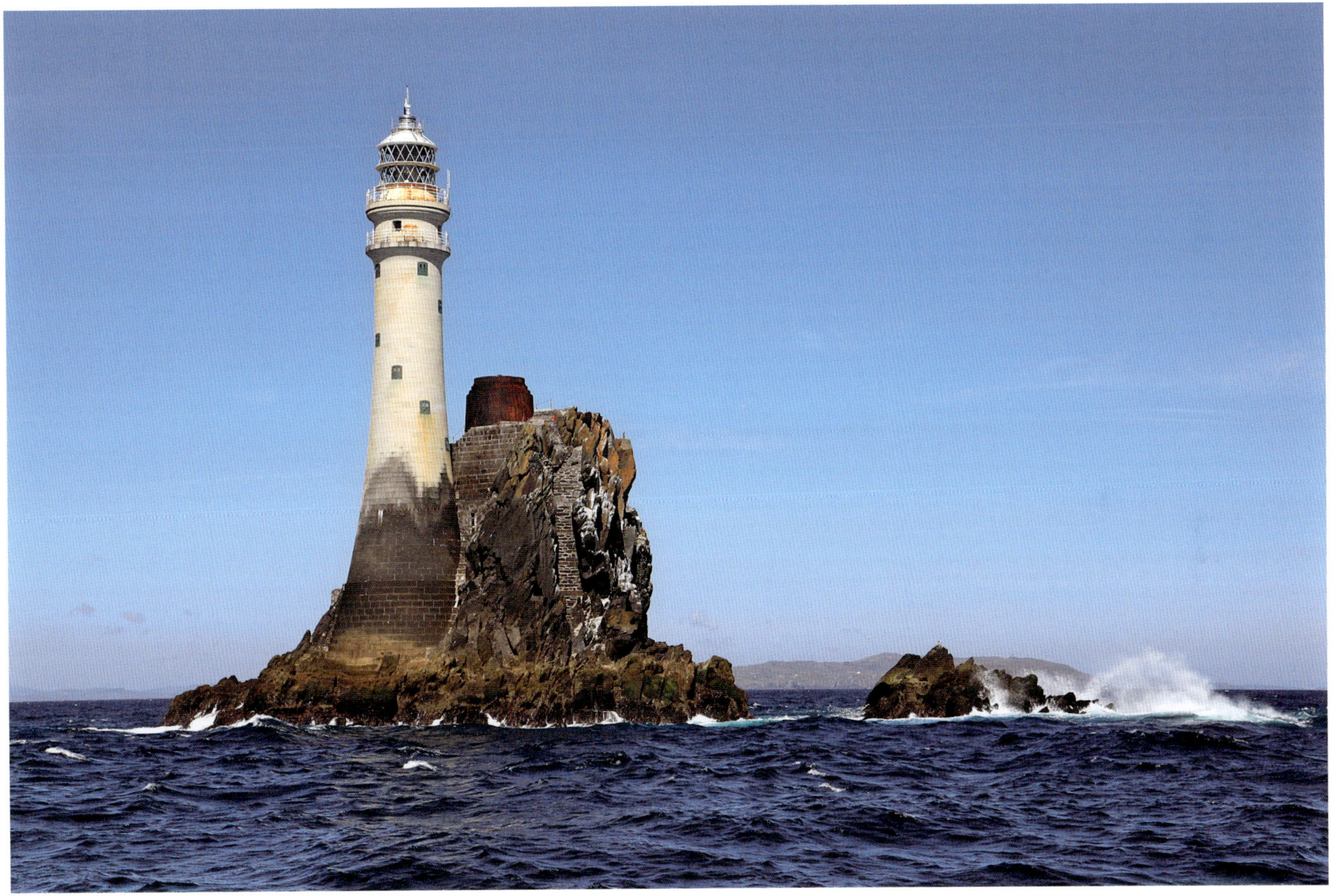

Left page: Sheep's Head Peninsula
Right: Fastnet Rock

The Dagda and the Morrígu

No wonder she fell for him. He was handsome, strong, fertile and most of all a good lover. His staff was made of iron, one end rough, bringing death, the other one smooth, bringing the dead back to life. His cauldron was never dry, eaving nobody wanting, and there were pigs that kept getting fat and roasted, trees that always bore fruit. The Dagda controlled the crops, the seasons, the stars, ruling over the tribe of the goddess and over wisdom and time. She liked his unruly beard and the way his woolen shirt always left a bit of his body uncovered. Sometimes in battle, she let her hand slip through the gap touching his skin like a breeze, and she could feel how he rallied his strength; together they were invincible. They fought the demons who had caused disorder and darkness in Ireland, and sometimes they fought each other.

The Dagda built a mound fort in the bend of the river with a window through which the sun would shine on the morning of the shortest day, so that they knew when the year was turning, and he lived there, at least until his son tricked him out of it. The Dagda's harp had two names—summer and winter—three strains—joy, sorrow and sleep—and she was a bit wary of it. He closed his red eyes when he played it, and she was sure he looked at something she couldn't see.

She, the Morrígu, had many names and was many things: an old woman, a fair maiden, a wolf, an eel, a screech and most often a crow. She was willful, deceitful, faithful and often jealous. She pursued the men she loved and the men she hated without mercy. Her beauty was as blinding as was her rage, and to love her and to hate her must have felt the same. Of course, she had children, by gods, humans, allies and enemies. But who would call her mother? She never dwelt in the mound of the Dagda, never tended a fire, a hearth, and her only homely gesture was to wash the bloodstains from the shirts of the ones who were going to die. She could change people's fate, and that she had no fear made her reckless and lonely.

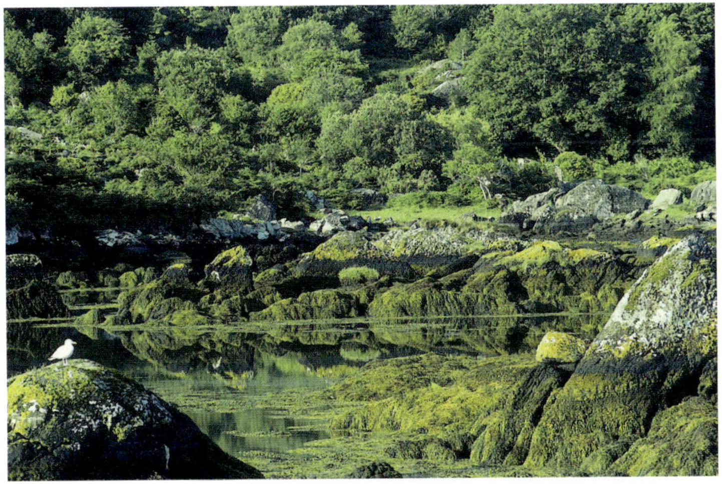

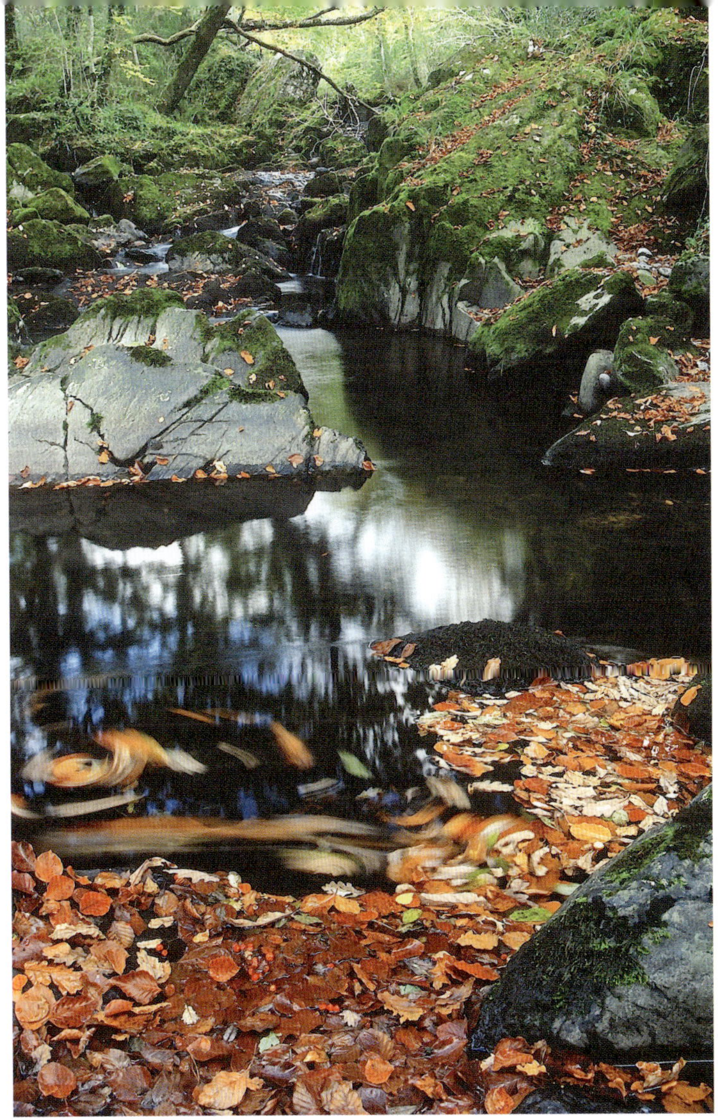

Left: Kenmare River
Right: Glengarriff Nature Reserve

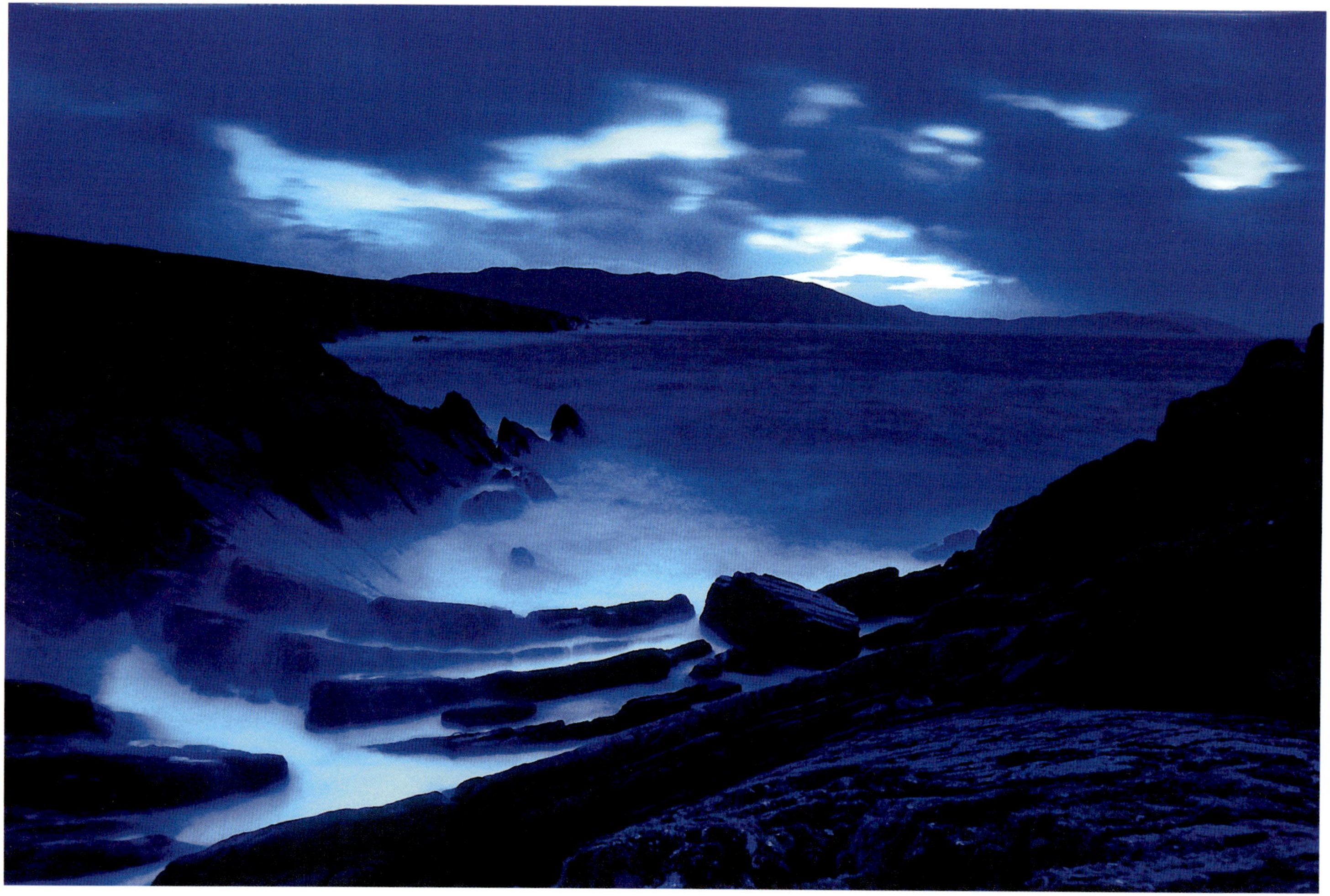

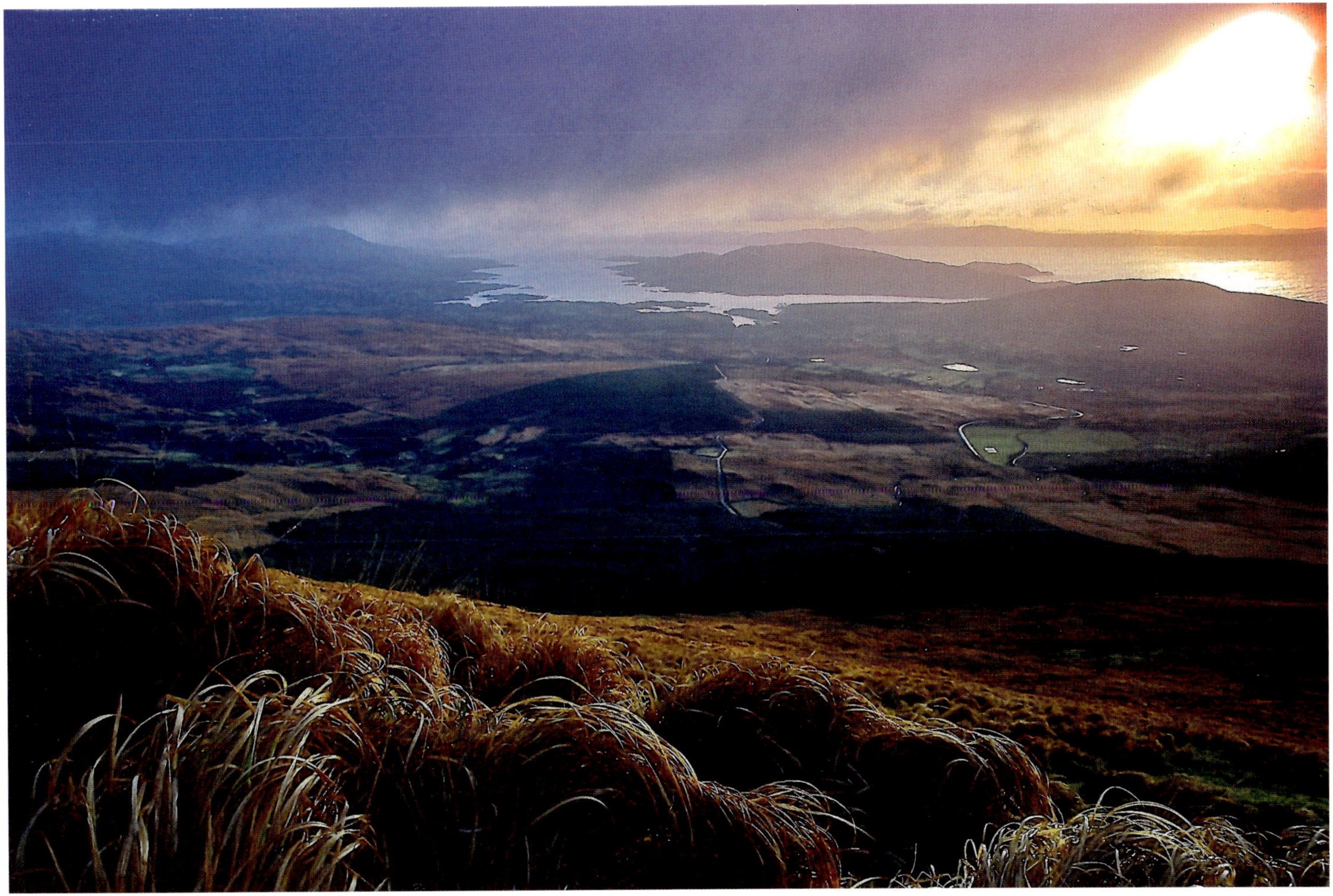

Left page: Coulagh Bay
Right: Beara Peninsula

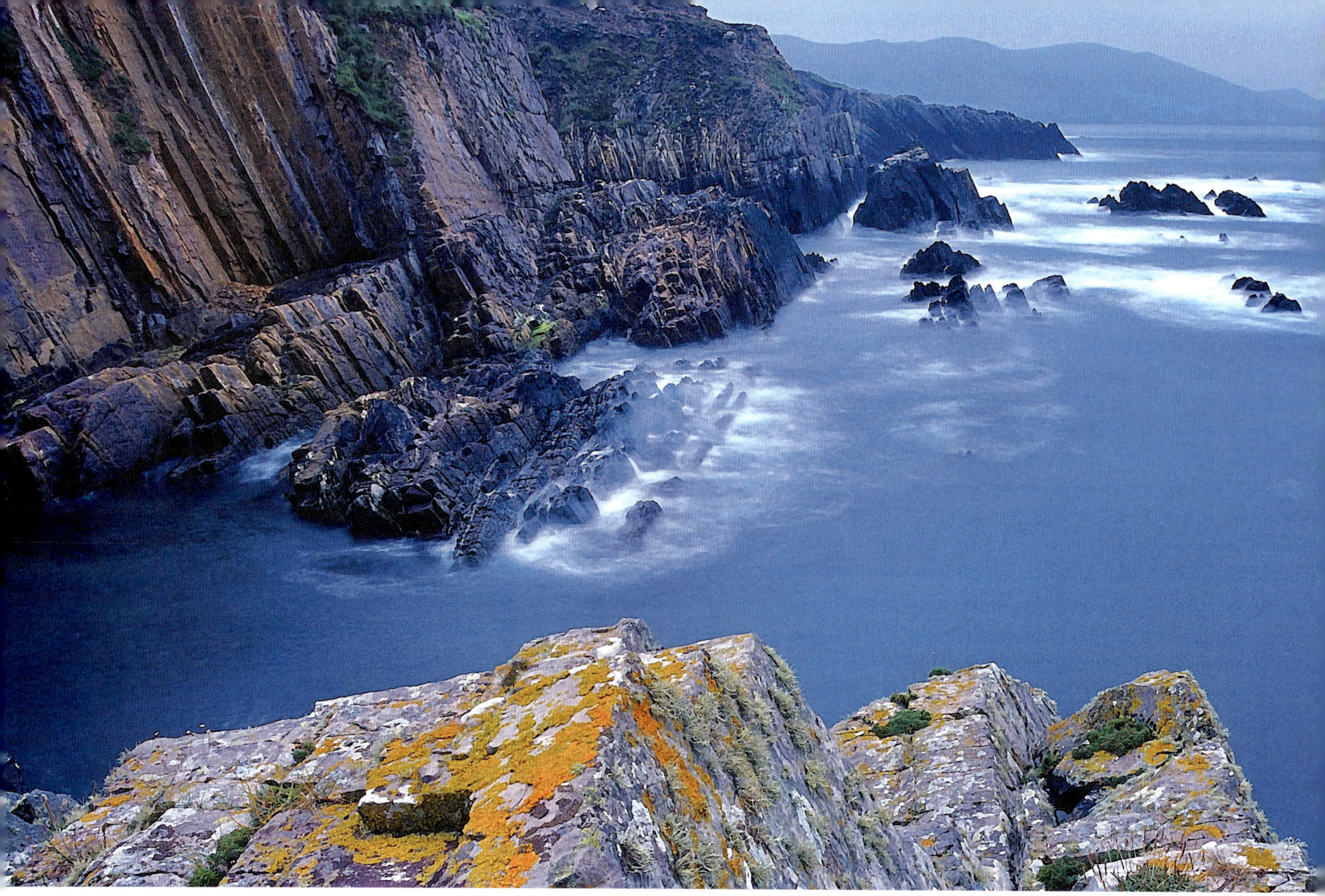

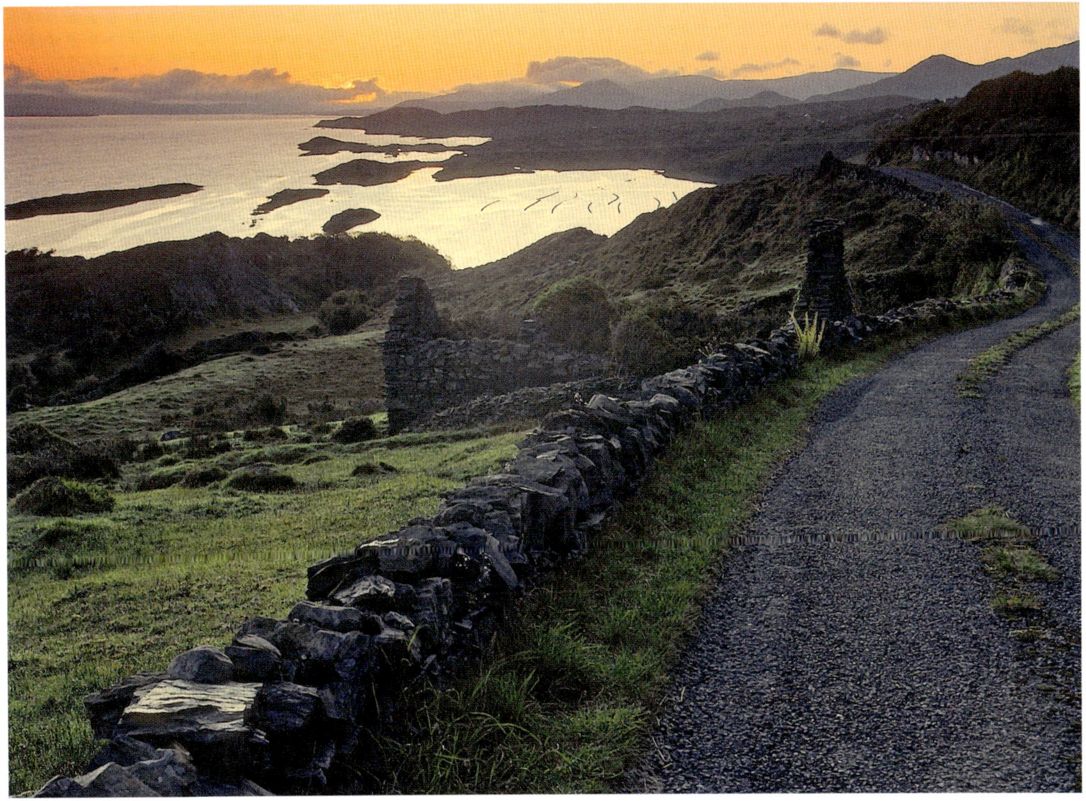

Left page: North Coast Beara Peninsula
Right: Ardgroom Beara Peninsula

Boann's Way

Boann was sweet to look at and playful like a little white calf. Men couldn't take their eyes off her; she knew that. Only Nechtan, her husband, remained indifferent; he was a bit of a bore. To flirt with the servants, the guardsmen, the lords wouldn't catch his attention, nor when she amused herself with the flute player or the three cupbearers who minded his well. She wondered how far she would get with the Dagda. To be honest, it was easier than she had thought. She just let her eyes go soft when she caught his look and remained silent. Men didn't like too much talk, she knew that.

But she hadn't expected that she would feel like that when the Dagda touched her. For the first time, she was herself; he was her one desire. "I'm pregnant," she said, when she caught her breath again.

The Dagda groaned. His wife, the Morrígu, was not called the jealous for nothing, and she was the goddess of battle and fate.

"What are you going to do?" Boann asked.

The Dagda looked at his mace with which he could kill nine men in one stroke. Then he took his harp and made the sun stand still for nine months. And so Boann's son Aengus, the god of love, was conceived and born on the same day.

Only Nechtan and his three cup-bearers were allowed to come close to the well of wisdom. Boann liked to take her little dog there to rummage in the hazel grove.

"No women allowed here," the first cupbearer said when she strolled by.

"No dogs allowed here," the second one added.

Dabilla, the little dog, wagged its tail. The three men smiled, and while they petted the dog, Boann slipped past them. She walked around the well against the course of the sun, as she had seen the men do.. Was there a rumble of a distant thunder? Bubbles rising to the surface of the well? The water sprang up and blinded Boann in one eye. She fled, followed by Dabilla, and the water chased them through the hazel grove, down the hill, past the mound fort of the Dagda to the shore of the sea. It seized her, tore her asunder, scattered her body. Thus, the river Boyne was formed, and Boann became the landscape through which it flows. Dabilla, the little dog, was washed out to sea and turned into Rockabill, a pair of islands not far from Dublin.

The mound fort of the Dagda was named Brú na Bóinne, the Palace of the White Cow, as Boann, it is said, means white cow; and the reflection of the River Boyne in the sky is called "the Way of the White Cow" or the Milky Way.

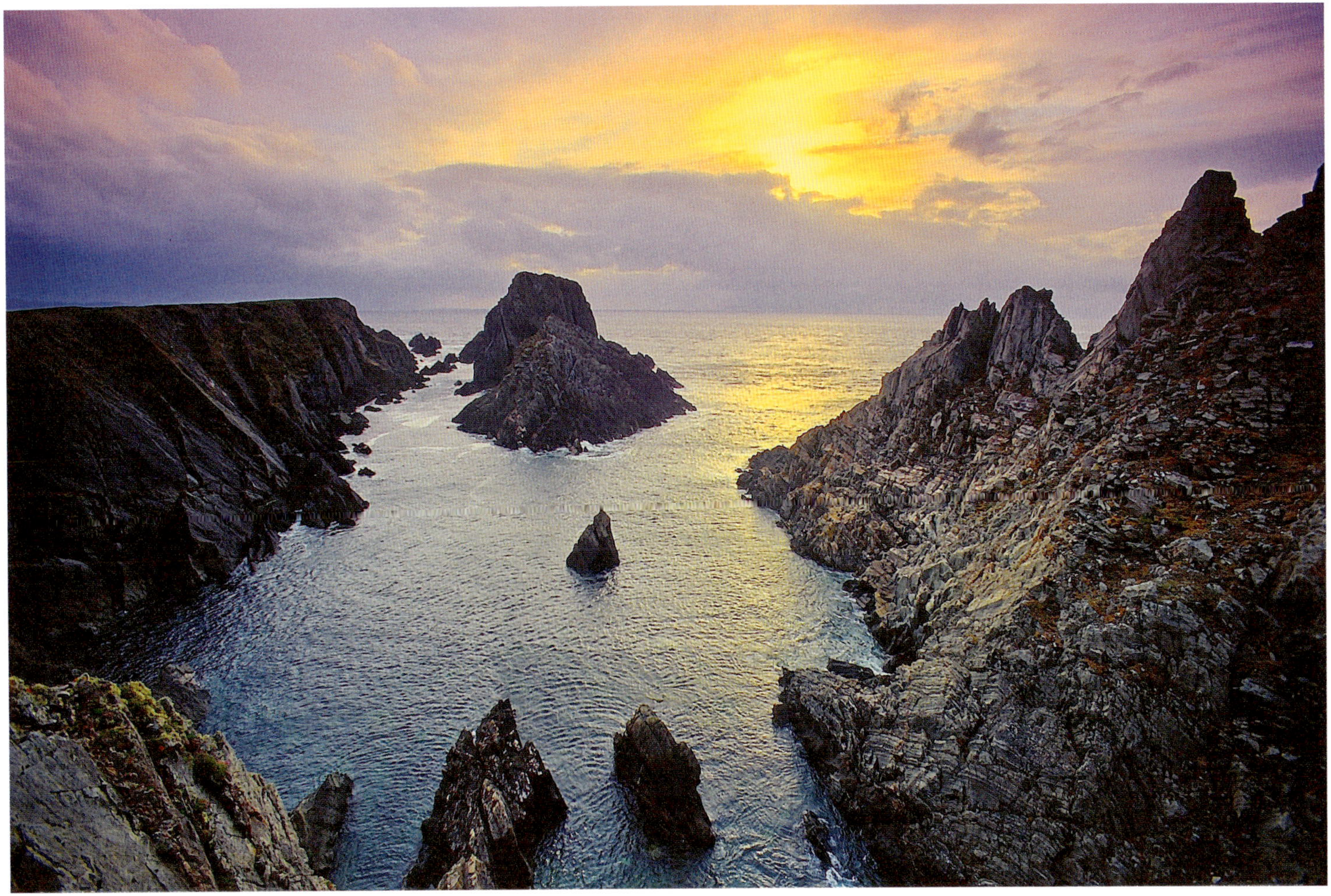

Malin Head

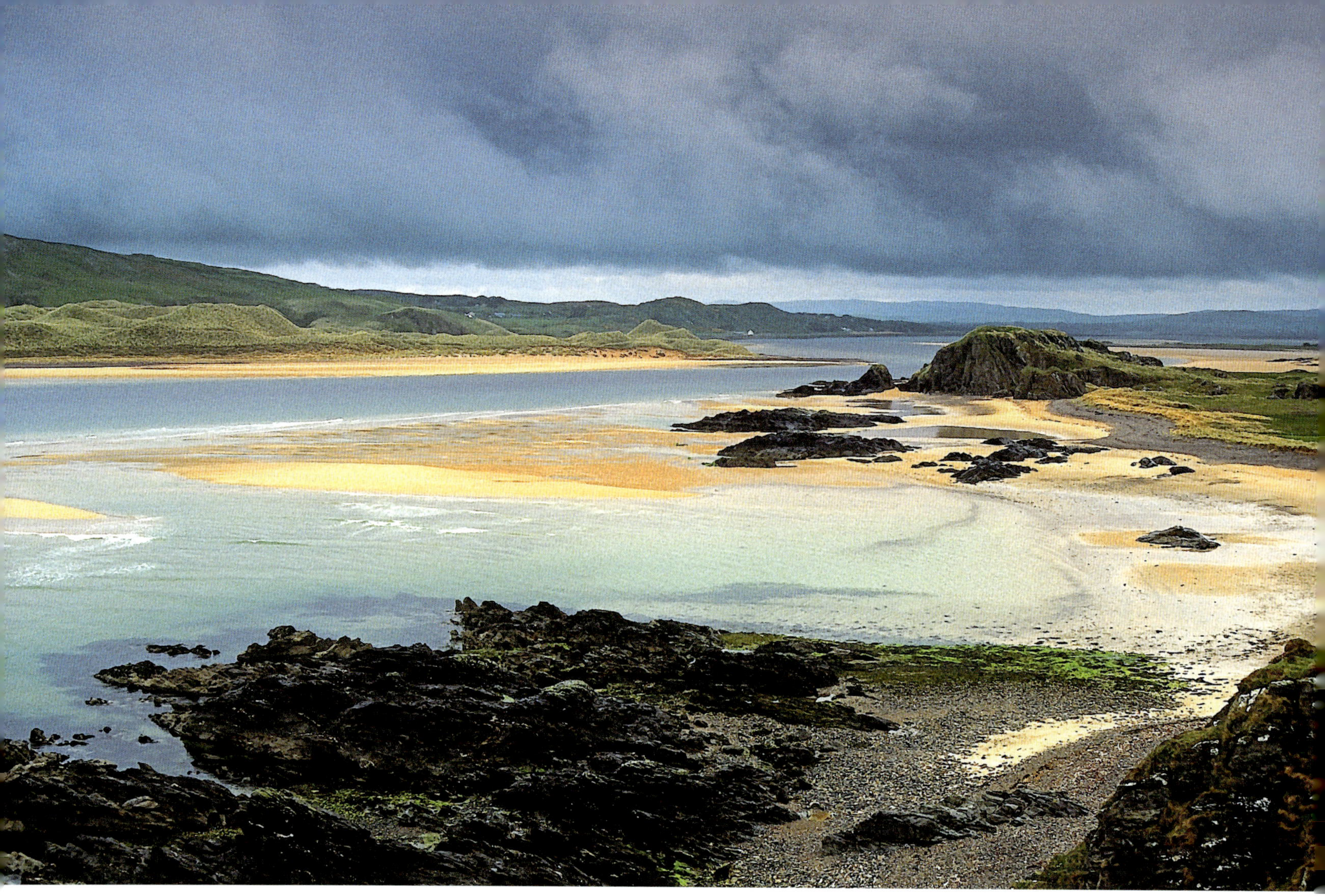

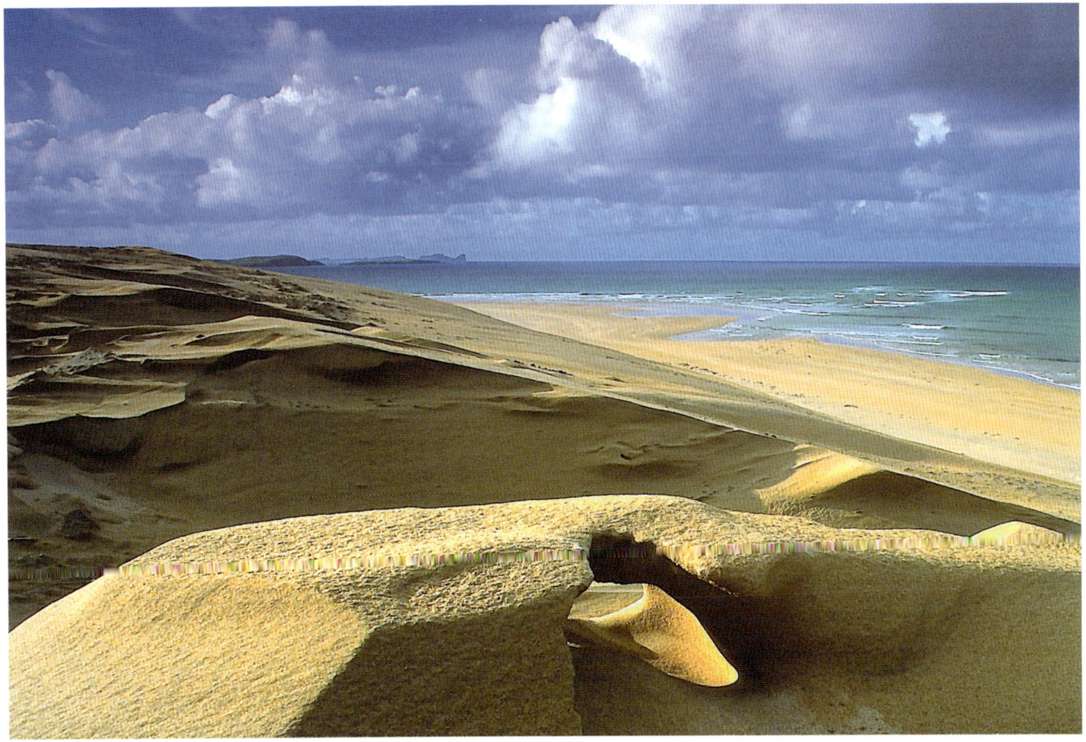

Left page: Trawbreaga Bay
Right: Ballyneess Bay

The Longings of Aengus

He was a good horseman, a good sailor, a good singer, well equipped by nature, just like his father, and sweet to look at, as was his mother. People liked him. When Aengus discovered that the Dagda had bequeathed all his possessions to his other children, he requested the kingship of Brú na Bóinne for a day and a night, and his father agreed. As the Irish language has no indefinite article, a day and a night meant the same as day and night. “And it is in days and nights that the world passes,” Aengus said, and stayed in the Palace of the White Cow for good. Others say, Manannán mac Lir, the son of the Sea, incited Aengus to expel the Dagda from Brú na Bóinne with a spell. As the Dagda heard about this, he laughed: “I would have given the fort to Aengus anyhow, but now sorrow and madness will follow him.”

Night after night, a girl with apple blossom in her hair stood at Aengus' bedside. He wanted her, but each time he tried to touch her, she vanished. Soon, he couldn't eat anymore, talk anymore, all his thoughts were of her; she was his one desire. His family started to worry. For one year, Boann, his mother, searched for the girl. Then his father, the Dagda, searched for a year. But only at the end of the third year, Bodb, Aengus' brother, spotted the girl on the lake of the dragon's mouth.

When Aengus came to the lake called Muskry today, he saw thrice fifty swans linked in pairs by silver chains. Every second Samhain, the night in autumn when the doors to the Otherworld open up, they would turn back into girls for a day.

“If you recognize her amongst the other swans, you can be with her,” the druid challenged Aengus. Aengus laughed. He didn't hesitate a moment, but turned into a swan and, with his beloved, he flew back to Brú na Bóinne. There, it is said, the enchanted singing of the two made all who heard it fall asleep for three nights and three days. Others say Aengus never found the girl with the apple blossom in her hair and is still walking the island in search of her.

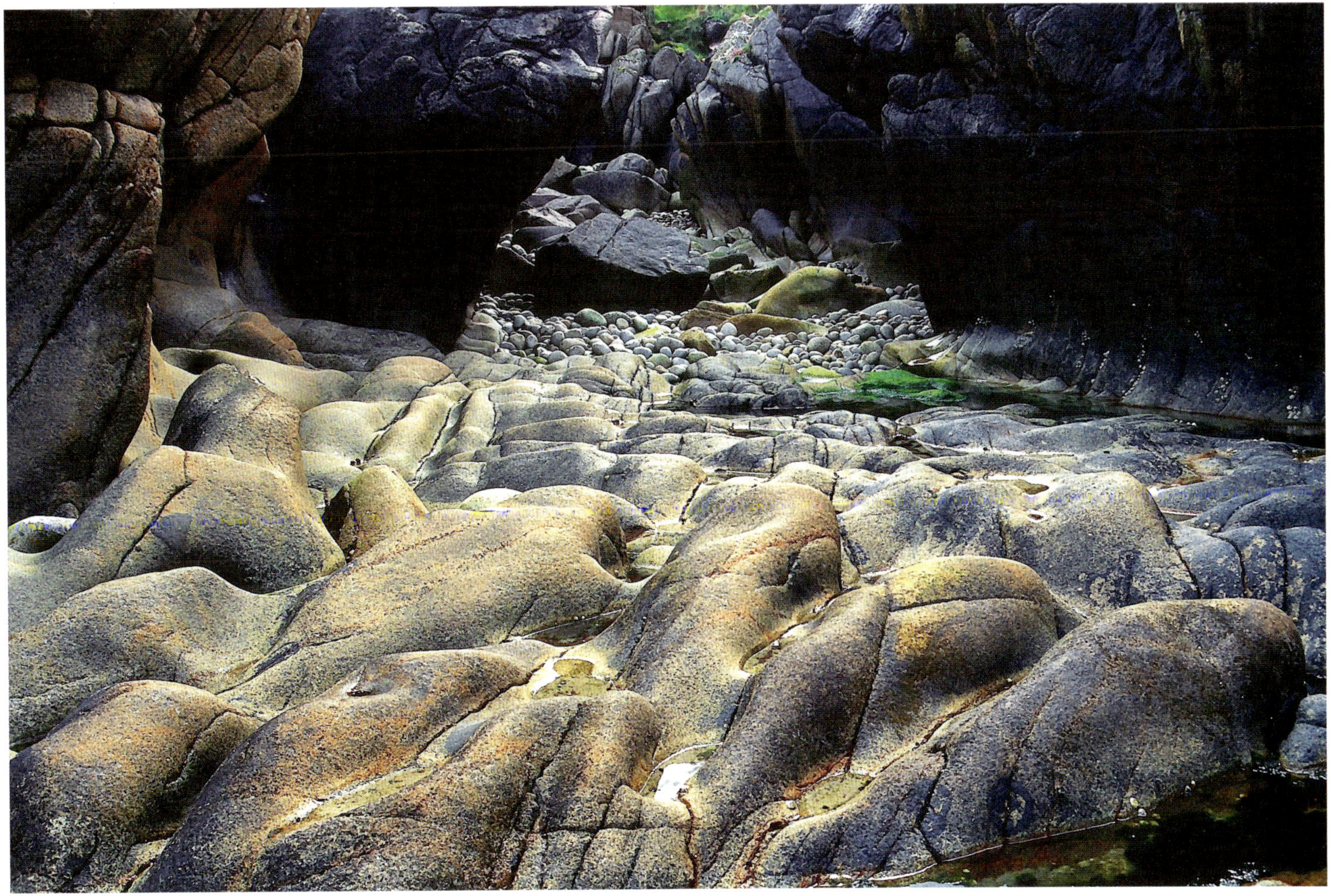

Lenan Head

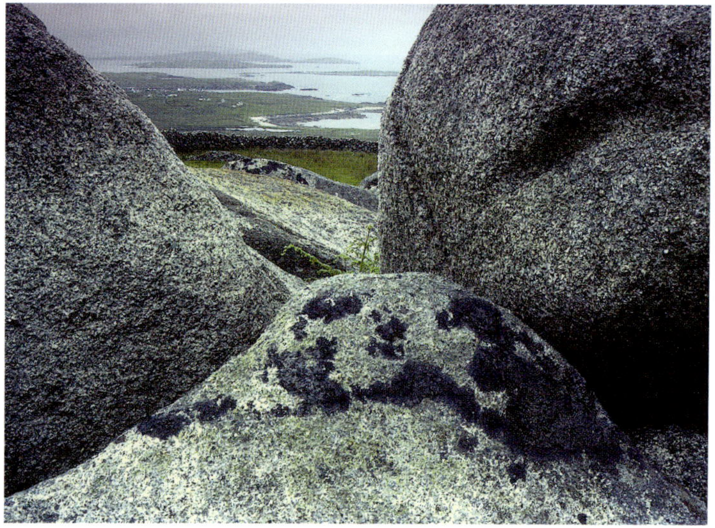

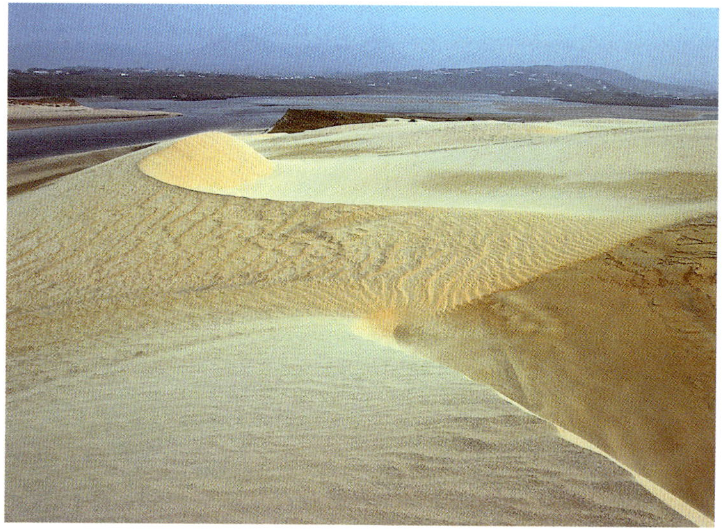

Left: Derrybeg
Right: Ballyness Bay

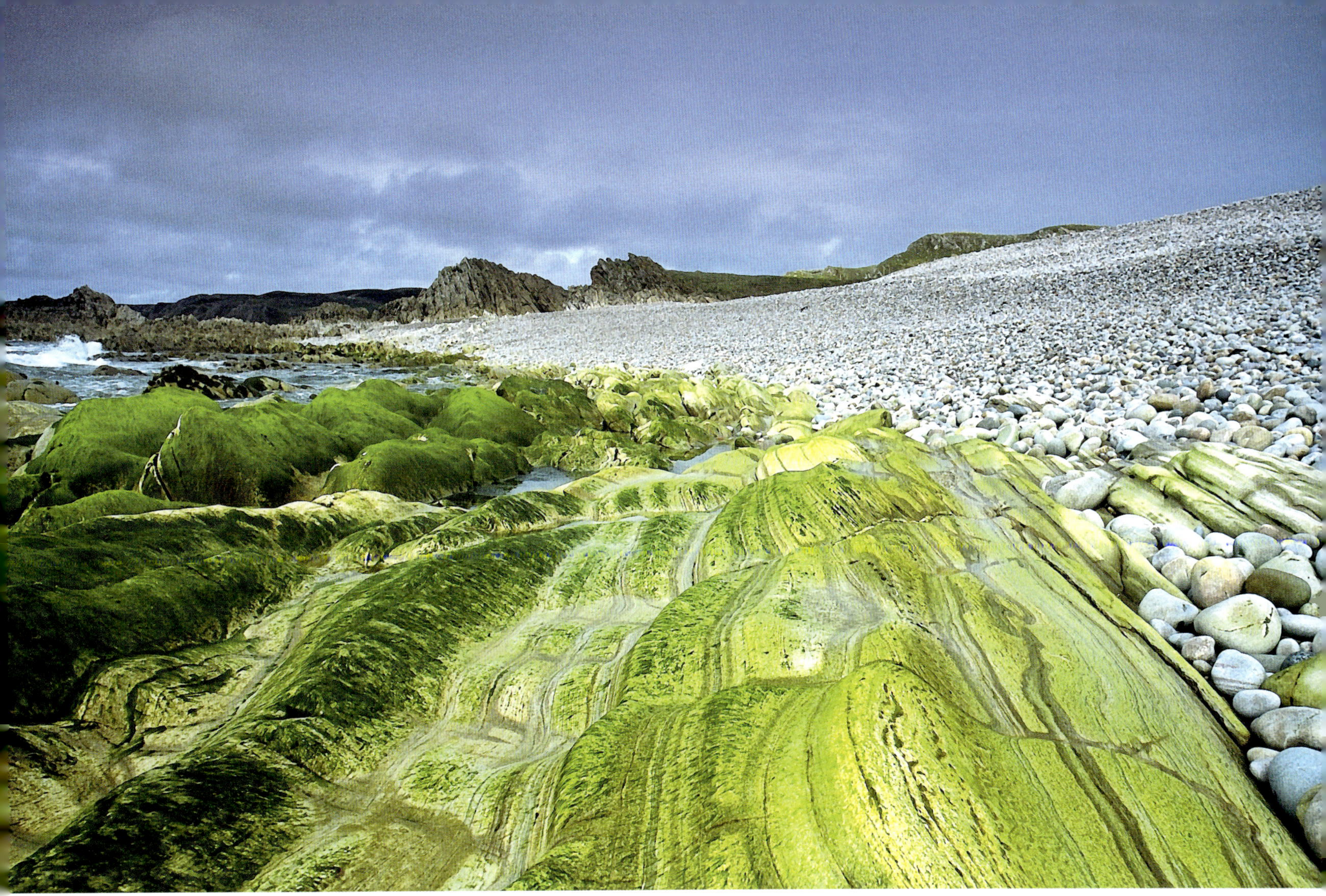

Doagh Isle, Inishowen

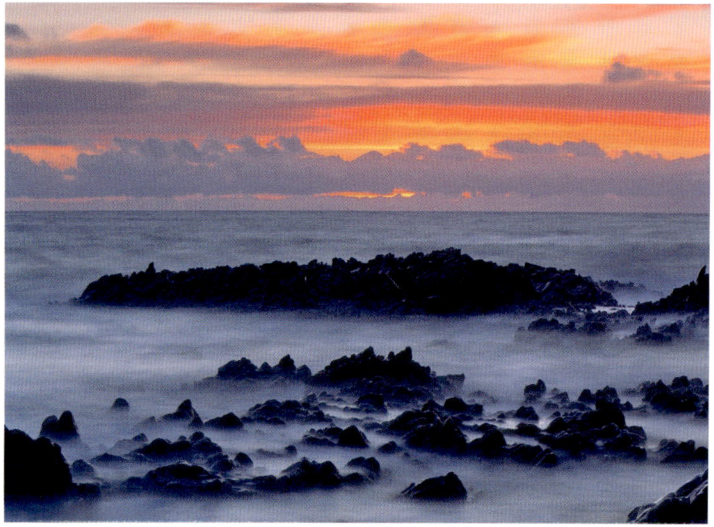

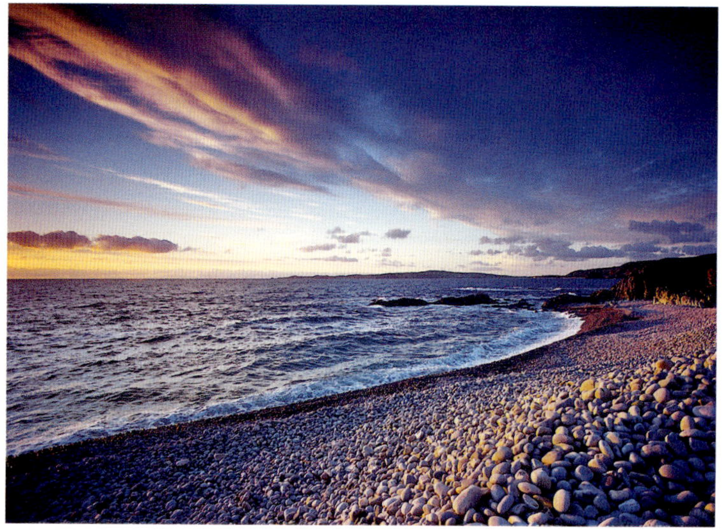

Left and right: Pollan Bay

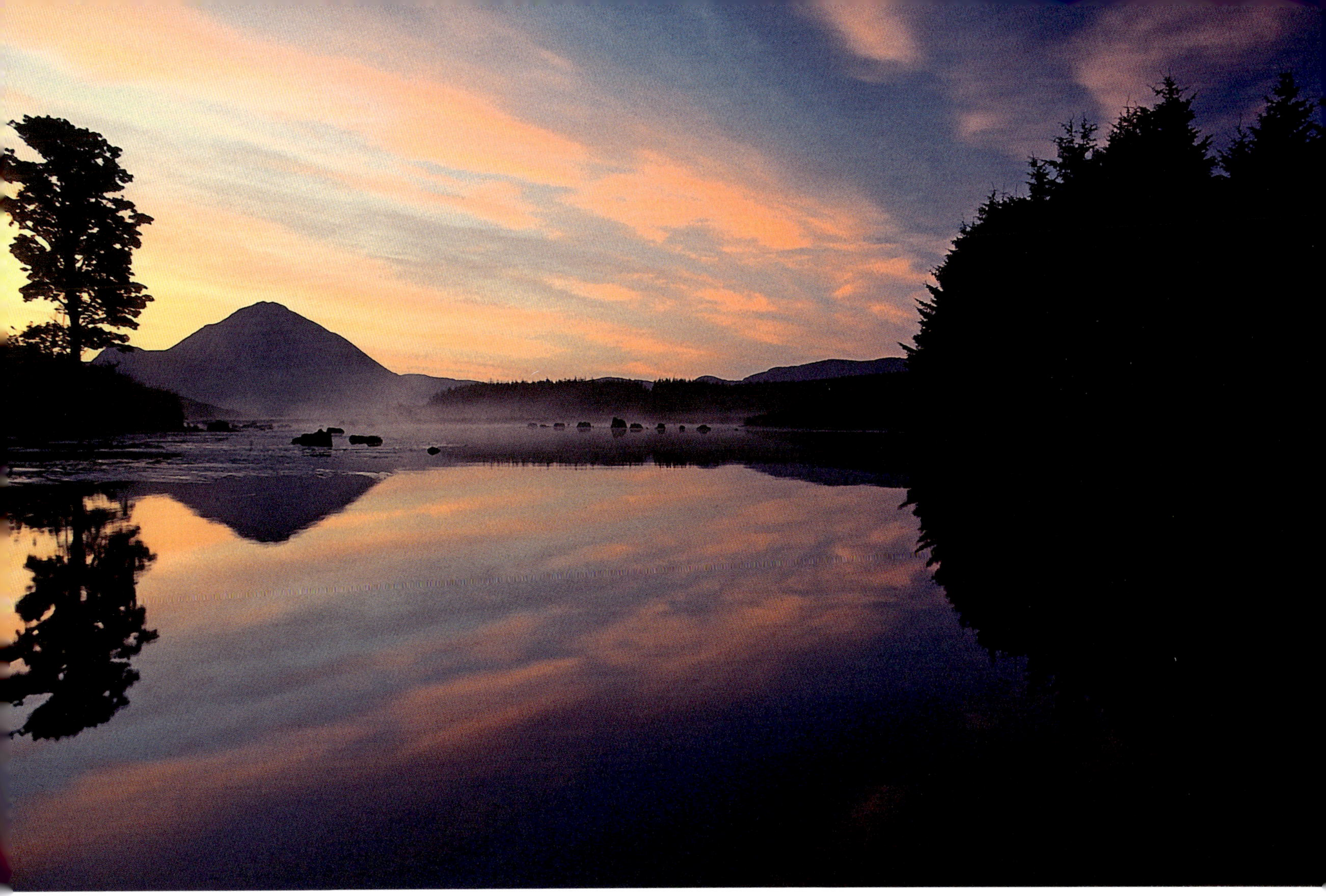

Mt. Errigal

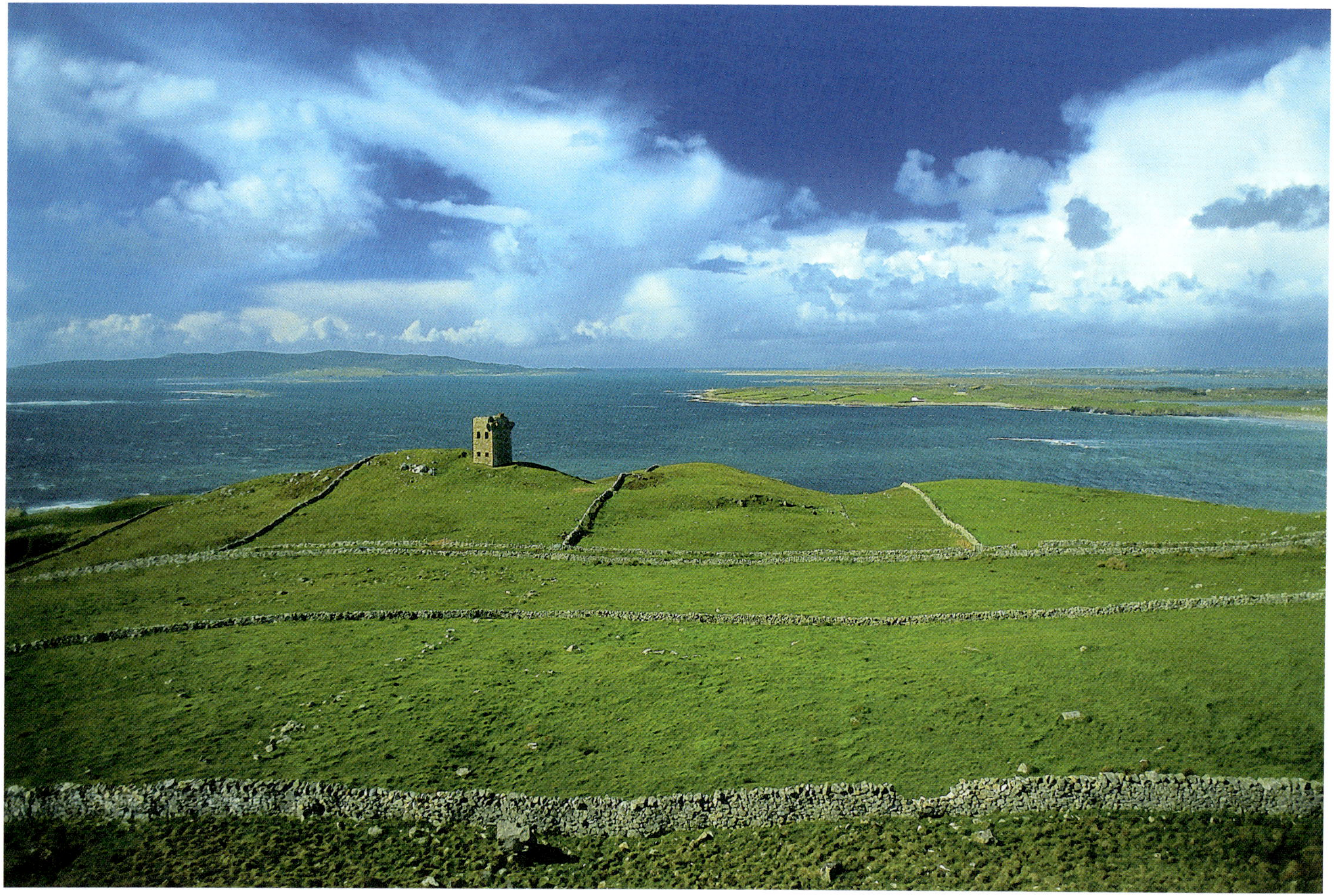

Deirdre's Sorrows

Her father was a storyteller, and from the very beginning, there was too much talk: That she was going to be the most beautiful girl on the island, that kings and lords would fight over her, that much blood would be shed on her account, that people would be forced into exile. Some demanded that she be killed at birth. But Conchobar, the king of Ulster, beguiled by the prospect of her beauty, wanted her for himself and gave the child to a woman, a poet no less—as if there wasn't enough fabrication already—to raise her in secret until she was ready for his bed.

One winter morning, Deirdre watched a raven in the snow, tearing at its prey. "Hair black like a raven, skin white as snow and blood-red cheeks—these will be the colors of the man I love," she said.

The woman, the poet moaned with delight. "I know him," she said, "he is not far."

"I will be ill until I have him," Deirdre declared, and the woman arranged for Deirdre to meet him in secret. Naoise was a young hunter at Conchobar's court. He knew he was in trouble when Deirdre said she had chosen him, but she taunted him until he took her. They couldn't stay at Conchobar's court. Together with Naoise's two brothers, they fled across the water to live in a secluded place, where they hunted and fished, and possibly had children.

Conchobar was very cross. He sent Fergus mac Róich out to track Deirdre and Naoise down and to promise them a safe return home. Fergus convinced the couple in exile, giving them his word of honor. Even after he had been tricked out of his kingship by Conchobar's mother, he had remained loyal to the king, but now he was deceived once again. When Conchobar heard that Deirdre's beauty was unspoiled, he had Naoise and his brothers slaughtered even before they reached his court at Emain Macha. "Enough now," said Fergus, and set fire to Conchobar's palace before he defected with three thousand men to Connacht, offering his services to King Ailill and Queen Maeve. Conchobar forced Deirdre into marriage.

A year went by, but for all his royal splendor, Conchobar couldn't make Deirdre lift her head or stop grieving. Cruelly, he decided to send her to the very man who had killed Naoise, and when she set out, he taunted her. "Enough now," Deirdre said very softly and let herself fall off the chariot, dashing her head against a rock.

A yew tree grew out of her grave and across the country until it reached the branches of the yew tree on Naoise's grave; and yew trees, it is said, live for thousands of years.

Left page: Crohy Head

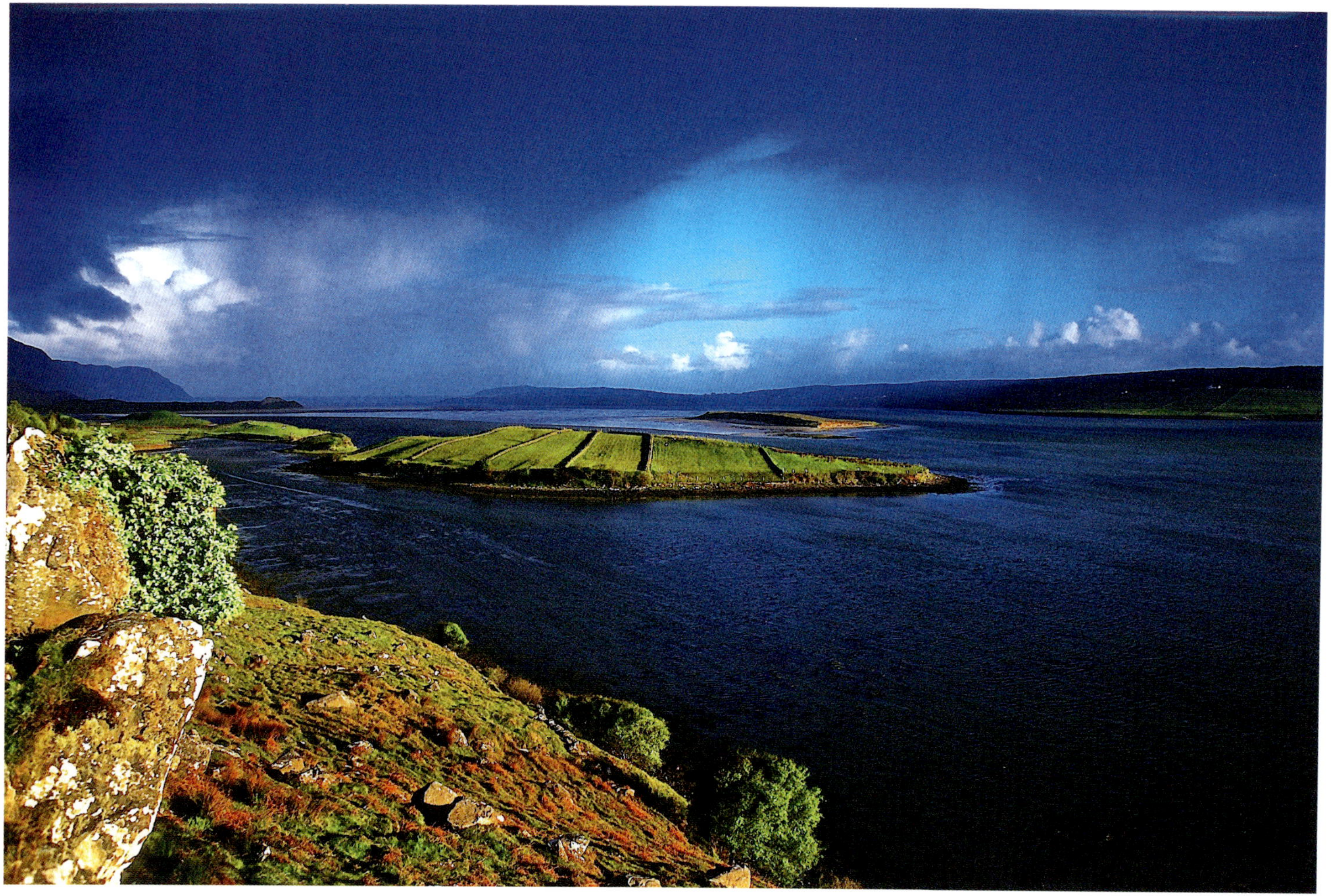

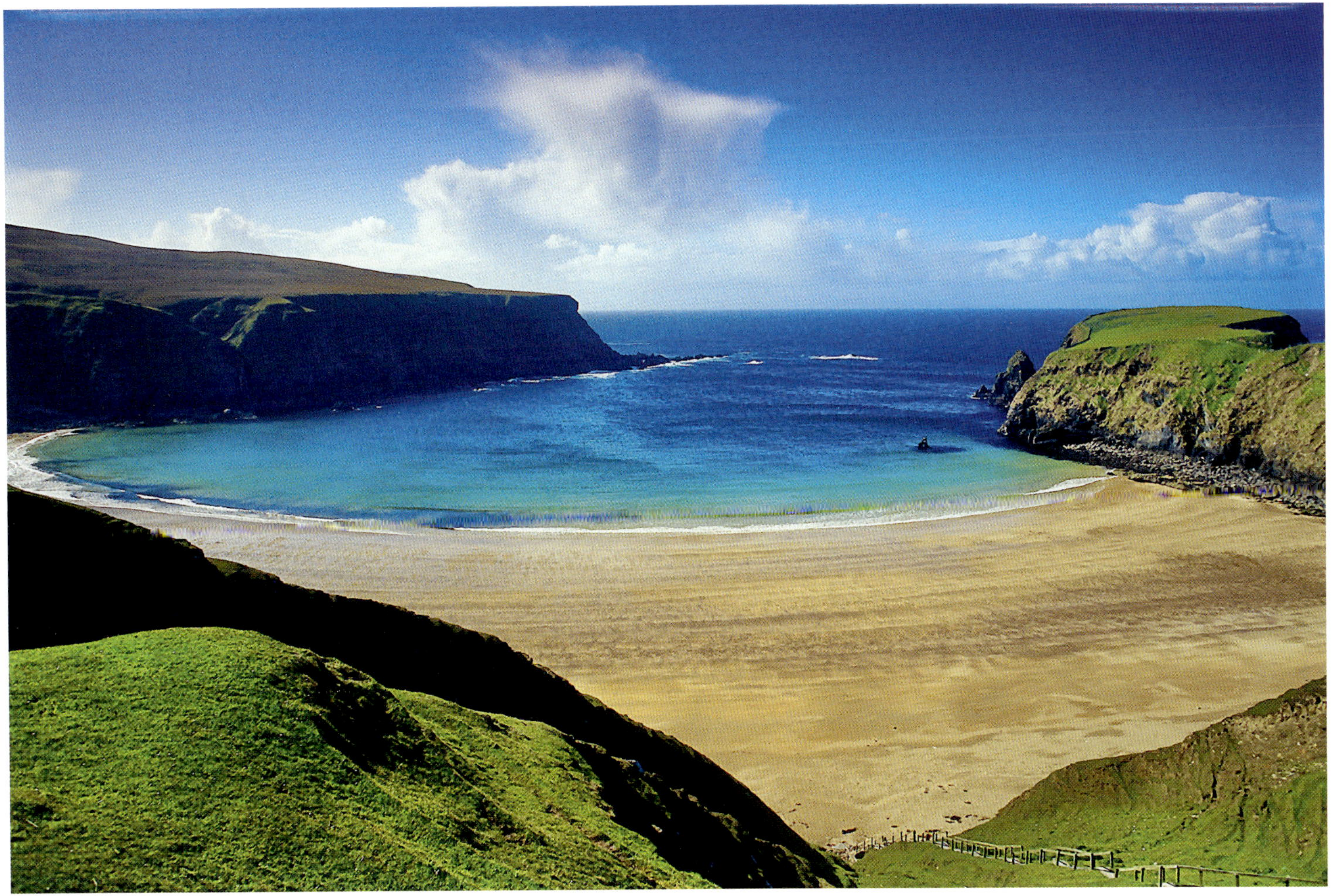

Left page: Loughros Bay
Right: Malin Beg

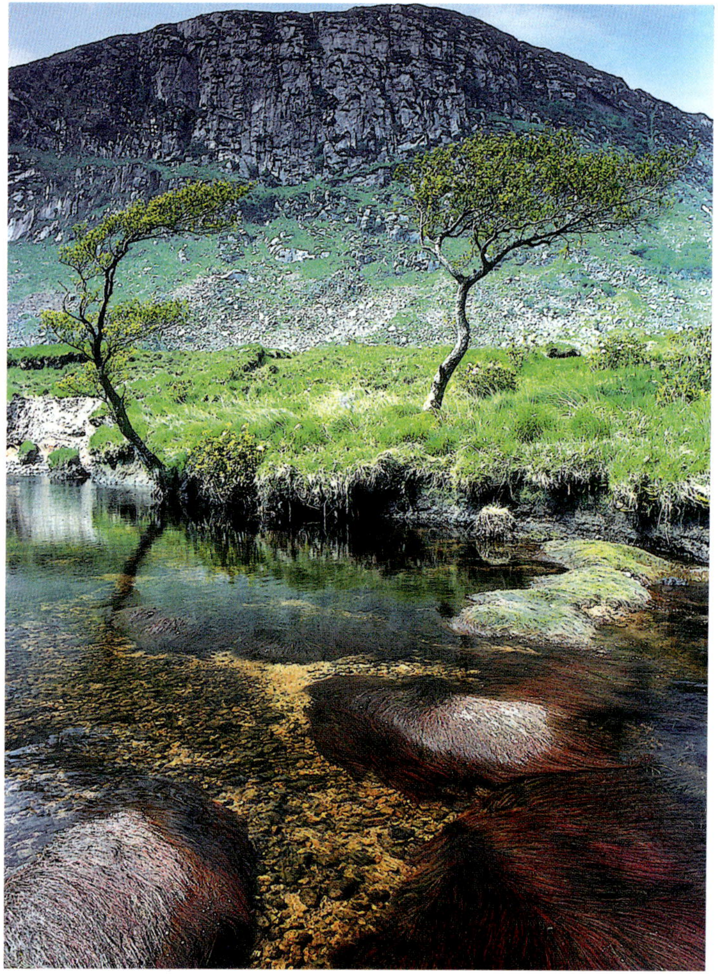

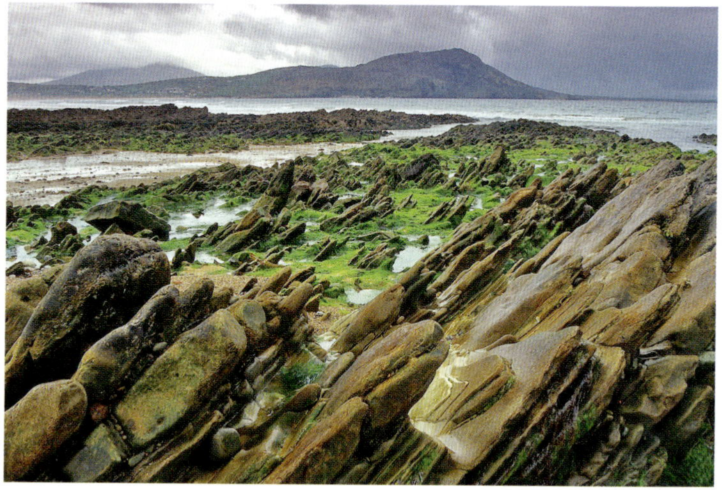

Left: Glenveagh National Park
Right: Pollan Bay

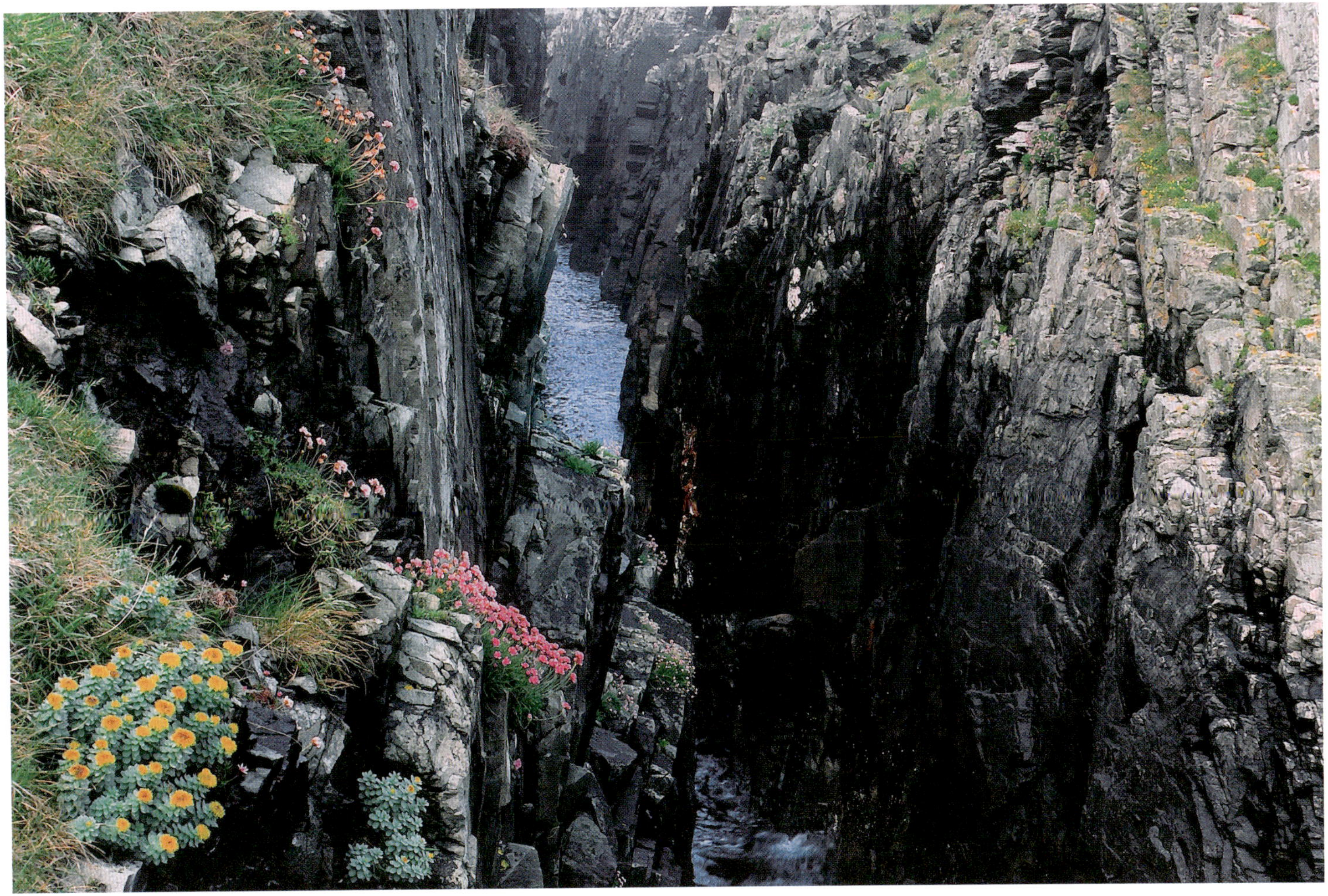

Malin Head

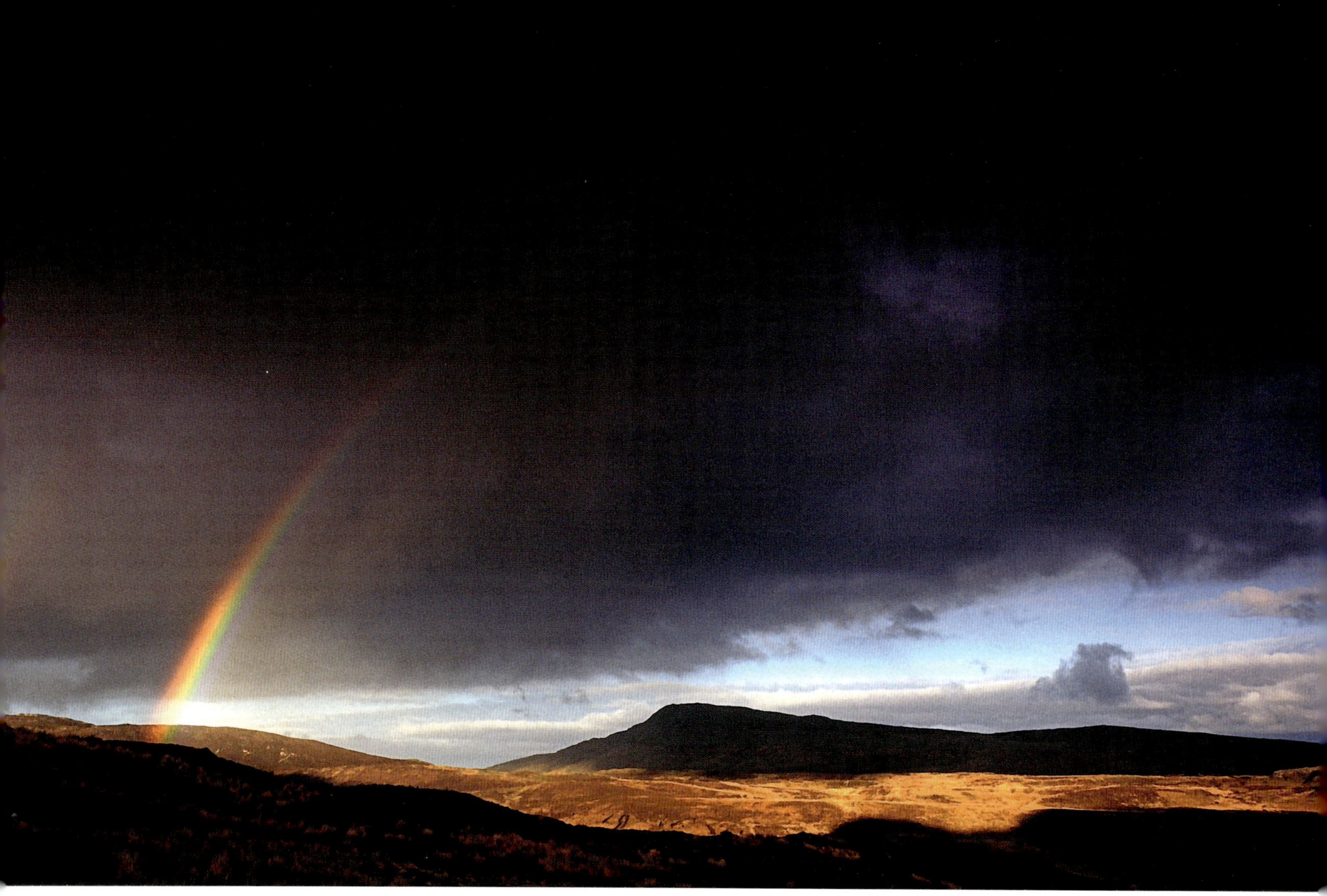

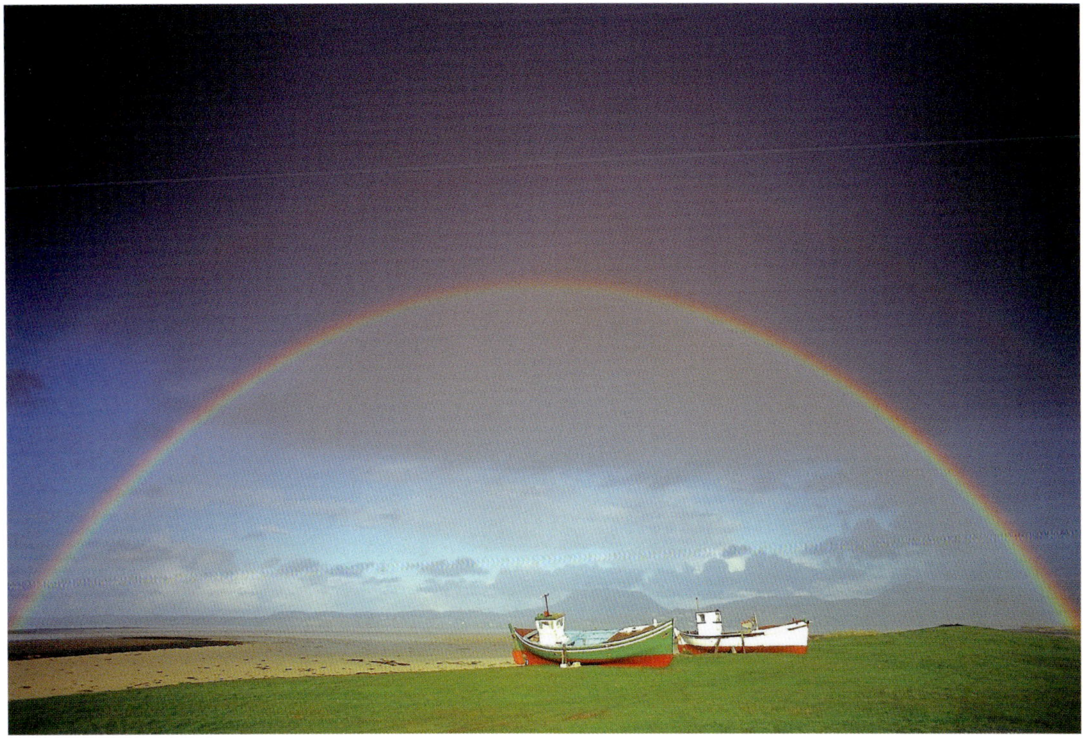

Left page: Inishowen
Right: Ballyness Bay

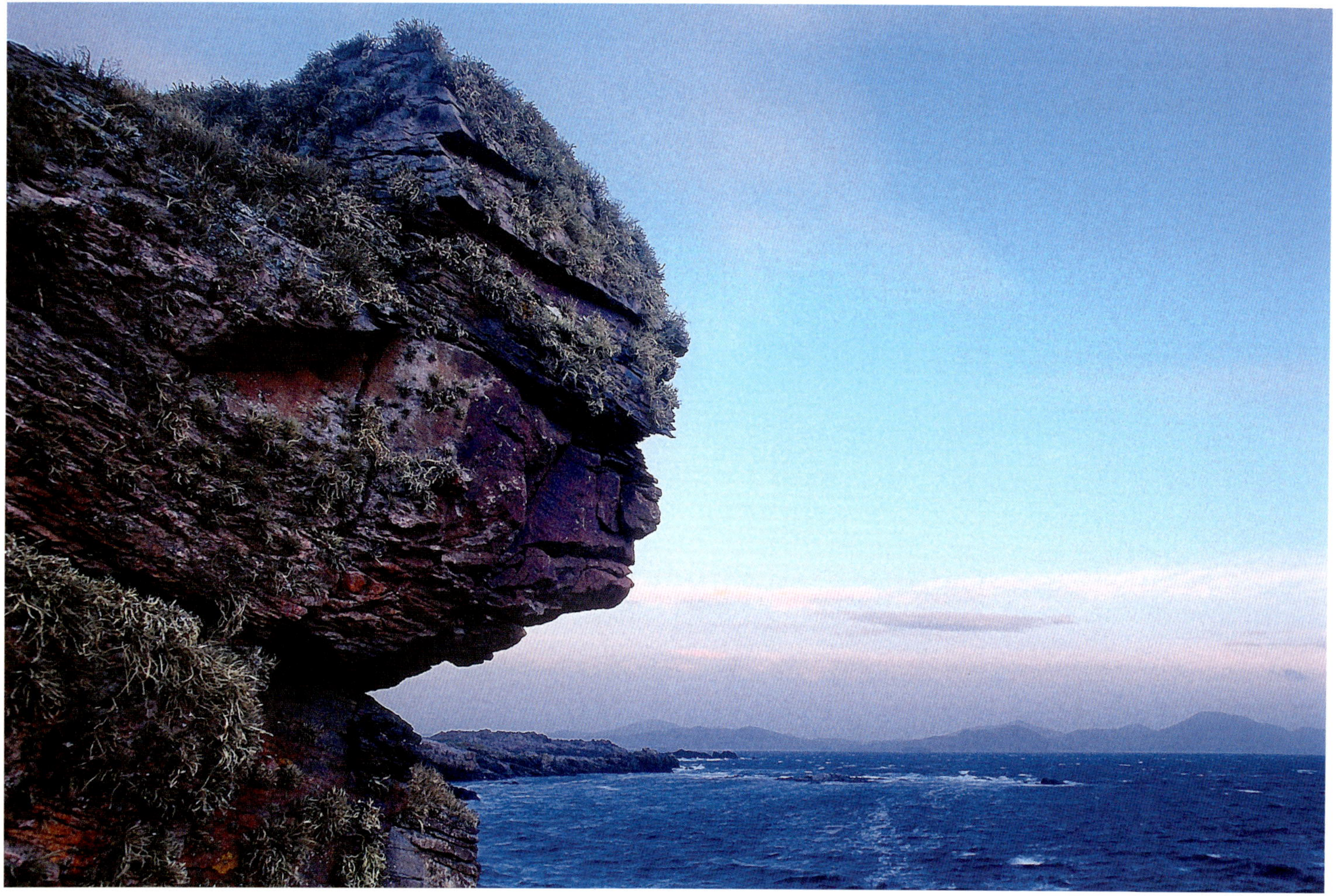

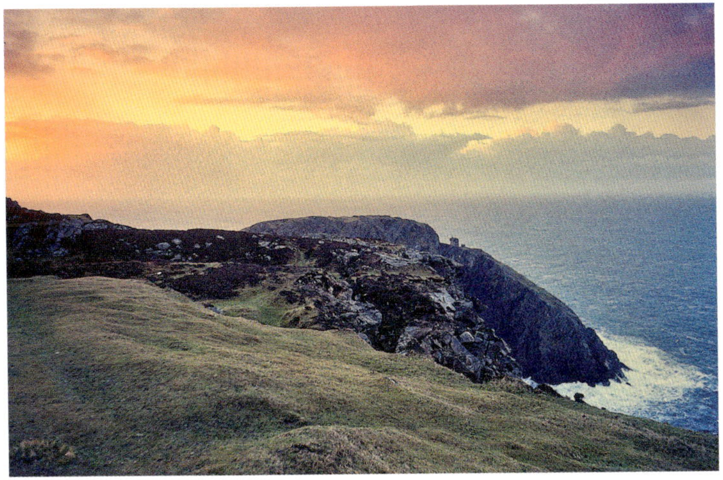

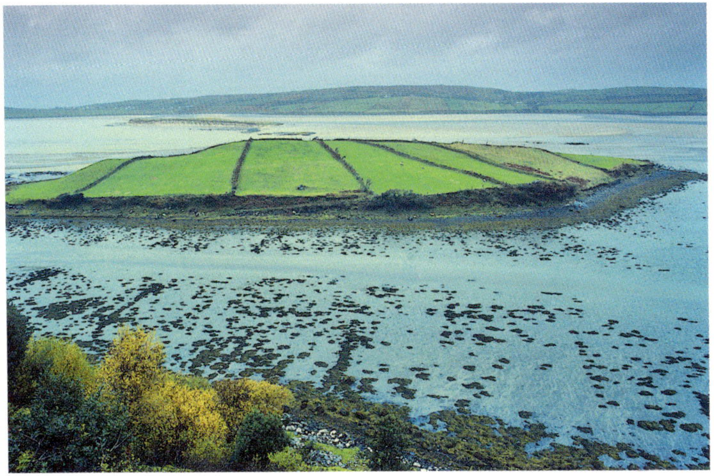

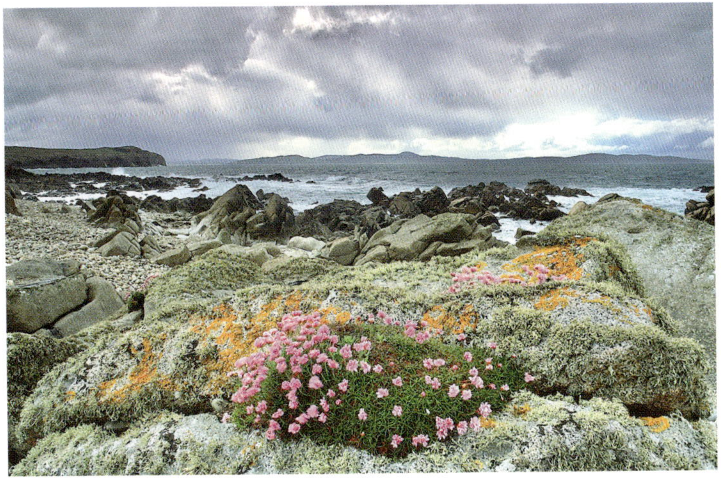

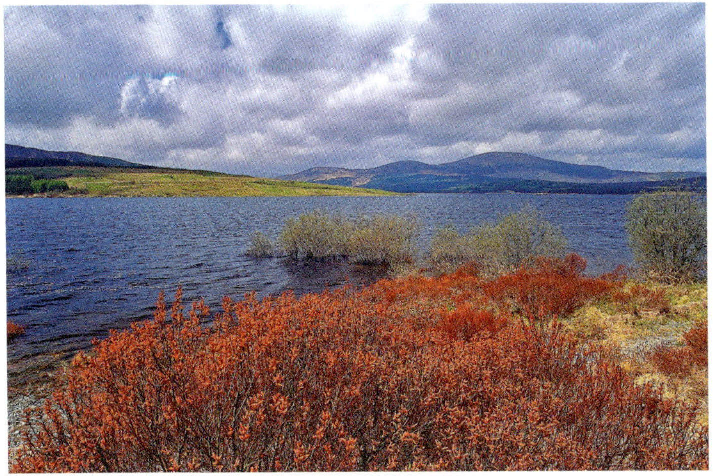

Left page: Malin Head
Right: Donegal Landscapes

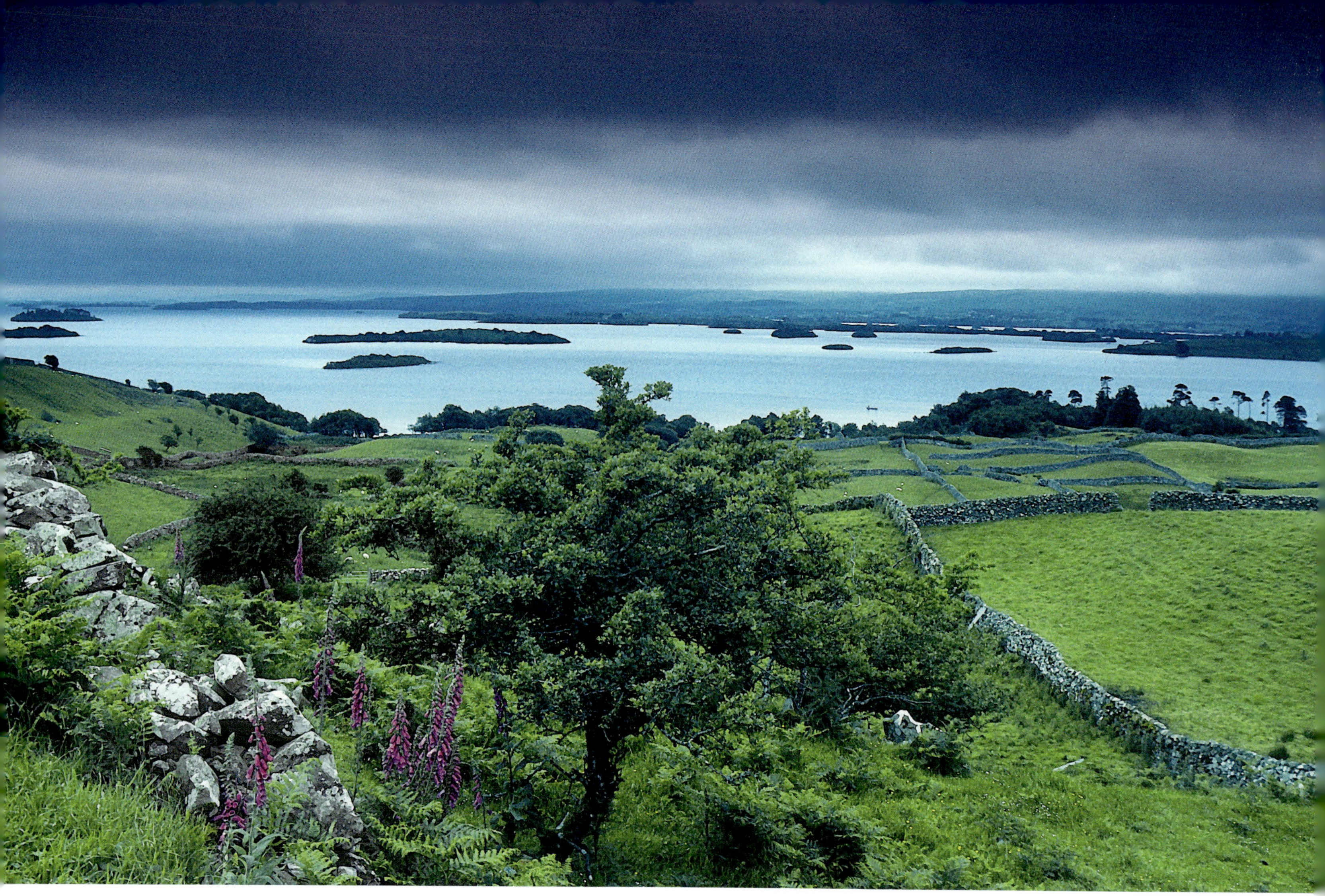

The Pangs of Ulster

Crunniuc mac Agnomain was rich and lived with his sons in a far-away place in the mountains of Ulster. One day, while he was home alone, he saw a woman running through the woods, and she was a beautiful woman, he thought. She came to his house and immediately set to work. By evening, she had everything tidied, and then she lay with him. She stayed on, and during that time, there was no lack of food, clothing, or anything else in the house.

A fair was being held in Ulster and everyone went, including Crunniuc dressed in his finest clothes and in high spirits.

"It would be better not to boast or say anything," the woman warned.

"Why would I boast?" he asked and set off.

At the end of the day, the king's chariot and horses were brought to the field, and the people said that nothing was faster than those horses.

"My wife is faster," Crunniuc said.

Immediately, he was brought before the king, who sent a messenger to fetch the woman.

"It is hard for me to go with you to help my husband," she said, "for I am with child."

"Hard? If you do not come, he will die."

When they reached the fairground, her labor pains began. "Help me," the woman pleaded. "Wait until my child is born." But she found no mercy.

"Very well," she said, and then she raced against the chariot of the king. When she reached the end of the field, she gave birth to twins, a son and a daughter.

"I am Macha," she said, "the daughter of Sainrith mac Imbaith, and this place shall forever bear the name of my children: Emain Macha–the Twins of Macha. And all those who heard my cry shall suffer from the same pangs in the time of their greatest need."

From then on, the men of Ulster were stricken with labor pains whenever they needed their strength the most. Only the boys, the women, and Cú Chulainn, the Hound of Ulster, were spared.

Left page: Lough Corrib

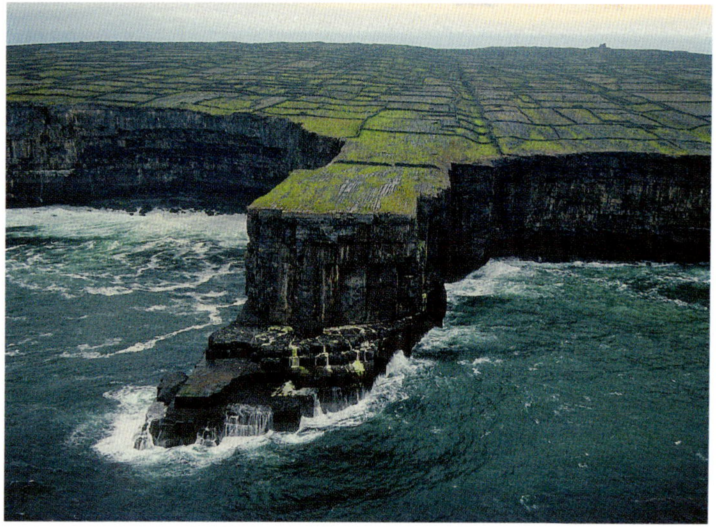

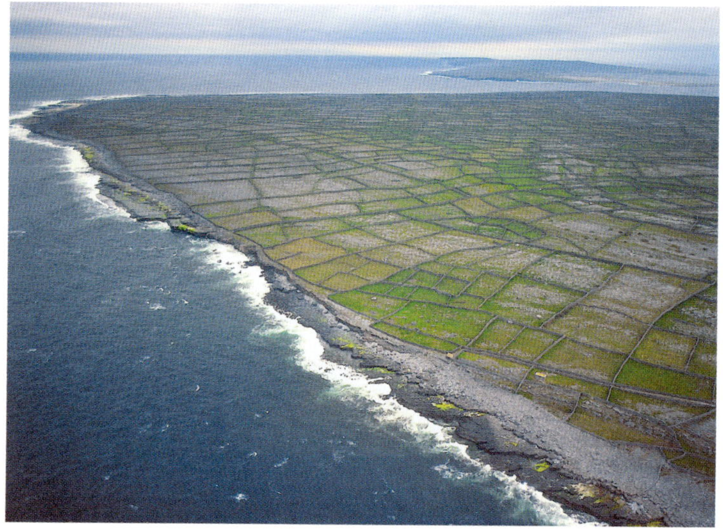

Left and right: Aran Islands

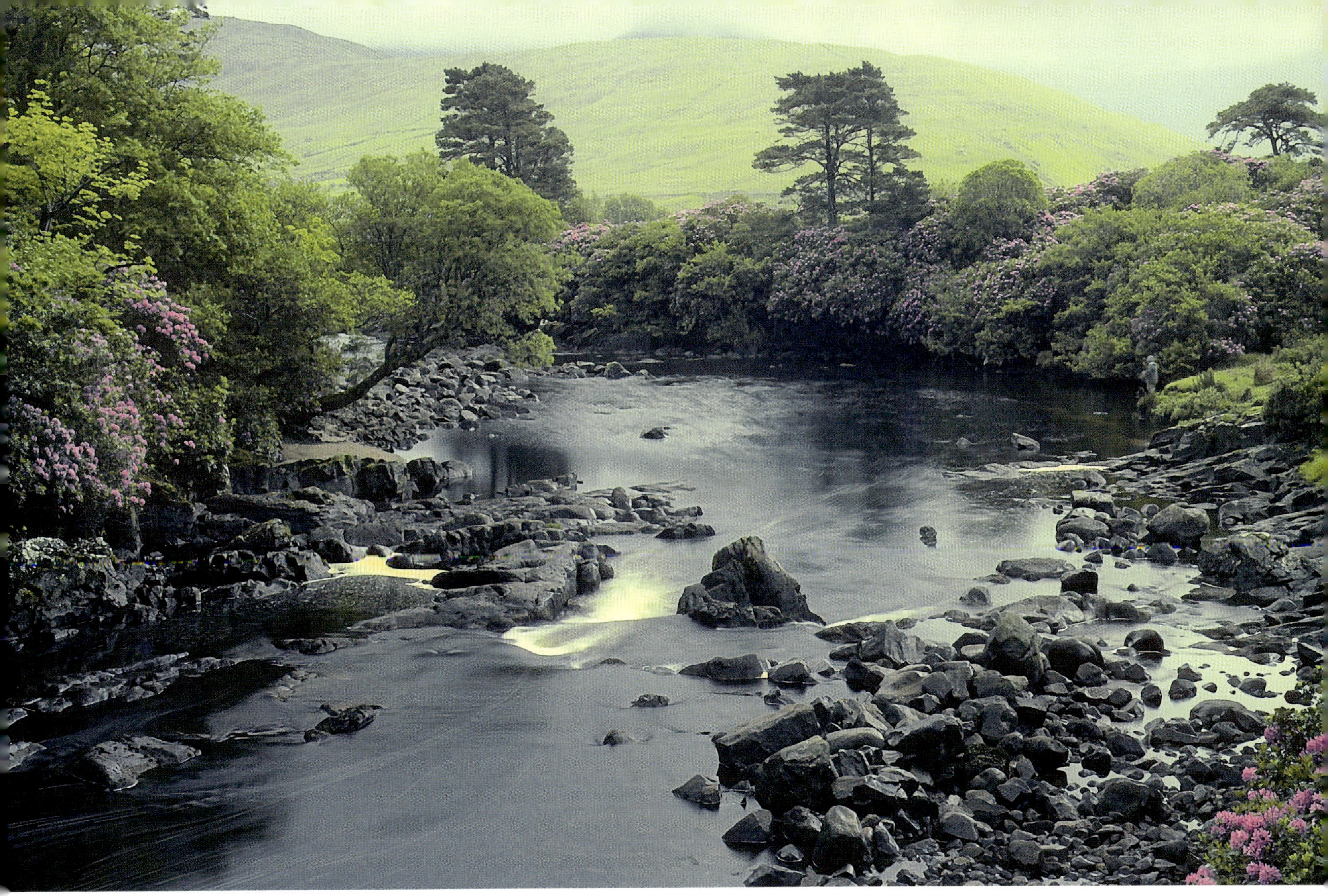

Erriff River

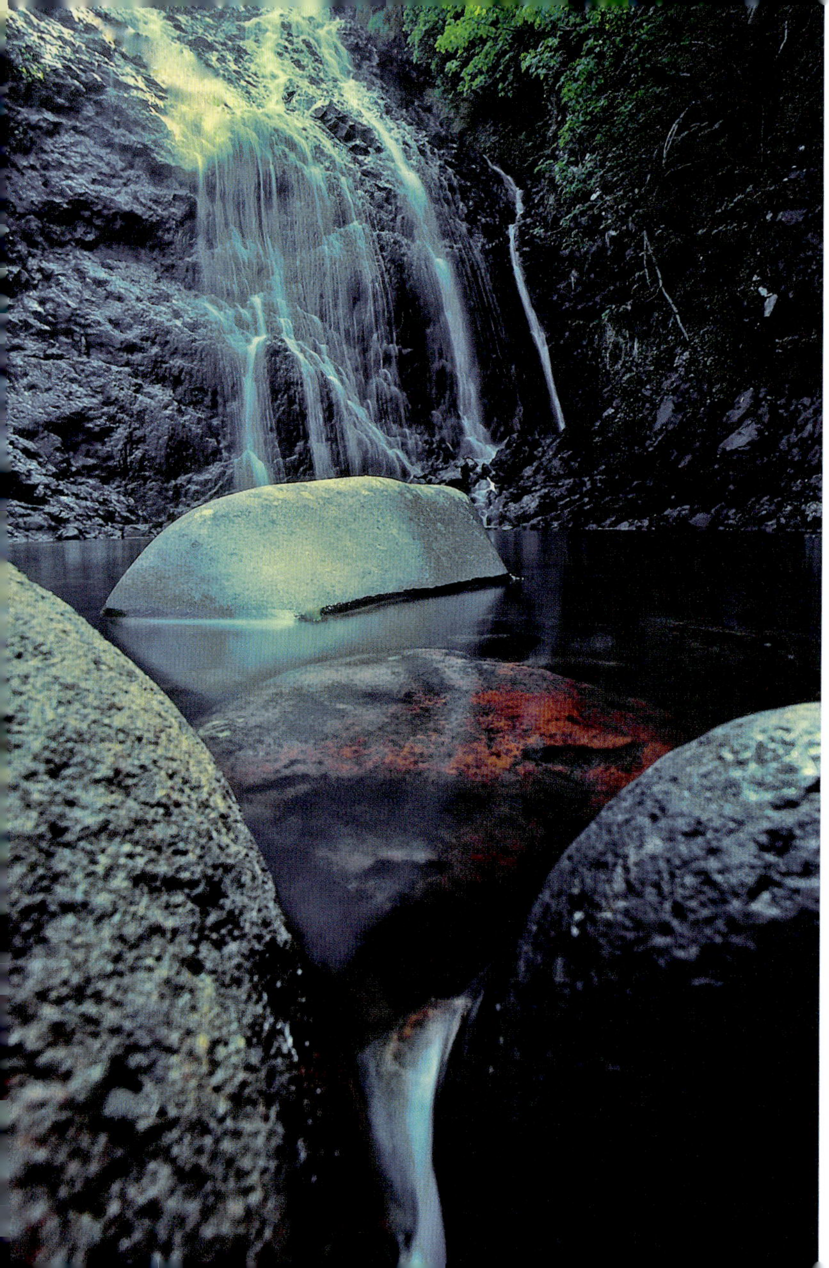

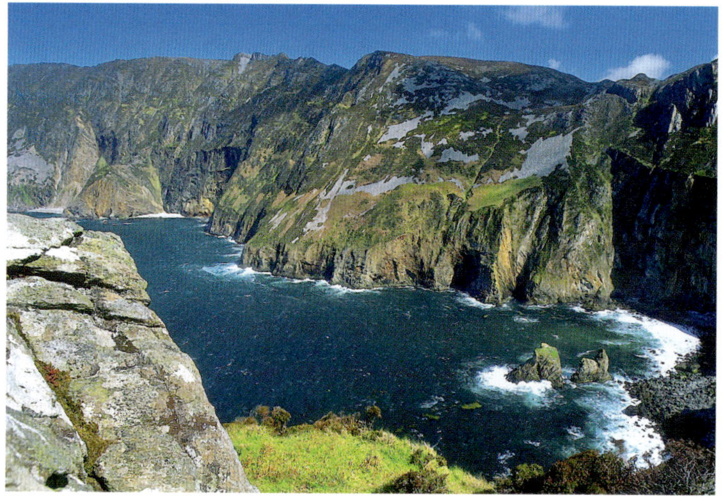

Left: At Loch Na Fooey
Right: Slieve League, Donegal

A Hero's Conceptions

A flock of birds was eating the pastures in the plain of Emain down to the ground, and the men of Ulster mounted their chariots to chase them away —nine flights of birds, each pair linked by a silver chain—and Deichtine, the sister of Conchobar, drove his royal chariot. The birds flew over the hills to the South, and the men of Ulster followed them until they reached the river Boyne. There, night and snow forced them to take shelter in a little hut. A couple who lived there made them welcome. While the men ate and drank, the woman of the house gave birth to a boy, and Deichtine nursed the child. The next morning, the hut and the couple were gone, so Deichtine took the baby with her to Emain Macha, as if it were her own. She was very sad when it died.

Thirsty from lamenting her loss, she asked for a drink of water. From the cup, a tiny thing slipped into her mouth, and she swallowed it. That night, she dreamed of a man who said he was Lugh, the bright one, the rightful, the skillful, the one with the long arm, and that he had slept with her down South in the little hut. The boy she had nursed was his, and now she was pregnant with the very same child, and it should be called Setanta.

As Deichtine grew heavy with child, the people of Ulster talked about not knowing the father, and some said that Conchobar himself, in his drunkenness ... So he gave his sister in marriage to Sualdam mac Roich. But she was ashamed to share his bed, pregnant as she was, and got sick until the life in her spilled away. She was whole again, a virgin, when she went to her husband, and as she got pregnant again, she gave birth to a son and called him Setanta.

The men of Ulster argued over who was going to raise the child; every one of them wanted it. Eventually, Conchobar brought them before Morann, the judge. He decided that the boy should be raised by all of them to become a chariot-fighter, a prince as well as a sage, and he said that the boy would be cherished by many and win all their battles.

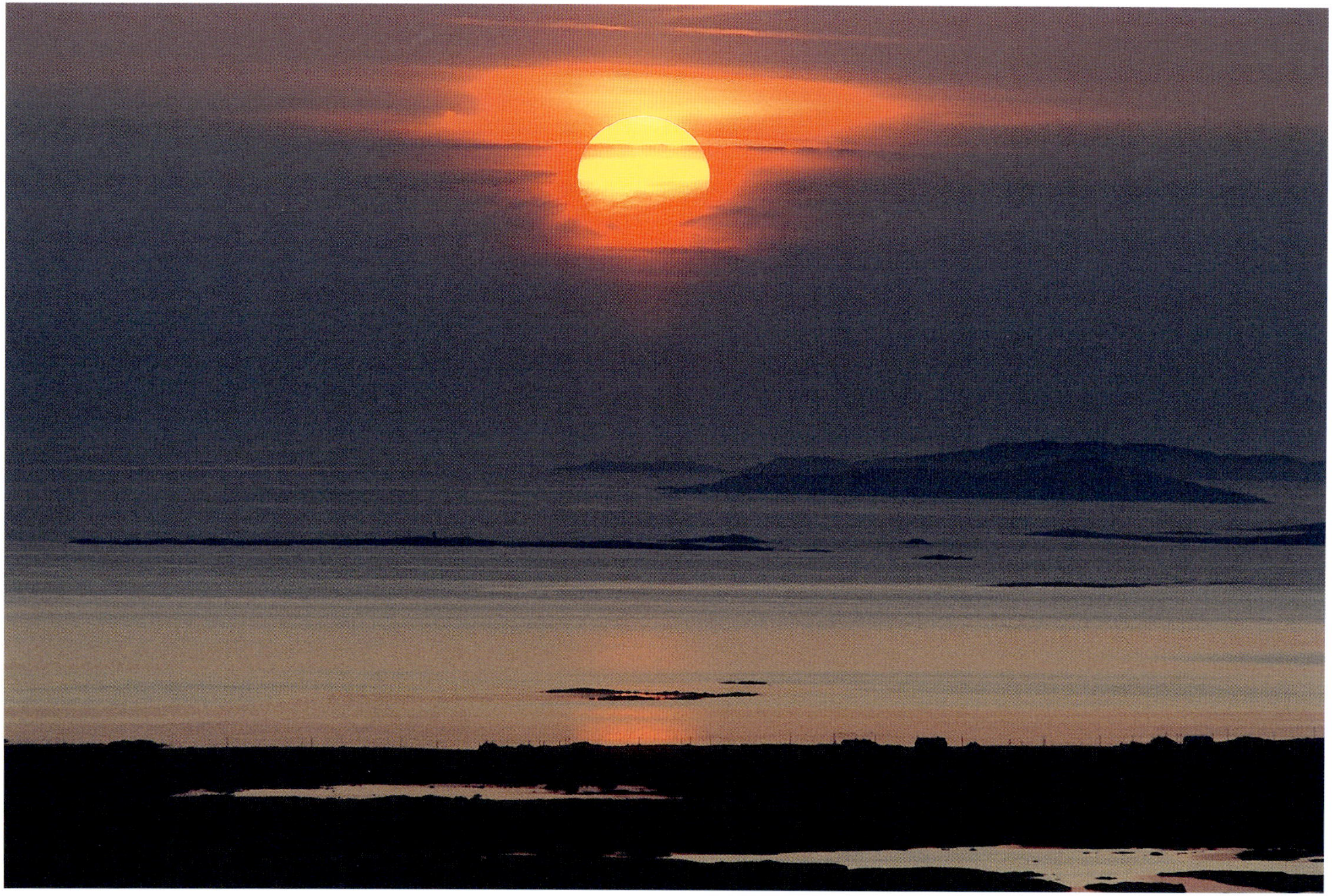

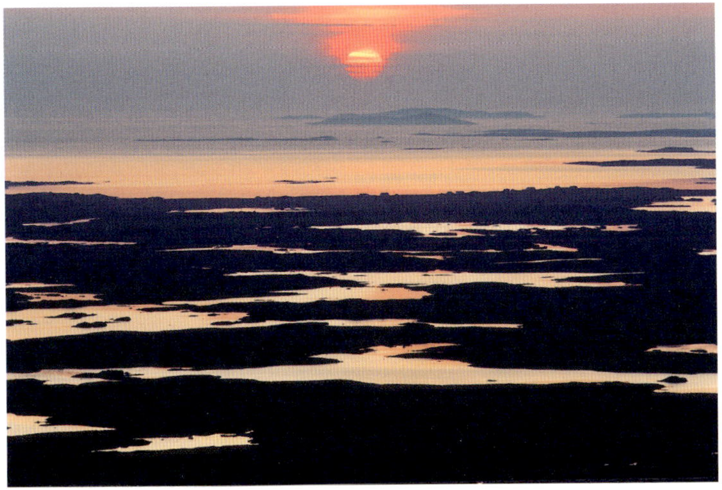

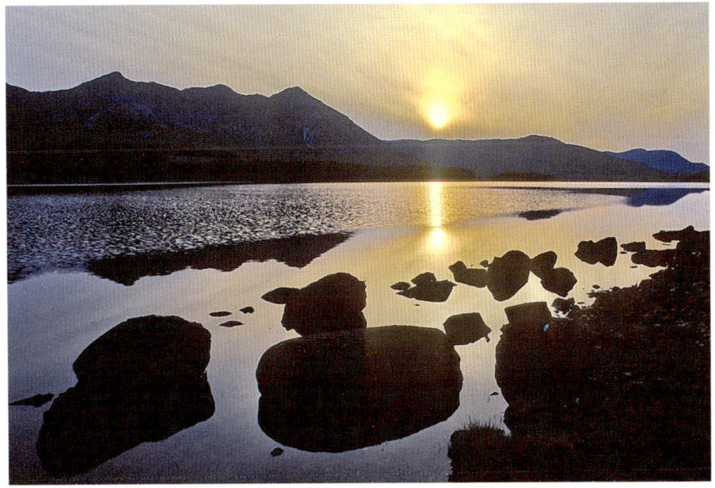

Left page and left: Ballyconneely Bay
Right: Lough Inagh

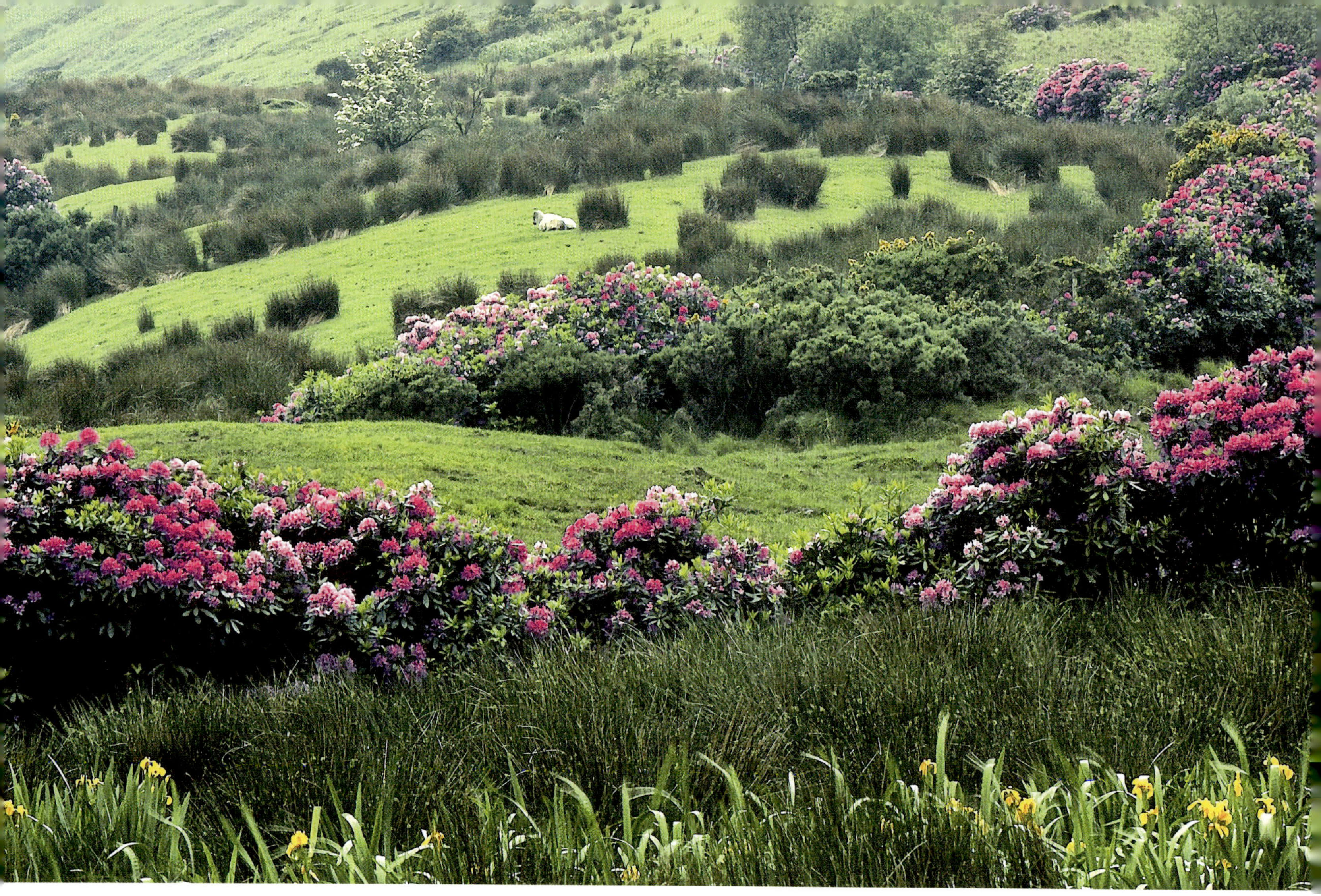

A Hero's Childhood

In his sixth year, the boy Setanta overheard Cathbad, the druid of Emain Macha, talk to his pupils.

"What is this day good for?" one of them asked.

"Whoever takes up arms for the first time today will perform great deeds...," Cathbad replied, and at once Setanta ran to the king to demand his weapons. "... and will have a short life," Cathbad finished his prediction.

"What is this day good for?" one of the pupils asked Cathbad sometime later.

"Whoever mounts a chariot for the first time today will perform great deeds."

At once, Setanta ran to the king and demanded his chariot. "And," Cathbad continued, "his name will never be forgotten in Ireland."

On his first outing with his chariot, Setanta caused all kinds of mischief. He killed the three sons of Nechta Scéne: the Cunning, the Deceitful, and the Greedy, and brought back their heads. Behind his chariot, he led a wild stag, and over his chariot flew a flock of wild swans. When the men of Ulster saw that, they grew fearful. So Conchobar sent out the women. They bared their breasts, and the boy lowered his eyes with shame. The first vat of water into which they plunged him burst, the second just heated up, and when he emerged from the third, Queen Mugain gave him a blue cloak with a silver brooch and set him on the king›s lap. That was going to be his place for all time.

Culann, the blacksmith, invited Conchobar, the king, to dine, and since the smith was poor, the king took only fifty men with him. On the way, they saw Setanta playing ball against the boys of Emain. Three times fifty, he struck down in his seventh year.

"Come with us," said Conchobar.

"First, I have to finish the game," Setanta explained.

Later, when the boy arrived at the blacksmith's house, Conchobar had forgotten about him and was already seated at the meal. The smith had let loose his guard dog. It took three chains to hold the beast, with three men on each chain. The boy was still tossing the ball and striking it with his stick. The dog lunged at him, and the men of Ulster thought he was lost. But the boy threw the ball into the dog's mouth, and the ball tore out its entrails.

"You are welcome here," said the blacksmith, "as the son of your mother, but for me, it is a bitter day. Without my dog, my house is defenseless, for it guarded my life, my honor, and my cattle."

"I will train a new dog for you," replied the boy, "from the same pack, and until it is grown, I will guard your life, your honor, and your cattle myself."

At that, Cathbad the druid said, "Cú Chulainn shall be your name from now on, the Hound of the Blacksmith."

Left page: Connemara

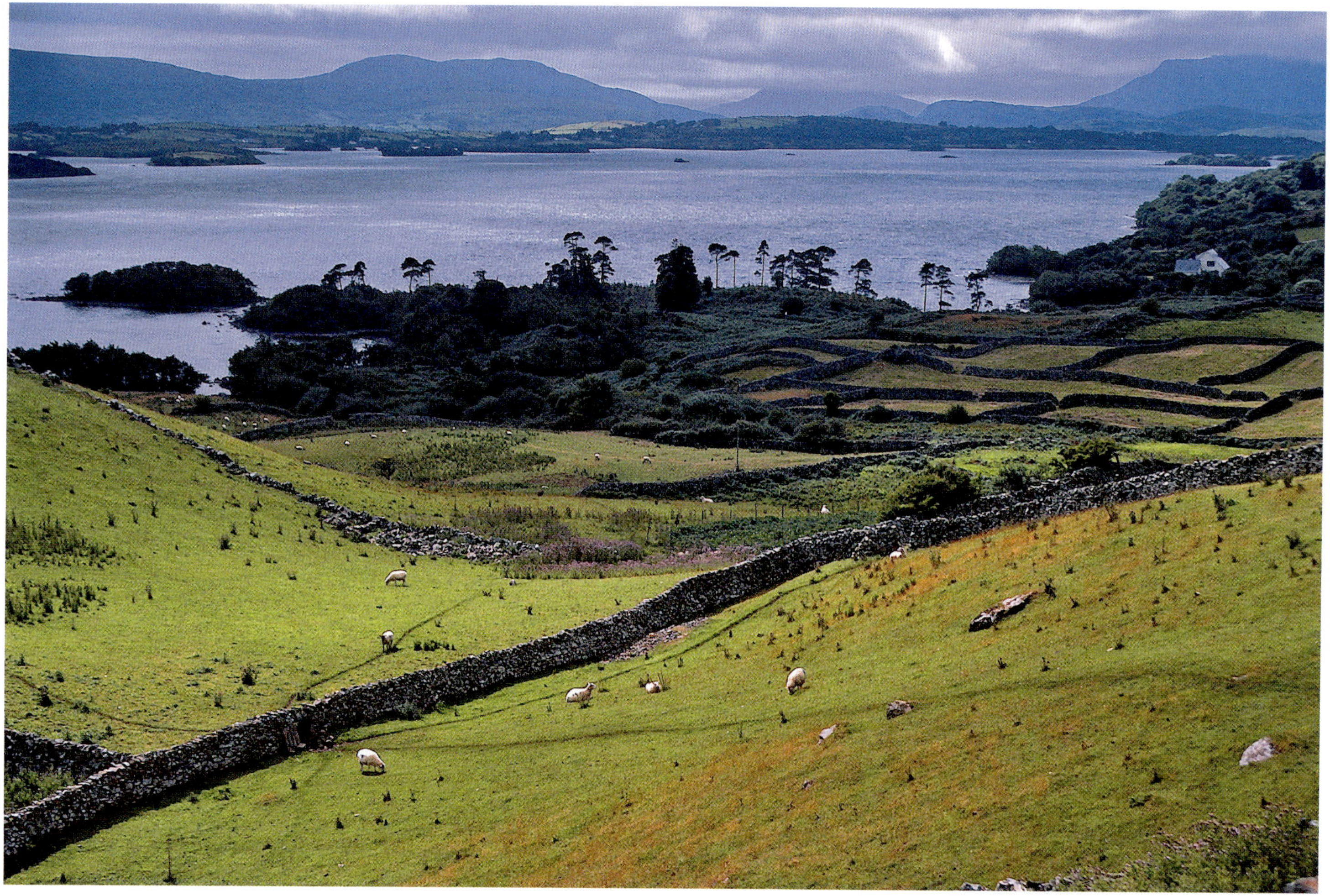

Cú Chulainn's Courtship

The men of Ulster were drinking and boasting, juggling apples (nine of them in the air, only one in your hand), throwing javelins across the hall, balancing full cups and other stuff on their swords' edges. Cú Chulainn, with his fair face, his fine figure, outdid them all, and the women were raving. "We'd better find a wife for this youngster," the men said, "before he ruins our daughters and brings our wives into disrepute." So, nine messengers were sent out to look for a suitable match for Cú Chulainn, but after a year, they returned empty-handed.

One day, Cú Chulainn went out by himself to meet Emer, the daughter of Forgall the Cunning. She sat in the garden with a troop of foster sisters, practicing embroidery and fine stitching. She recognized him, of course.

"May your road be blessed," Cú Chulainn greeted her, and when he caught sight of her cleavage, he added: "I see a country where I could rest my weapon."

"No man will travel this country until he has killed a hundred men at every fort along the river."

"I will rest my weapon in this country," Cú Chulainn said.

"No man will travel this country," Emer repeated, "until ..." She made a list of other fancy tasks that came to her head.

"I will rest my weapon in this country," Cú Chulainn insisted, and she extended her list.

"It's a deal," he said and went home.

"The Warped One," Forgall groaned when the girls told him about the conversation Emer had in the garden. Cú Chulainn was known for the ghastly spasms that distorted his body before battle. Forgall disguised himself as a Gaulish noble and brought wine and valuables to Conchobar as a tribute. He was made welcome at the court, and while watching the warriors performing their feats, he praised Cú Chulainn's skills but added that the young man would profit greatly from a bit of training with Scáthach, the Shadowy, in Alba across the sea. The very next morning, Cú Chulainn set out, not without saying goodbye to Emer, of course, who told him about her father's ruse to keep them apart. They promised to remain faithful to each other and pure until they met again.

Left page: Lough Corrib

The Training with Scáthach

Along his way to Scáthach, Cú Chulainn learned a few tricks, like walking on flagstones through fire until his soles were black, and how to coil on the spikes of a spear without bleeding. Over in Alba, he first met Scáthach's pupils. They told him she was on her island and that the pupils' bridge would take him to her. Three times the aspiring hero tried to cross the bridge, but as soon as he stepped onto one end, the other end flew up at him and threw him on his back. Eventually, the spasm warped his body, and with his salmon-leap, he reached the middle of the bridge and from there, the other end, so quickly that it had no time to fly up at him.

"Clearly," Scáthach said, "this boy already got some training," and sent her daughter Uathach out to meet him.

The girl returned with a glint in her eyes. "Clearly," Scáthach said, "the boy pleases you."

Uathach nodded.

"Then take him to bed tonight and sleep with him."

As darkness fell, everybody could hear them, and Scáthach's guards went for Cú Chulainn, but he defeated them all. After three days, Uathach explained to Cú Chulainn that he needed to leap into the yew tree where Scáthach rested and put his sword between her breasts until she promised him to train him, give him a dowry for his marriage, and tell him his future. And that he did.

Scáthach and her two sons went against Aife, the hardest woman warrior in the world, and Scáthach gave Cú Chulainn a sleeping draught to keep him safe. But he woke after an hour and joined the battle. Aife challenged Scáthach to single combat. Cú Chulainn insisted on being Scáthach's champion, and he fought Aife on the rope of feats until she had smashed all his weapons down to the stump of his sword. "Oh look," Cú Chulainn said, "your chariot with your horses and your charioteer have fallen into the valley."

Aife, who some say was no other than Scáthach's sister, looked around because she loved these two horses, the chariot, and the charioteer. In that moment, Cú Chulainn leapt at her and grabbed her breasts. As he held her to the ground, she pleaded with him, and he demanded hostages for Scáthach and to never attack her again. He also requested Aife's company in his bed this night and that she would bear him a son, whose name would be Connla.

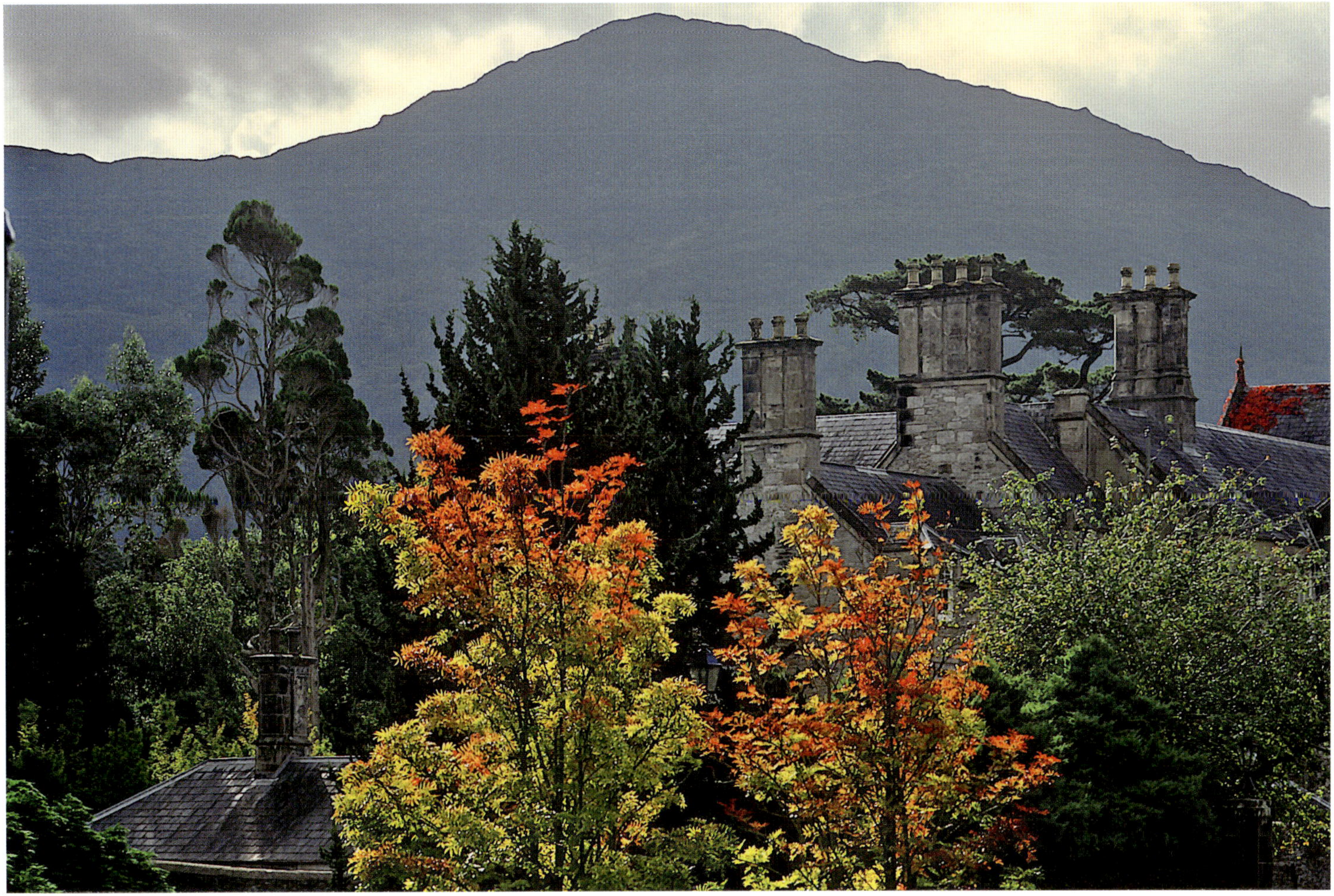

Muckross House

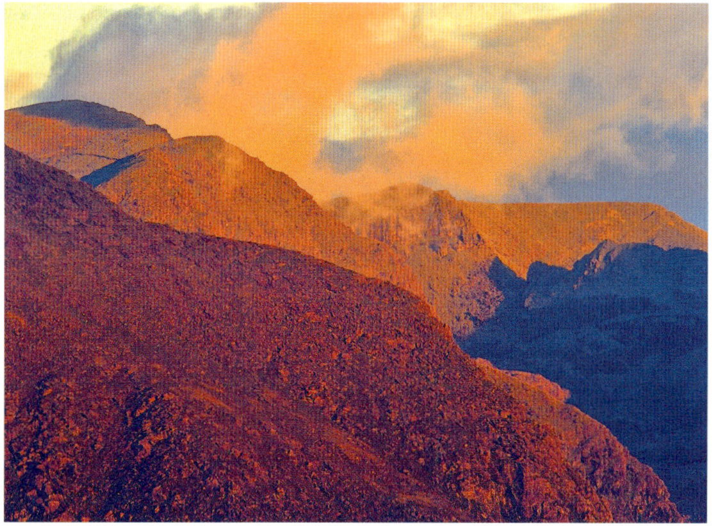

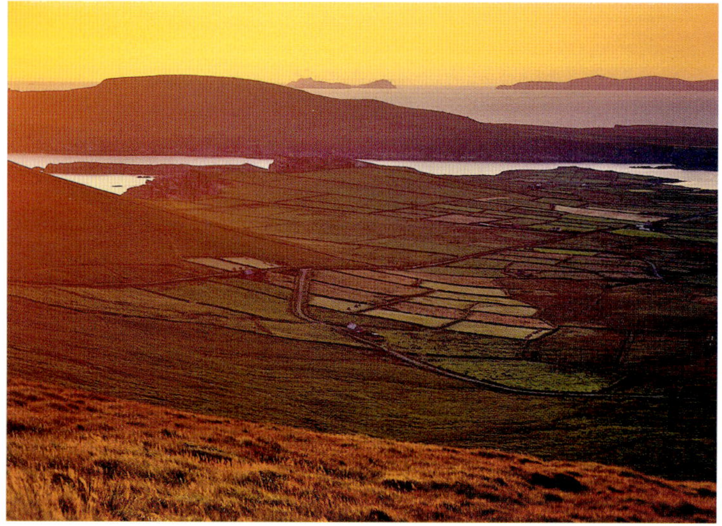

Left: MacGillycuddy's Reeks
Right: Portmagee

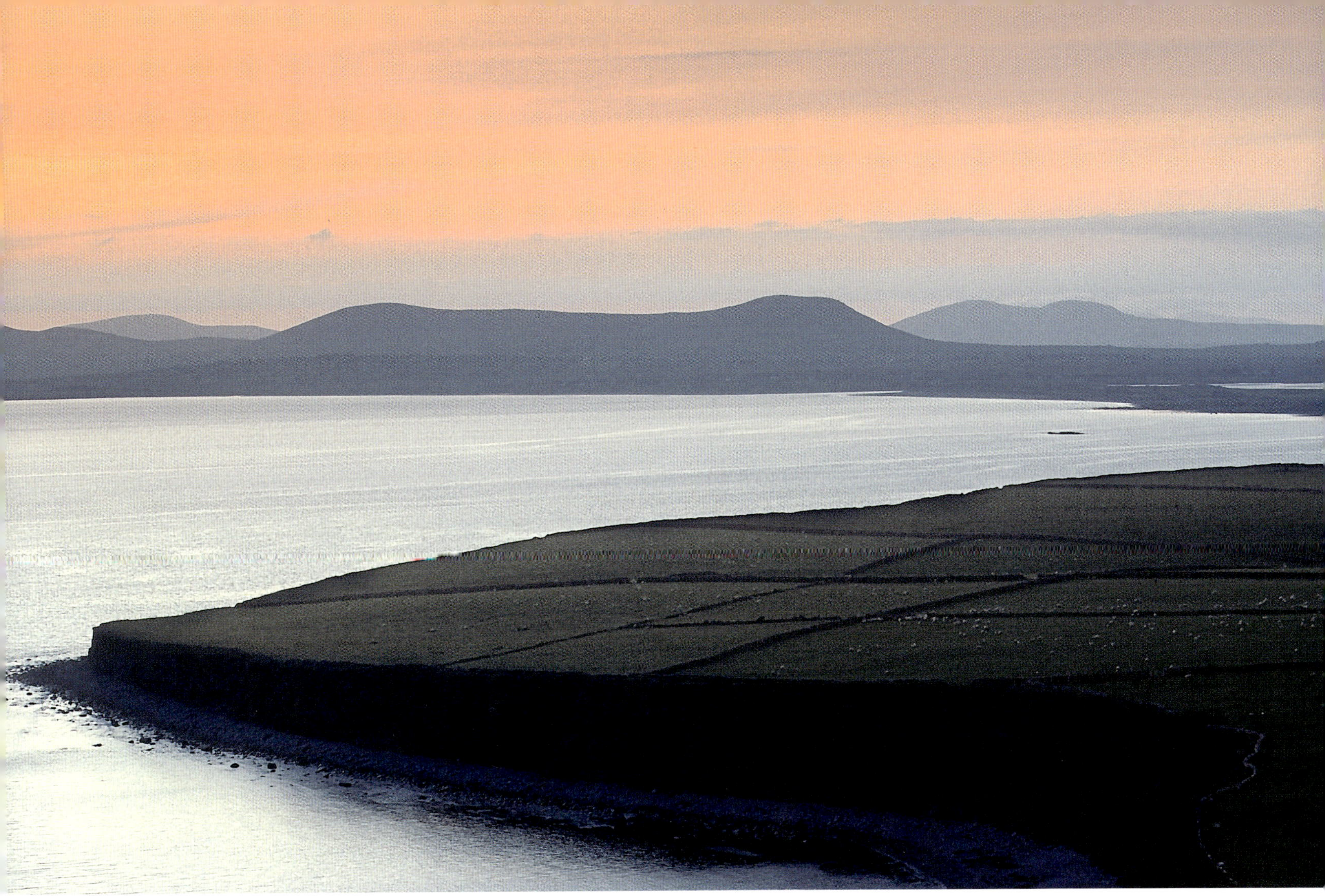

Ballinskelligs Bay

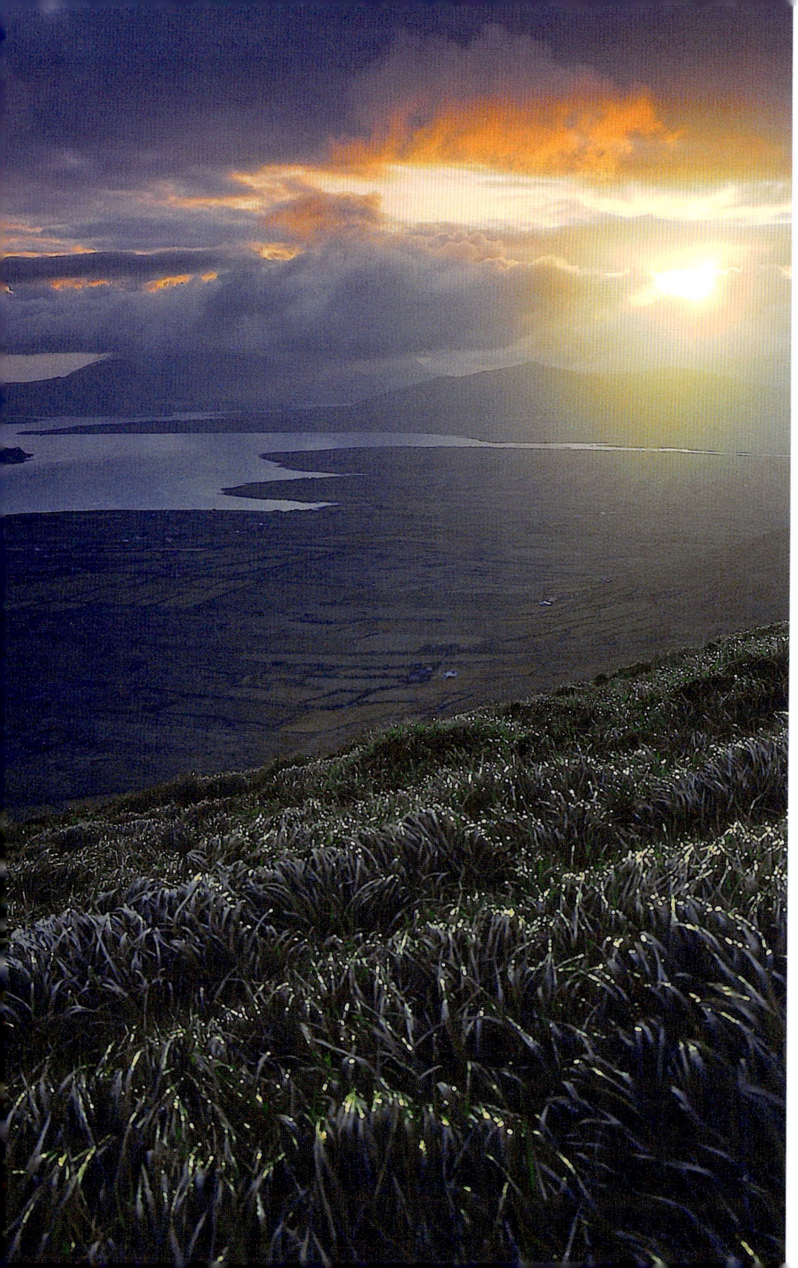

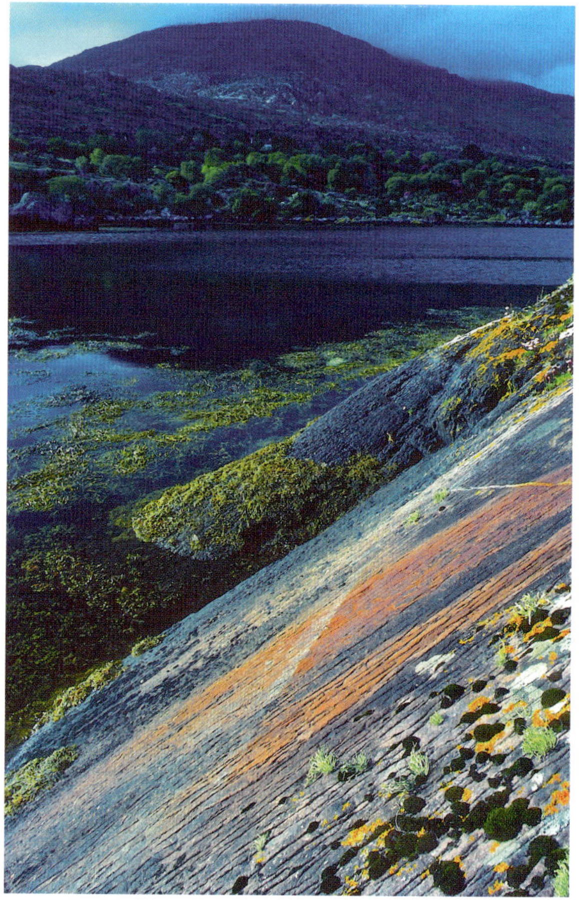

Left: Portmagee Channel
Right: Ardgroom

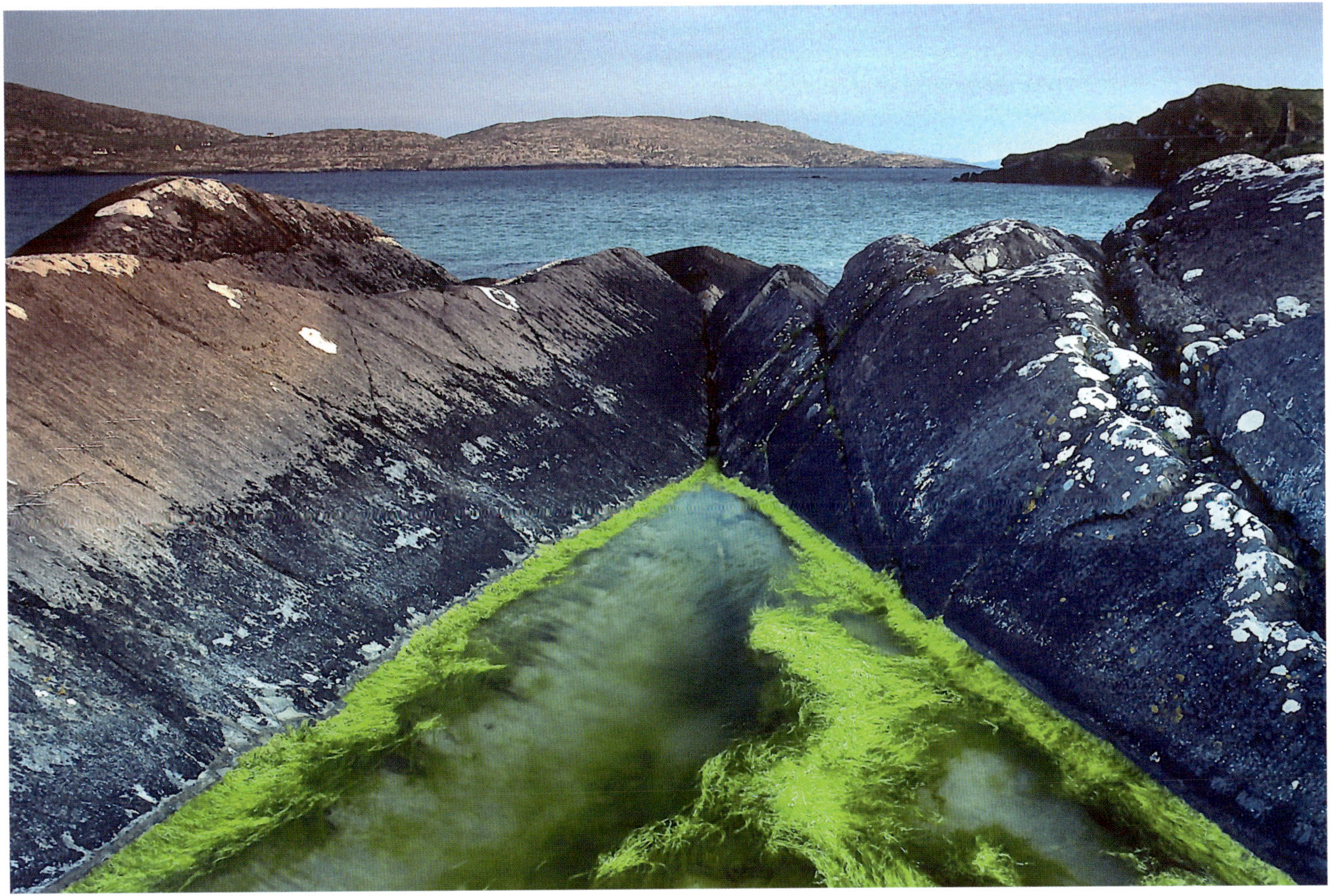

Derrynane

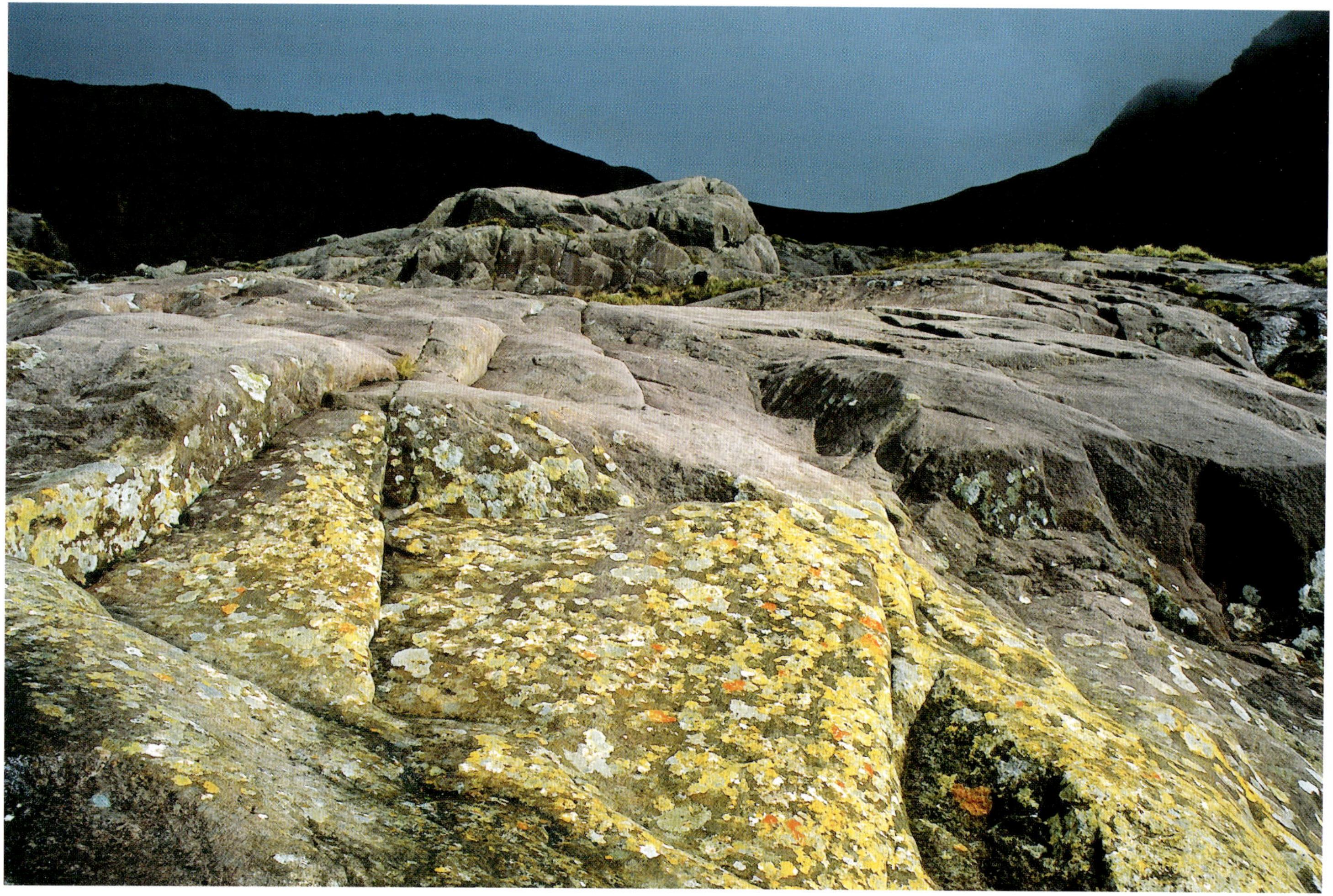

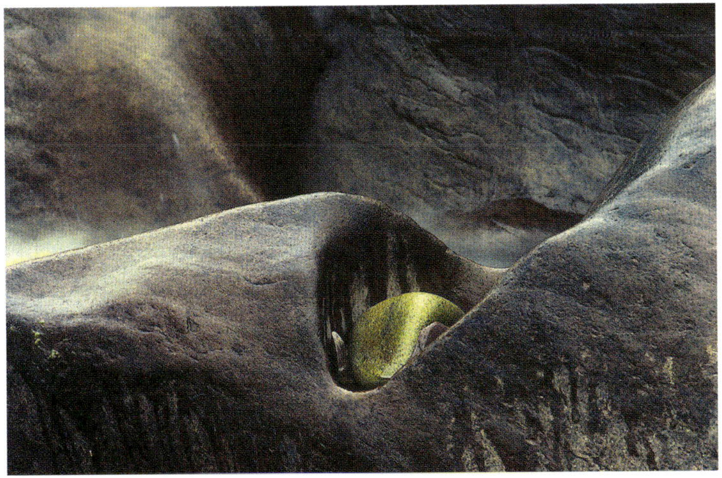

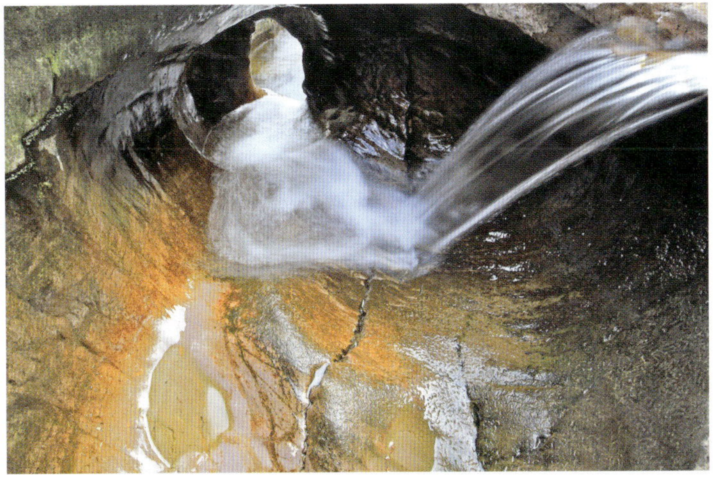

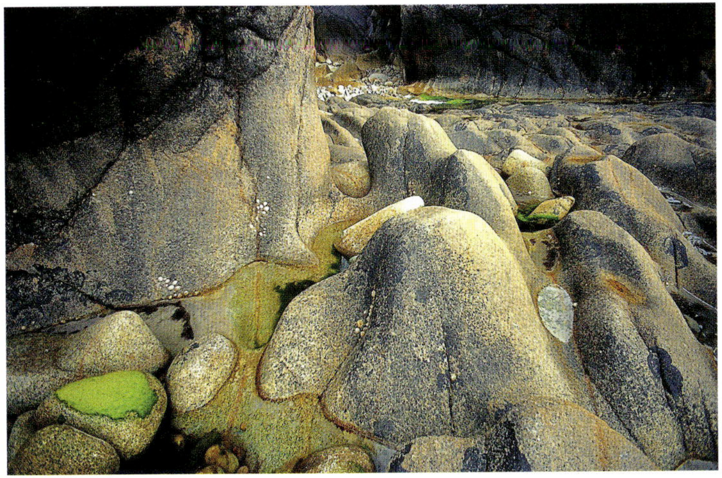

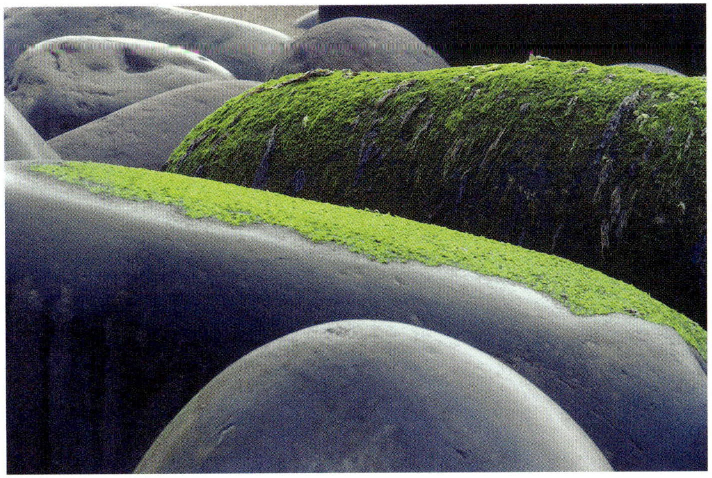

Left page: Conor Pass
Right: Sceneries shaped by water

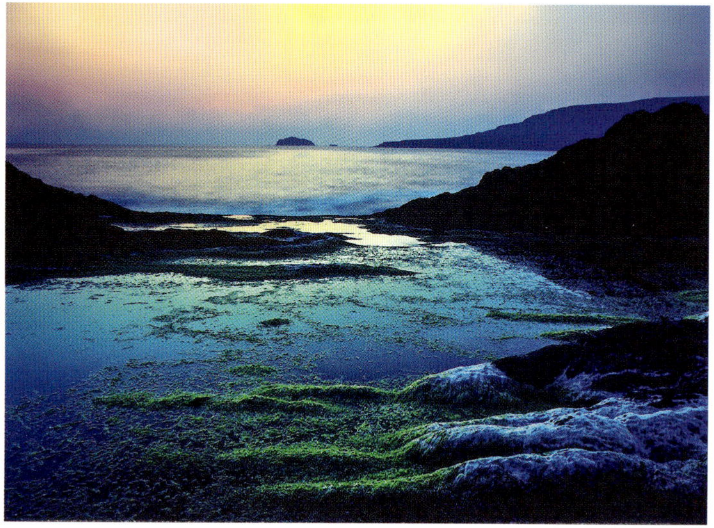

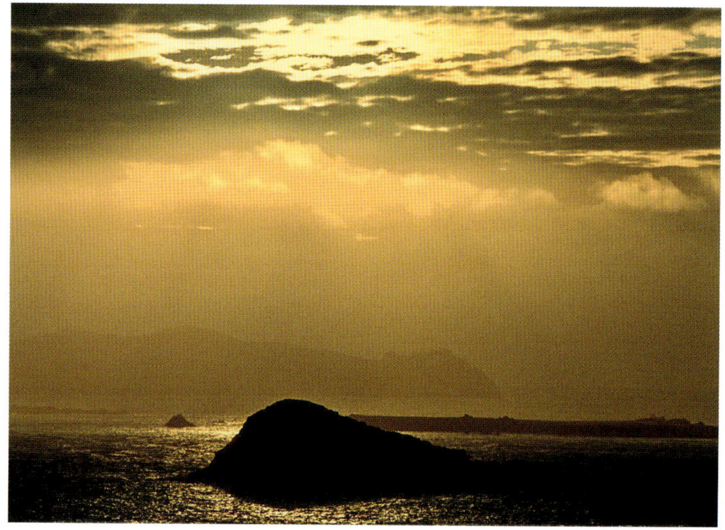

Left and right: Dingle Peninsula
Right page: Slea Head

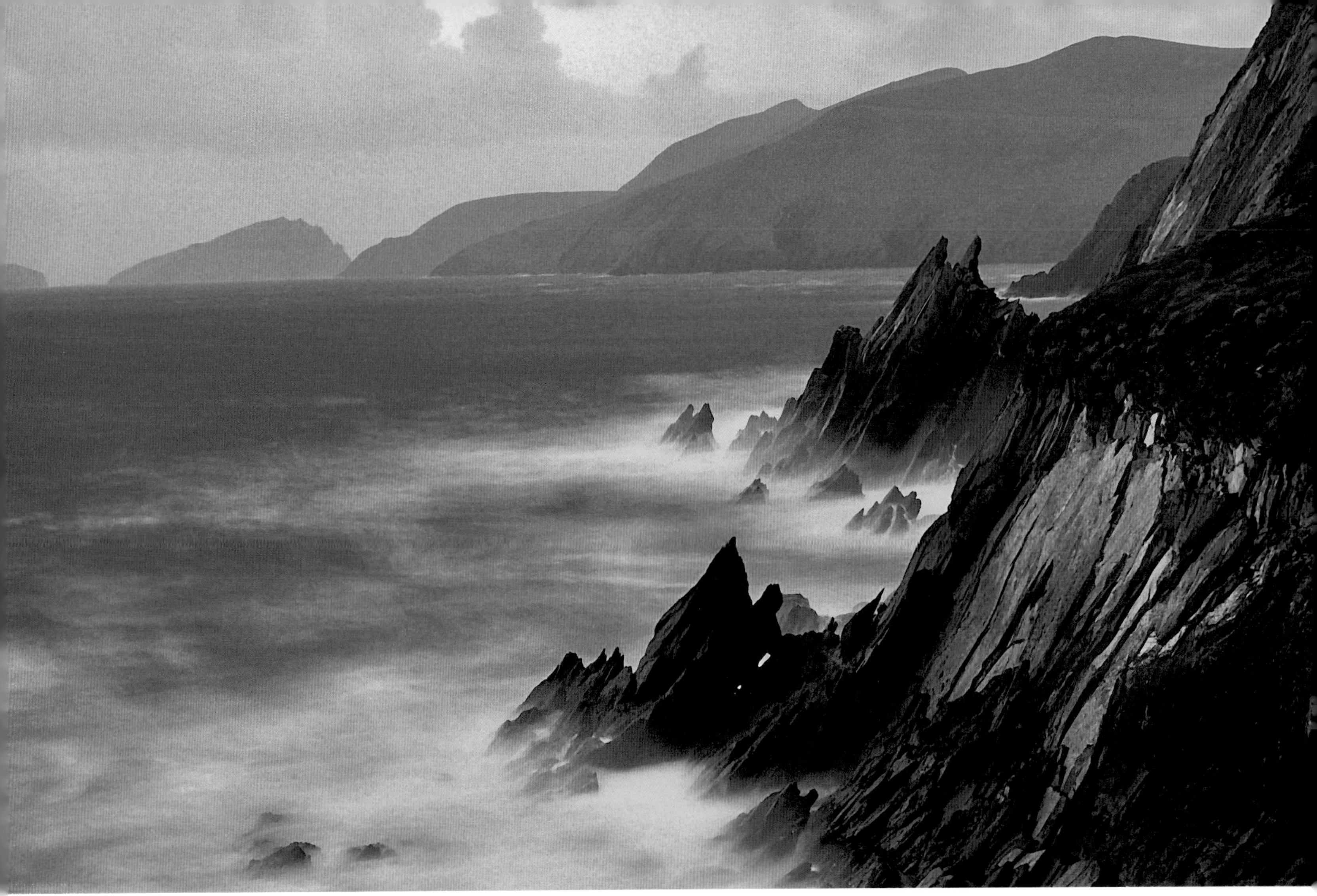

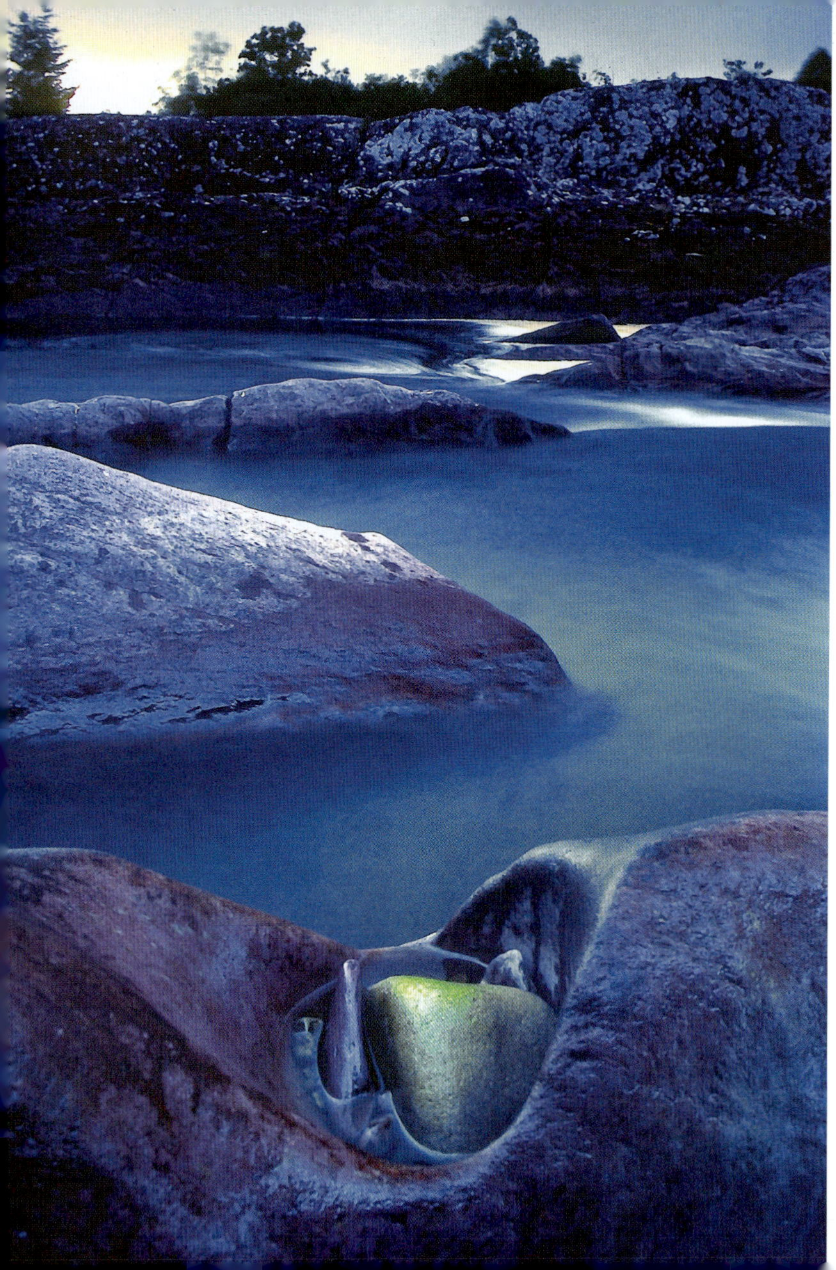

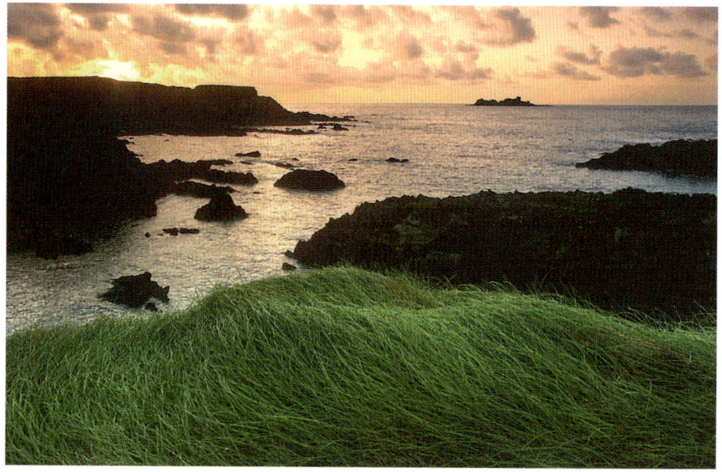

Left: River Sheen
Right: Toe Head, Southwest Coast
Right page: Gap of Dunloe

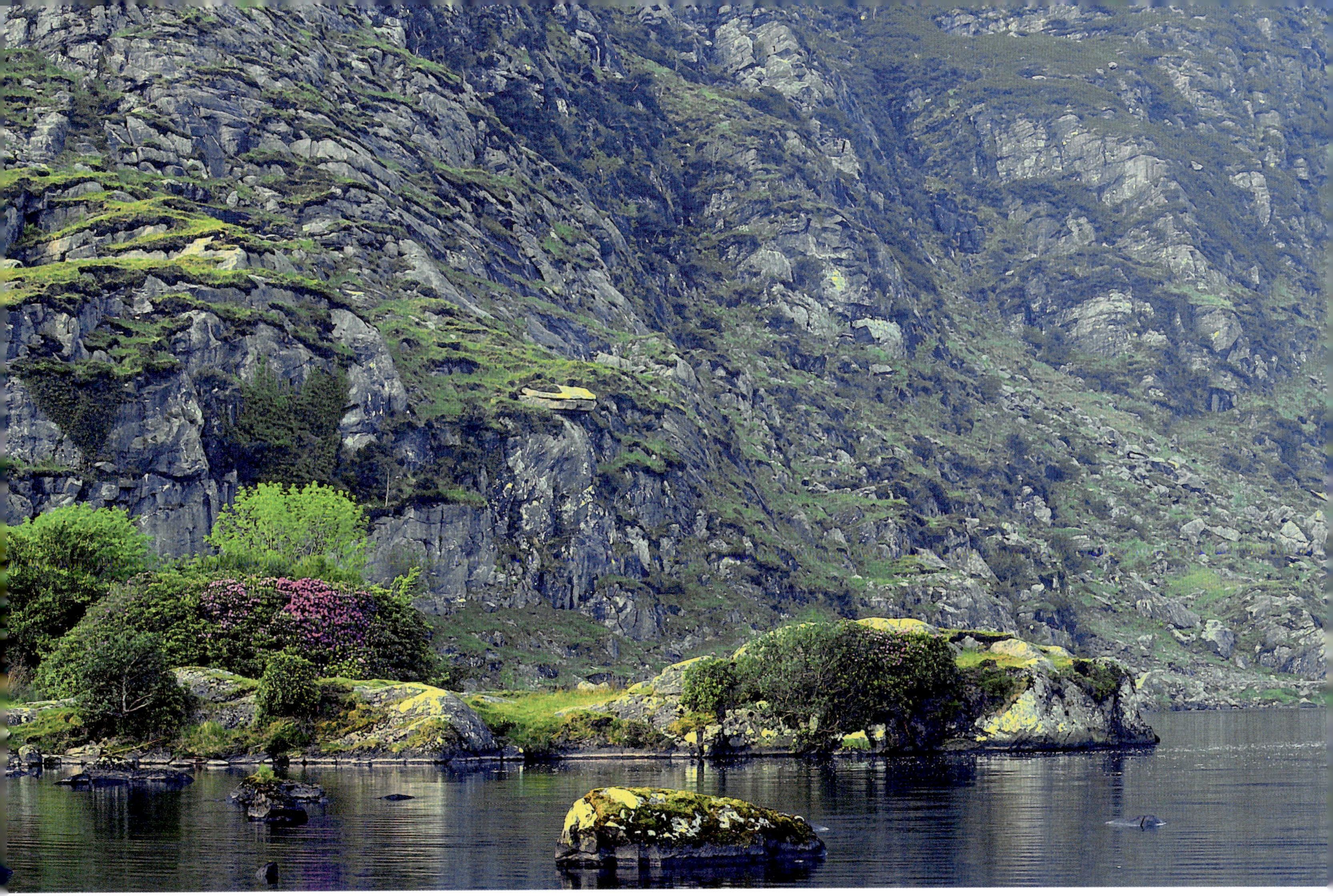

Cú Chulainn's Return

When Cú Chulainn had learned all that Scáthach could teach him, she told him his future: the names of all the men he would kill, the battles he would win, the wounds he would suffer— a life filled with triumph and women's love. Afterwards, he returned home.

Back in Emain Macha, he recounted his adventures before he went to see Emer. In his absence, Forgall had attempted to wed her to Cú Chulainn's foster brother, who was a great king. But when Emer told him that she was under Cú Chulainn's protection, he didn't dare to take her. Now, Forgall had put a guard around his fortress so strong that it took Cú Chulainn a year to get through it. Eventually, he performed his salmon-leap across the enclosures, killed every man in his way except Emer's three brothers, and made Forgall take flight and fall to his death. Then he took Emer and her weight in silver and gold and leaped back. "Not bad," she admitted, having grown tired of embroidery and fine stitching. And, on the way back to Emain Macha, it is said, Cú Chulainn accomplished the rest of the tasks on her fancy list.

There was one last hitch, however, as King Conchobar had the right to the first night with every girl in Ulster. "Cú Chulainn will not like this," Bricriu the Sour-Faced grinned. And as it happened, when the young hero heard of this, he grew so wild that the cushion burst under him, and the feathers flew all over the place.

"It's a bit of a nuisance," Cathbad, the druid, conceded. Neither could the king refuse to lie with the girl, nor would Cú Chulainn be restrained from killing him afterwards.

"We will have to find a solution", Conchobar said and sent Cú Chulainn out to gather all the cattle in the hills in order to get rid of him for a while.

The men of Ulster discussed the matter and decided that Emer should sleep in Conchobar's bed that night, but so should Fergus and Cathbad in order to protect Cú Chulainn's honor. They promised Cú Chulainn their blessings if he consented, and he—still panting from gathering all the cattle —did so. Ever after, he slept with his wife and they never parted again, it is said, but maybe just for the benefit of a happy ending.

Left above: River Sheen
Right above: Moll's Gap
Left below: Flowering splendour in the south-west
Right below: Ancient Forest at Derrynane

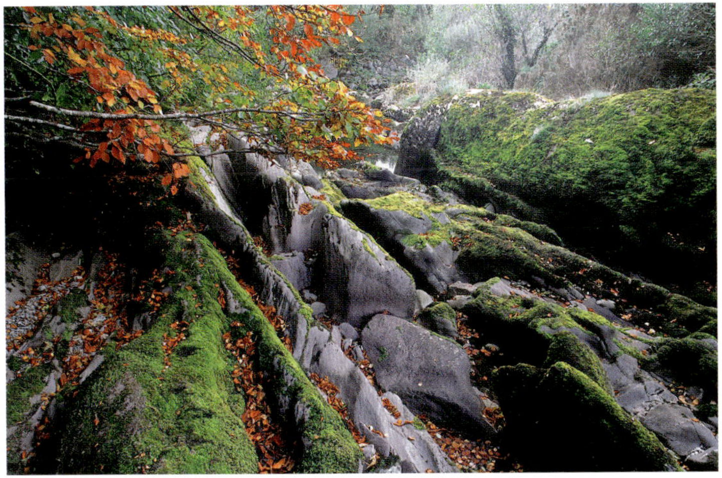

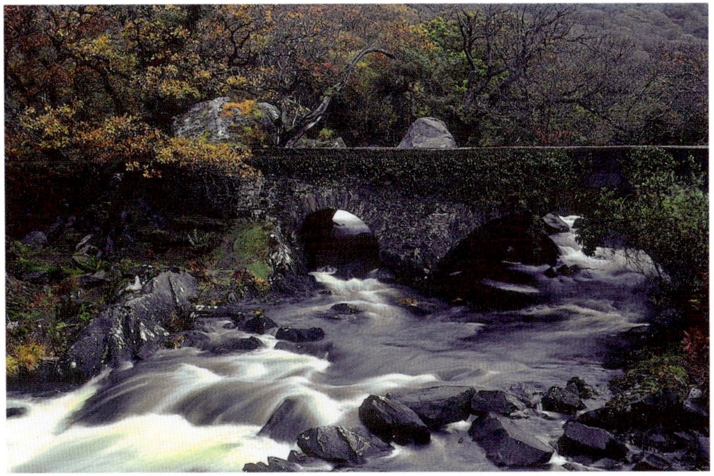

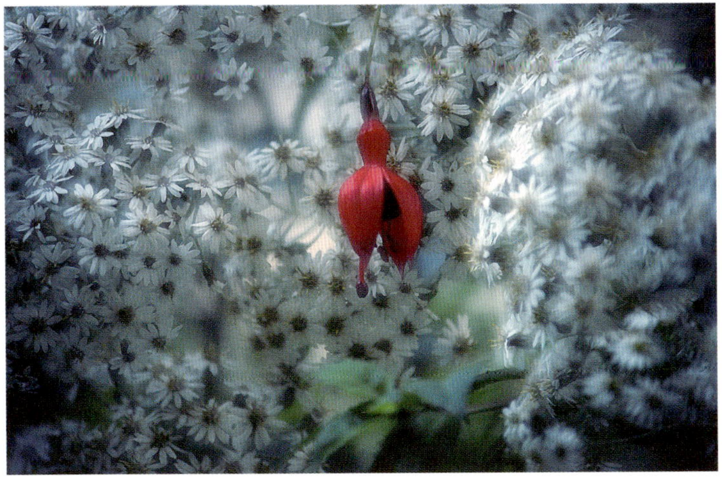

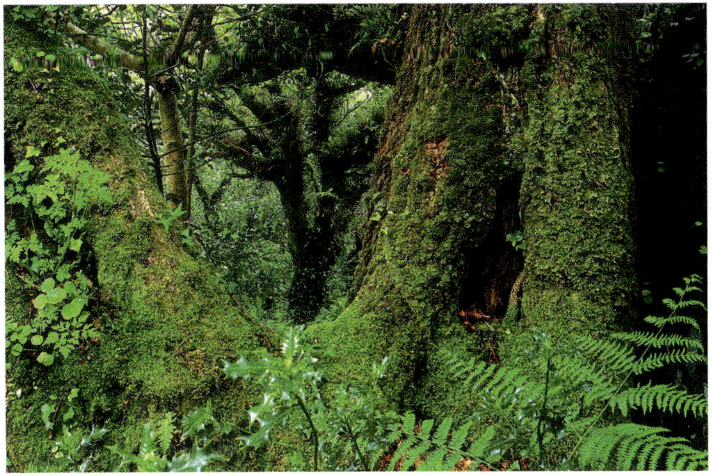

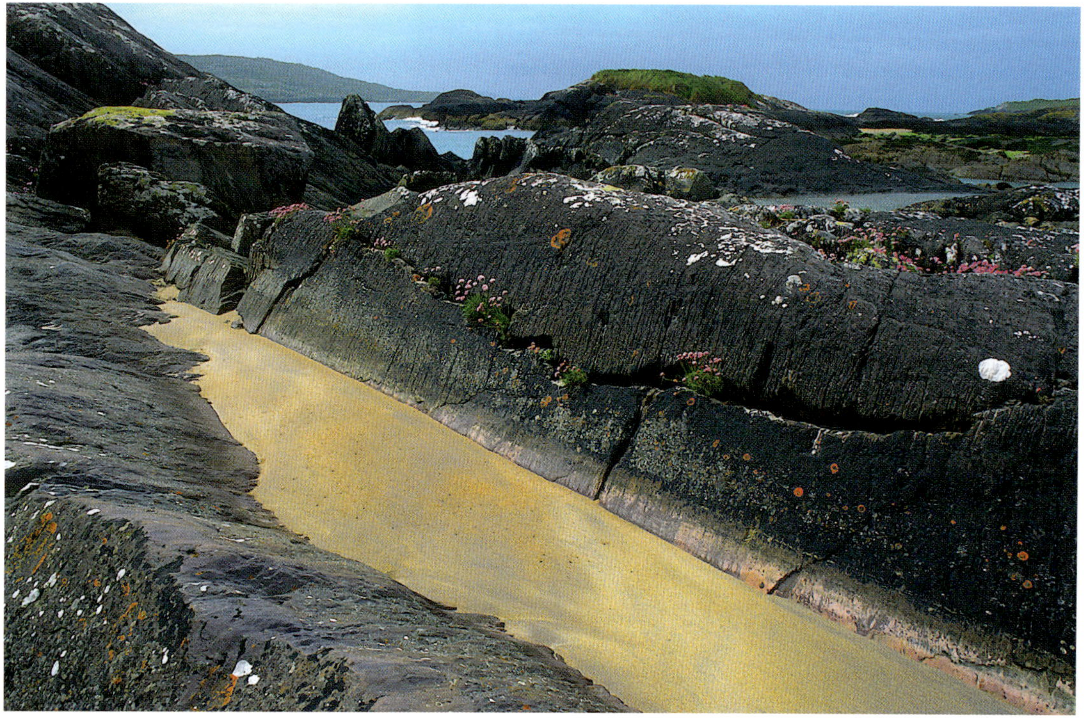

Rock formations in Derrynane National Park

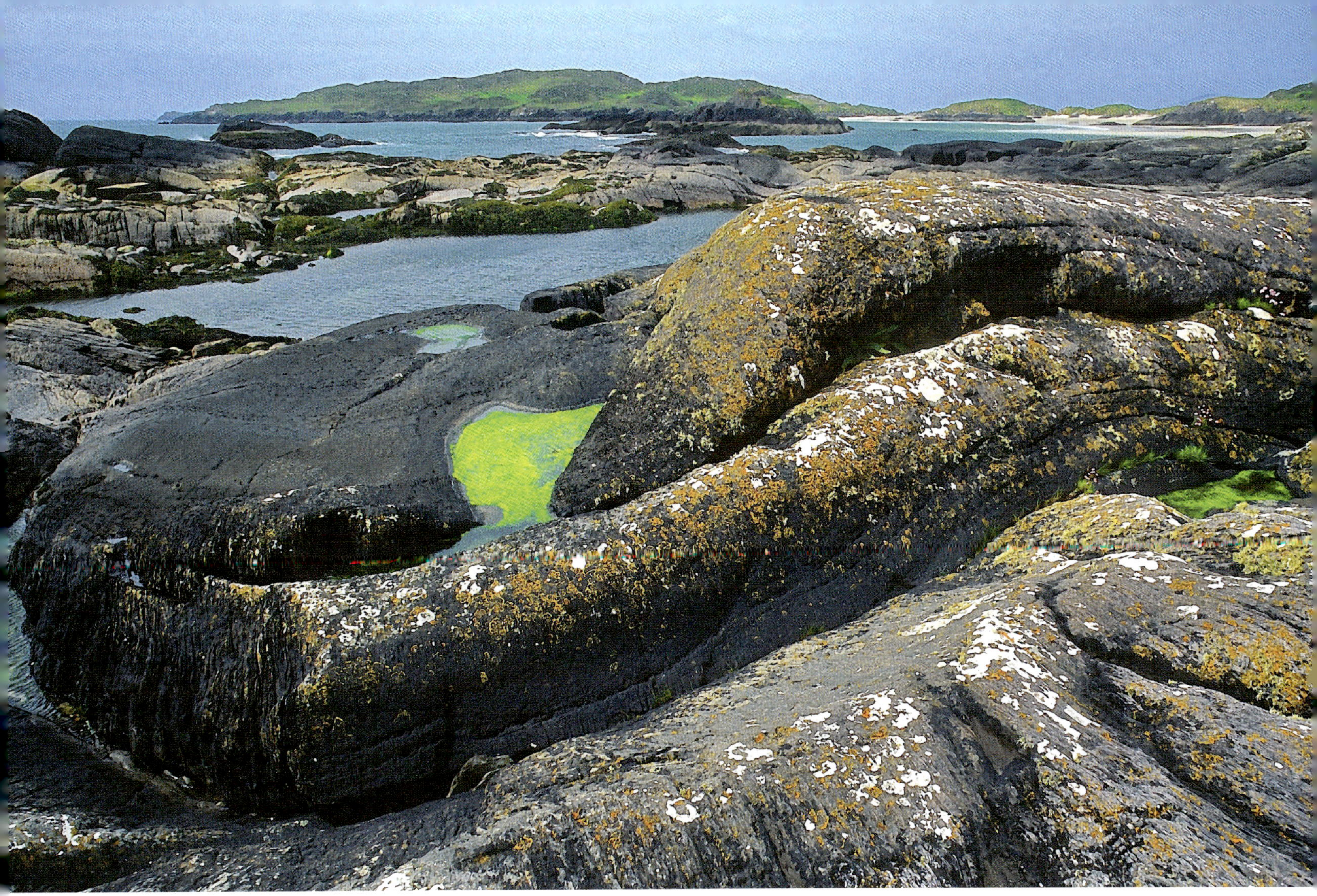

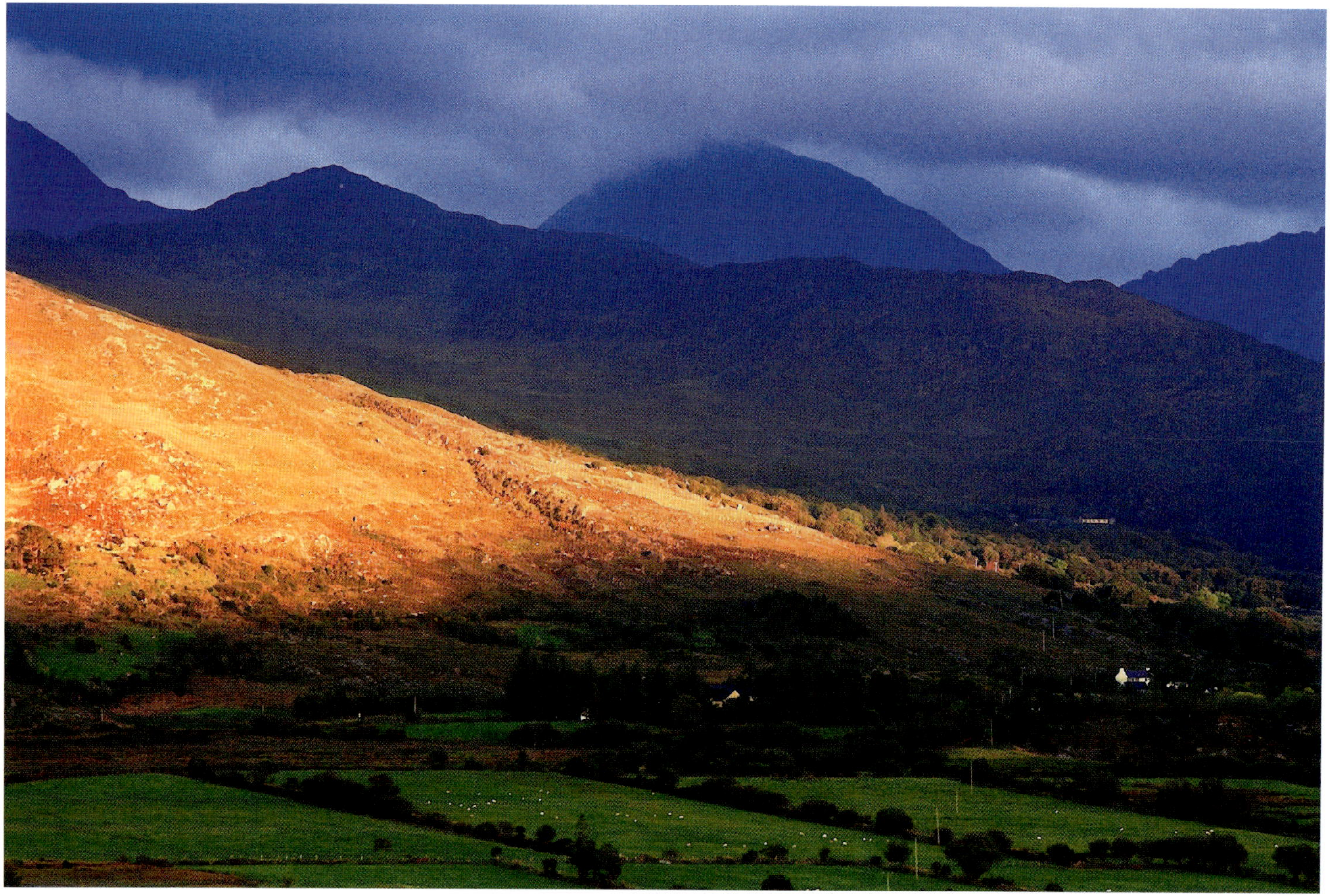

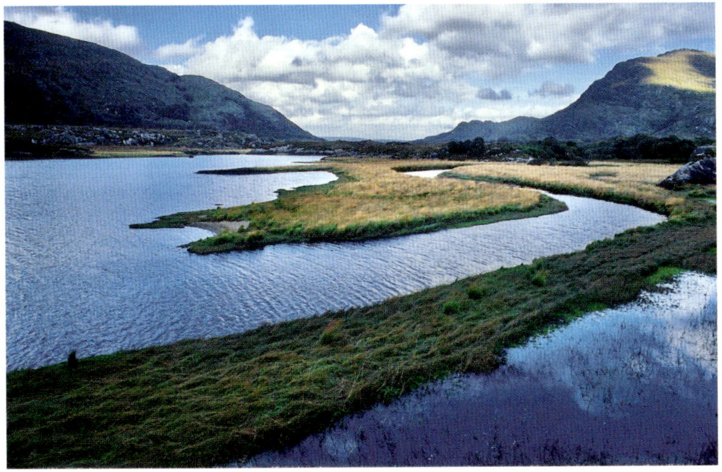

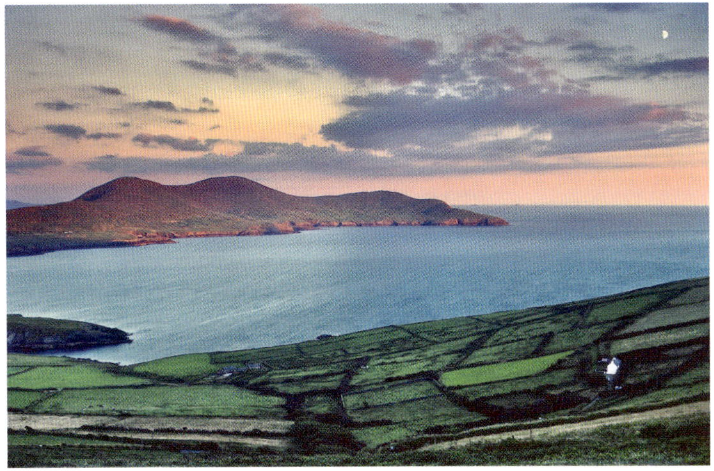

Left page: MacGillycuddy's Reek
Left: Killarney Nat. Park
Right: St. Finans's Bay

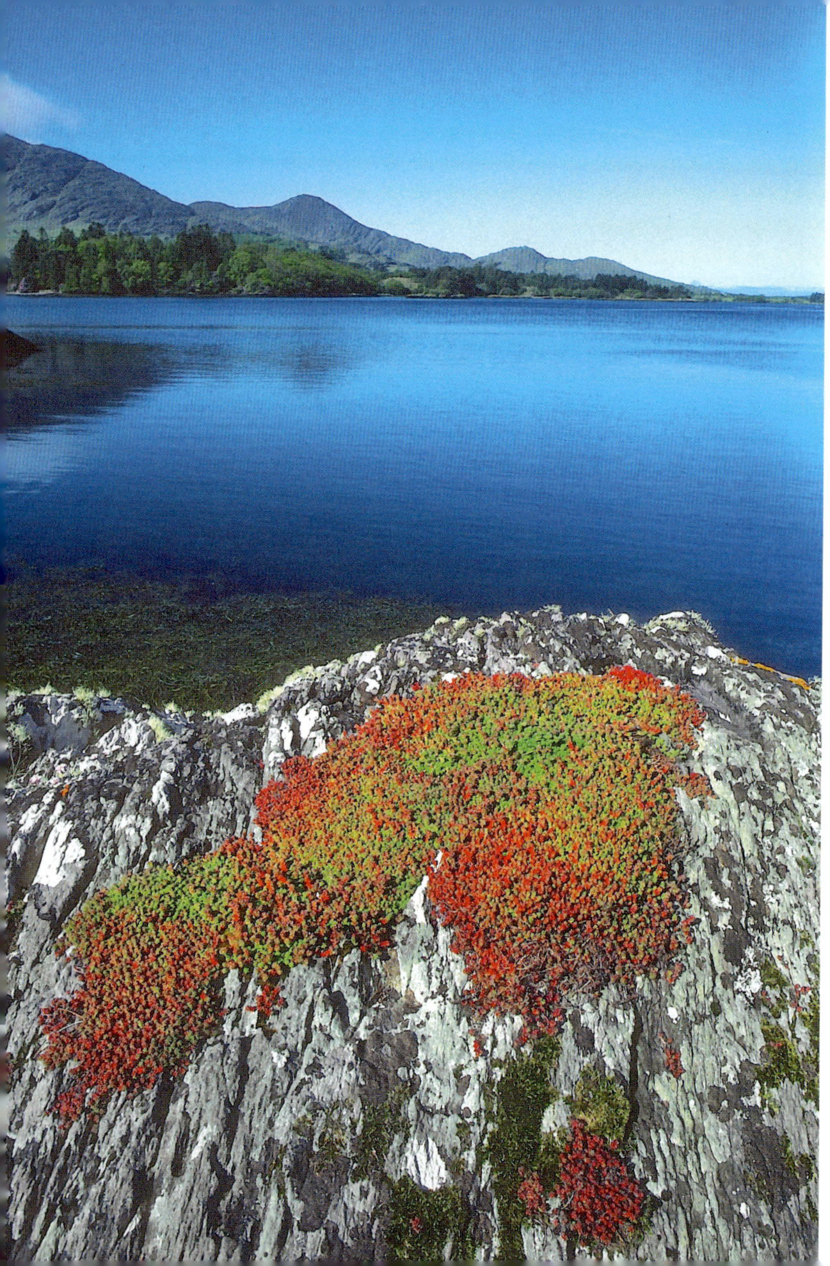

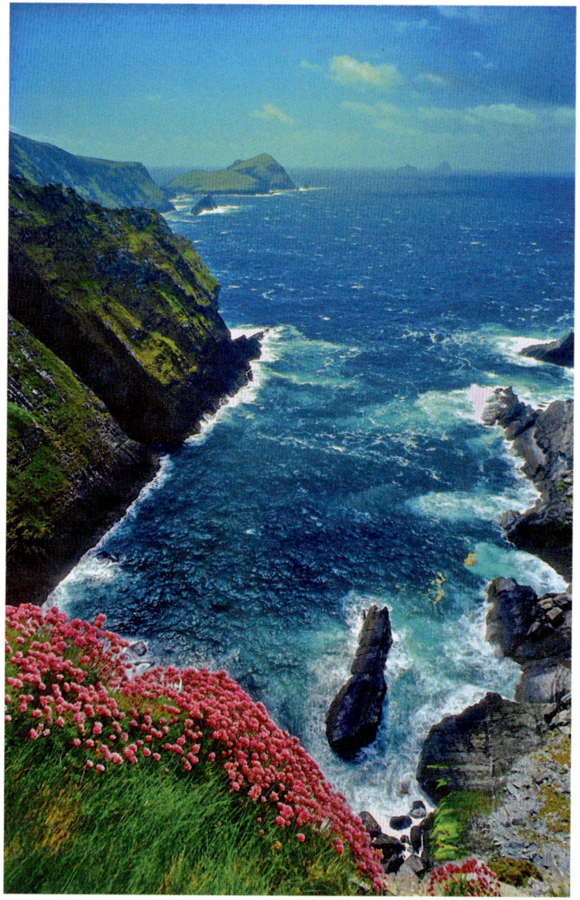

Left: Kenmare River
Right: Dromgour (Portmagee)
Right page: Caha Mountains

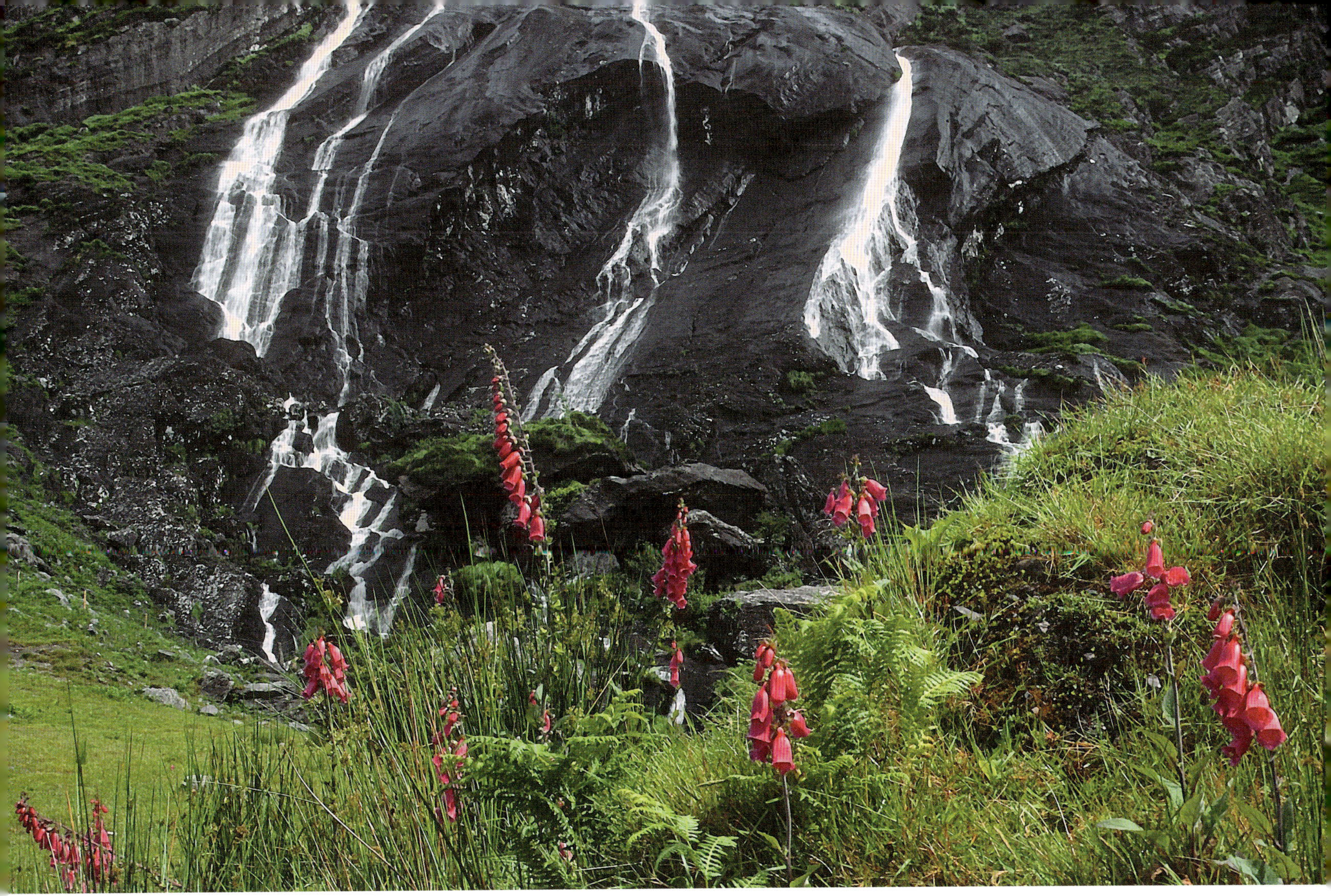

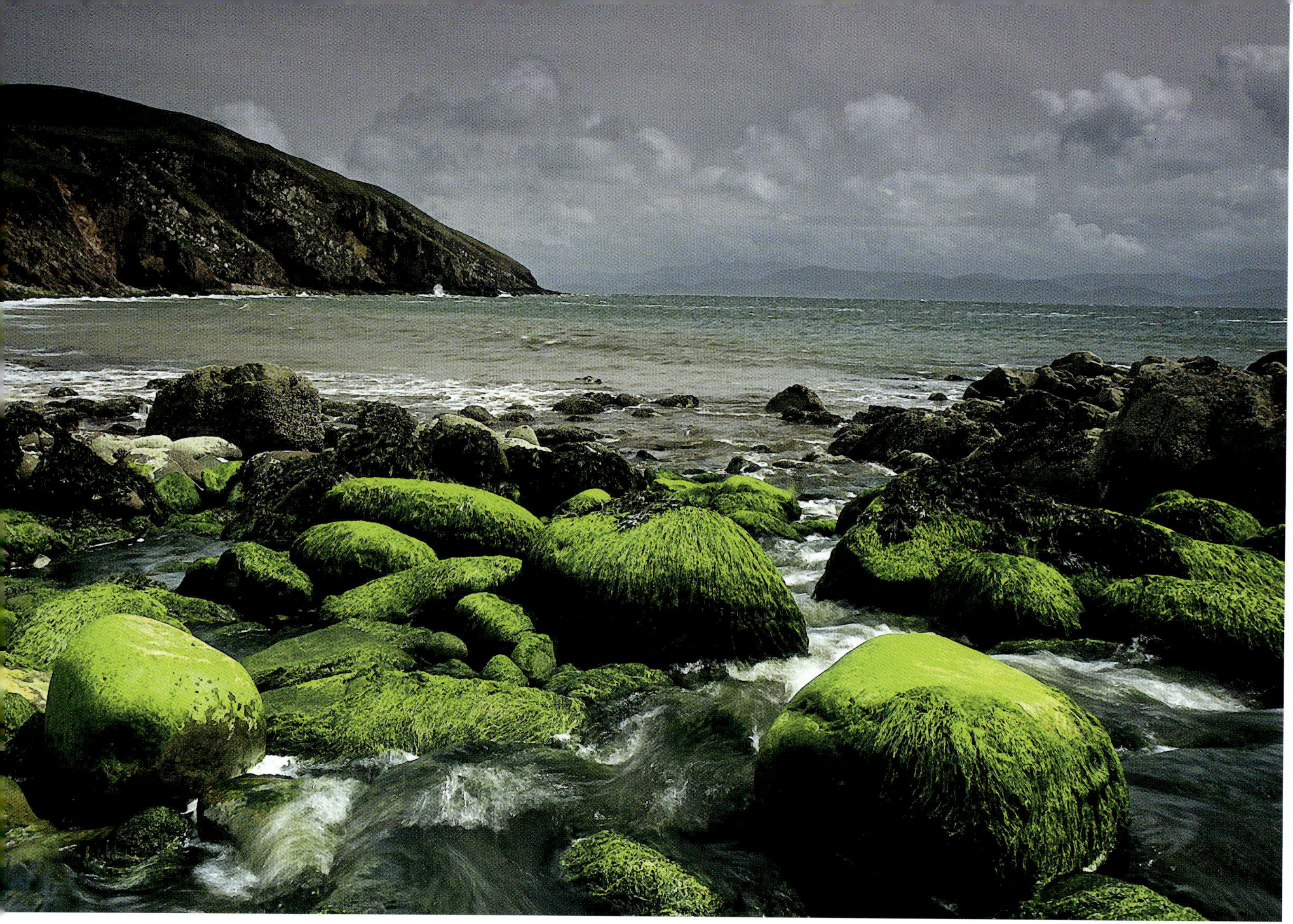

Dingle Peninsula

The Quarrel of the Swineherds[3]

They were friends, Friuch, who herded the squealing pigs of Ochall Ochnes, the king of the North, and Rucht, the swineherd of Bodb, who ruled over the plains in the South. They were friends, and when the oak and beech nuts lay under the trees of the North, the grunting one would drive his herd northward. When the wind shook the trees in the South, the bristled one moved southward.

But the people talked.

“Some claim you are mightier than me.”

“Surely, I am not weaker.”

“We’ll see,” said Rucht and cast a spell on Friuch’s pigs. No matter how much they ate, they would not grow fat.

The people in the North laughed when the skinny herd returned: “That was a bad day, Friuch; your friend is stronger than you.”

“Nothing is proven yet,” he grunted.

When Rucht next brought his sows northward, Friuch cast the same spell. Now, the people said their power was equal. But Bodb saw his skinny pigs and drove Rucht away. Friuch, too, was dismissed.

The two swineherds turned into birds—wings and claws. The first year, they sat in the trees of the North and quarreled, the second year in the trees of the South. Then they became swineherds once again. The people welcomed them back.

“Save your words,” they said. “We bring the lament of war and a flood of dead friends.”

Each went his own way. They became water creatures— a whale and a sea monster—and devoured each other first in the river Suir, then in the river Shannon. They became deer, and one drove the other’s herd away and destroyed his groves. As warriors—point and blade—they cut one another; as chimeras—shadow and shield—they frightened each other. Then they were two dragons who covered the other’s land in snow until they dropped from the sky and turned into maggots. Cruinnic and Tuinnic. One maggot fell into the spring of Cronn in Cuailnge, and a cow belonging to the king of Ulster swallowed it; the other fell into the spring of Garad, and the cow that swallowed it belonged to Maeve, the queen of the South. Thus, the two bulls were born: Finnbennach, the White-Horned, in the plain of Ai, and Dub, the Dark Bull of Cuailnge.

[3] The following chapters are based on The Táin translated from the Irish by Thomas Kinsella, Oxford University Press, London, 1970

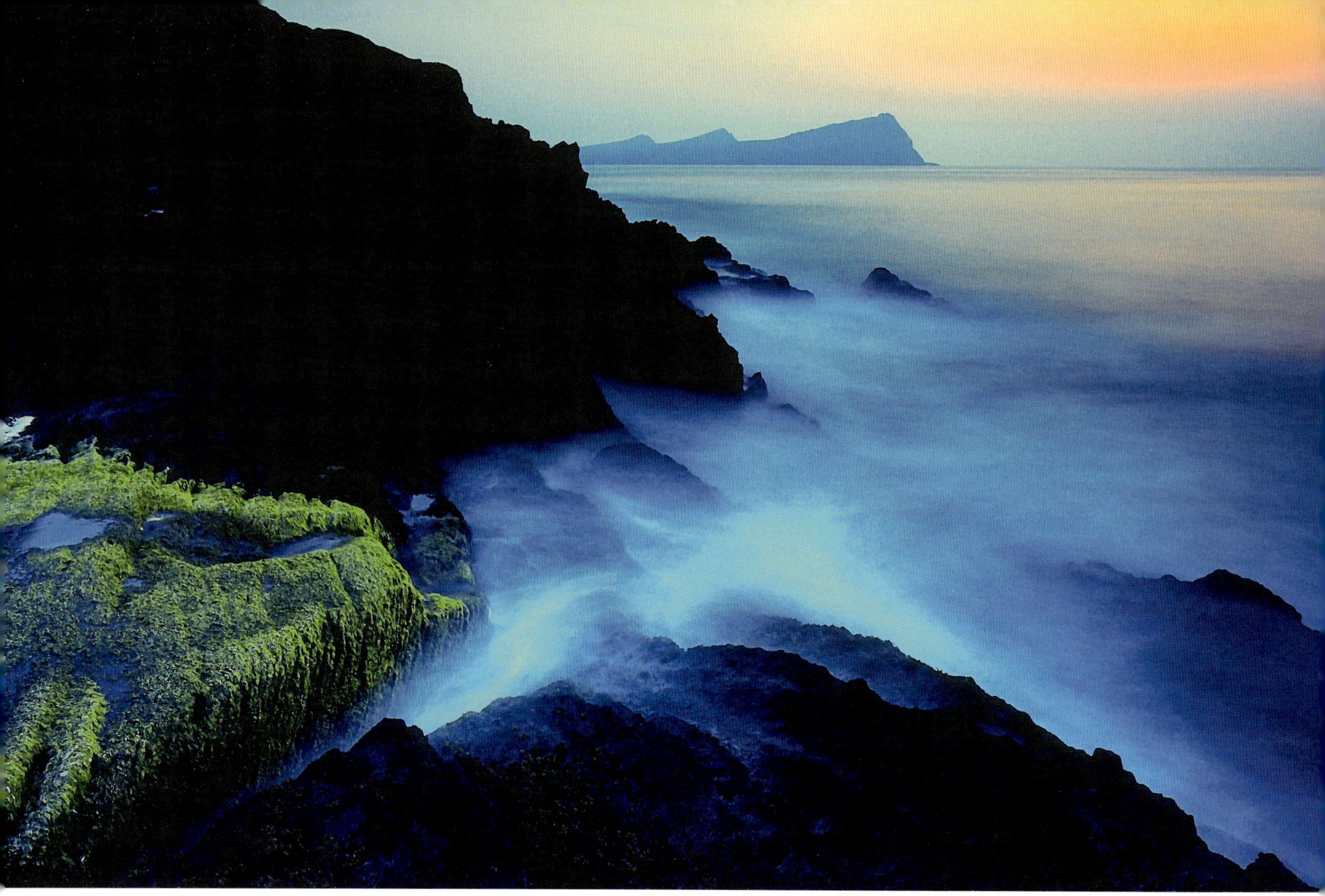

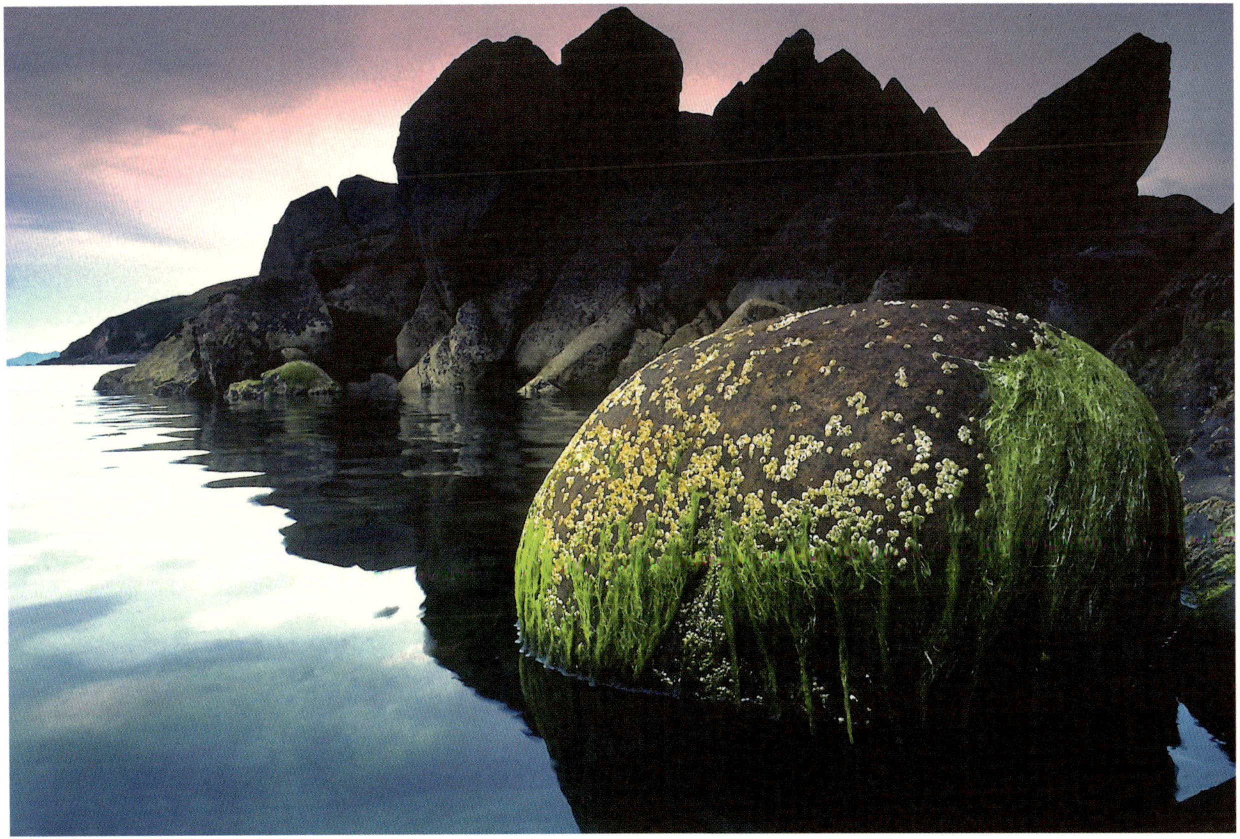

Left page: Dingle Peninsula, West Coast
Right: Dingle Peninsula, Southeast Coast

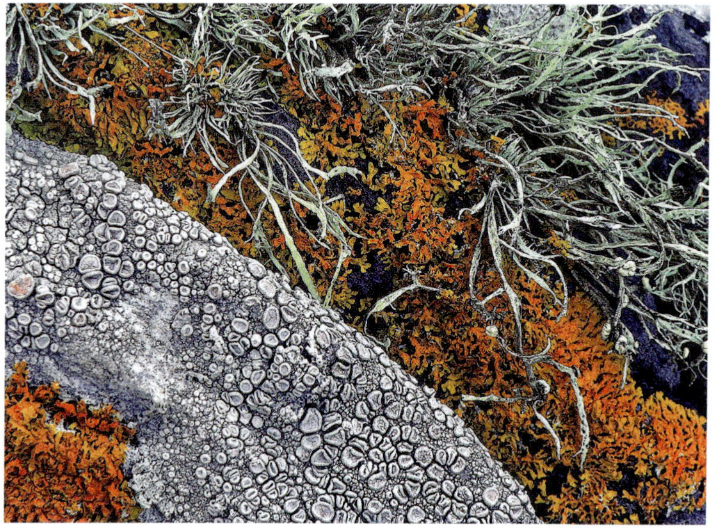

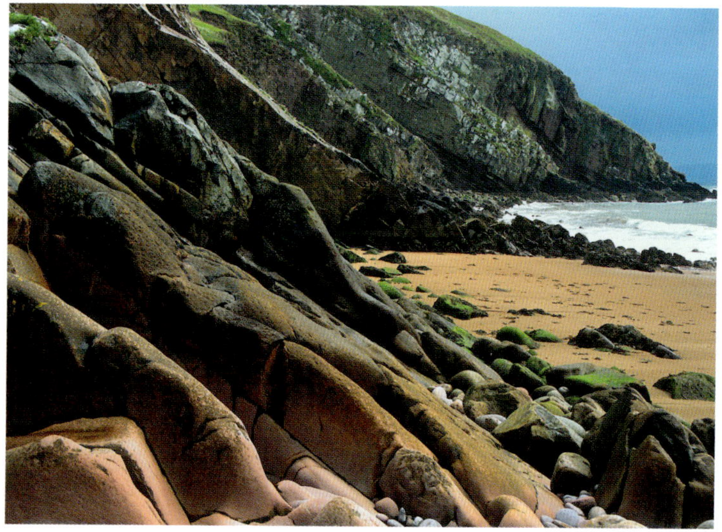

Left: Lichen
Right: Dingle Peninsula
Right page: Conor Pass

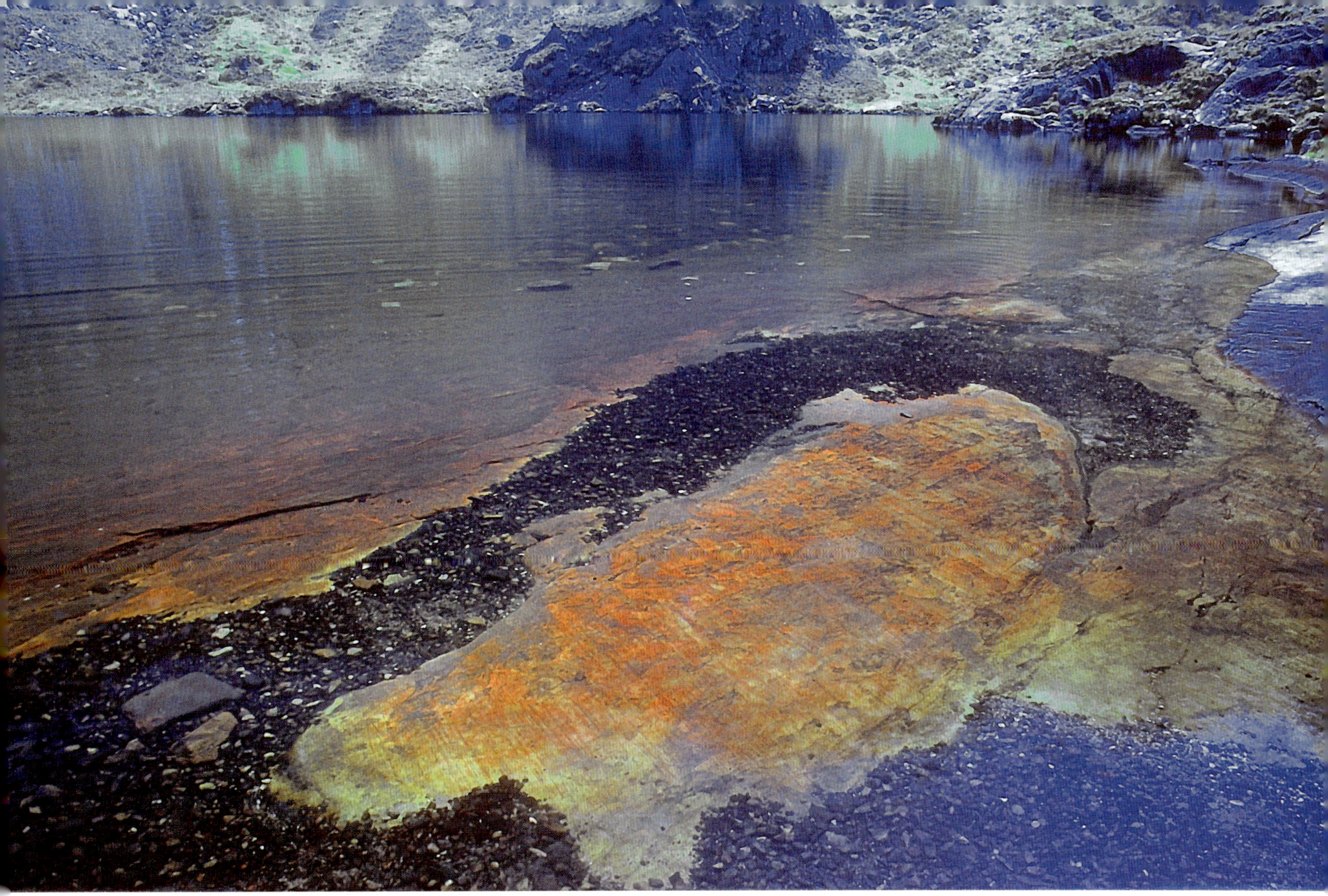

The Cattle Raid of Cooley— how it began

Ailill and Maeve rested on pillows in their royal bed at Cruachan, when Ailill, pleased with himself, remarked: "It's true, my dear, what people say: the wife of a wealthy man leads an agreeable life."

"Where did that come from now?" Maeve wondered.

"Just think how much better off you are today than on the day of your wedding."

"I was doing well enough without you."

"But, love, you had no more than your woman's belongings back then."

"I, the daughter of Eochaid Fedlech! I had a thousand and five hundred soldiers, ten more men for every paid warrior, and an entire province from my father. Suitors came from all the kingdoms, but I wanted none of them. I demanded more than any woman in Ireland before me: a man without stinginess, without fear, and without jealousy. For I am generous, magnanimous, a lover of all battles, and in the shadow of any man I have, another is already waiting."

The next morning, Ailill and Maeve began comparing their possessions: plates, pots and chests, precious rings and robes of every color, striped and mottled. They brought their herds from the pastures. For every sheep Ailill owned, Maeve had an equal one, and for every cow of Maeve's, Ailill produced a match—except for the white bull Finnbenach. He had been born to one of Maeve's cows, but the schmuck refused to belong to a woman and crossed over to Ailill's herd.

Maeve was distraught. She called Fergus mac Róich, the messenger, and asked him if there was a match for Finnbenach somewhere in Ireland.

"I know where to find even a better bull," said Fergus, who was also her lover. Thus, Maeve sent him to Ulster to ask Dáire mac Fiachna, the owner of the Brown Bull of Cuailnge, to lend it to her for a year. "When I return the bull, he shall have fifty yearling heifers. And if he comes with the bull, he shall have a portion of the fine Plain of Ai equal to his own, a chariot worth thrice seven bondmaids, and my own friendly thighs on top."

Dáire was overjoyed when he got this offer. He jumped on his cushion until it burst. The feathers flew all over the place. Fergus and his men were made welcome with food and drink, and they chatted.

"The men of Ulster are good," one of them said, pleased with himself, "to give us willingly what we might otherwise have taken by force."

"By all the gods I believe in," Dáire cried when he heard this, "nothing leaves this place without my permission."

Fergus returned empty-handed.

"Then," said Maeve, "we will take the bull ourselves."

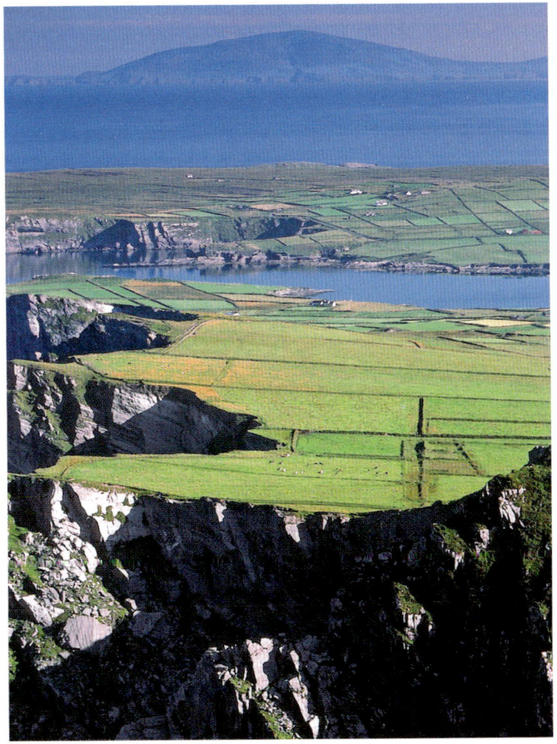

Left: Portmagee, Dingle in the background
Right: Derrynane, Ring of Kerry

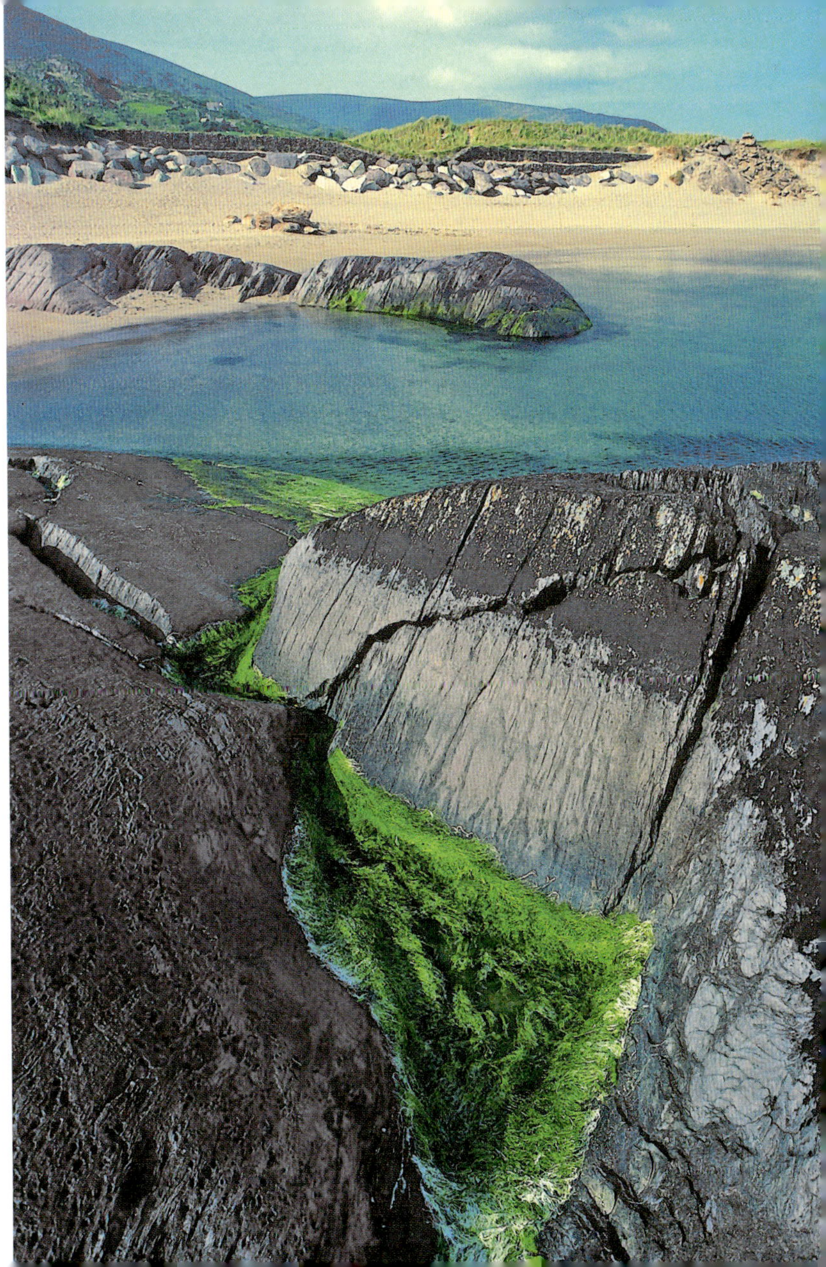

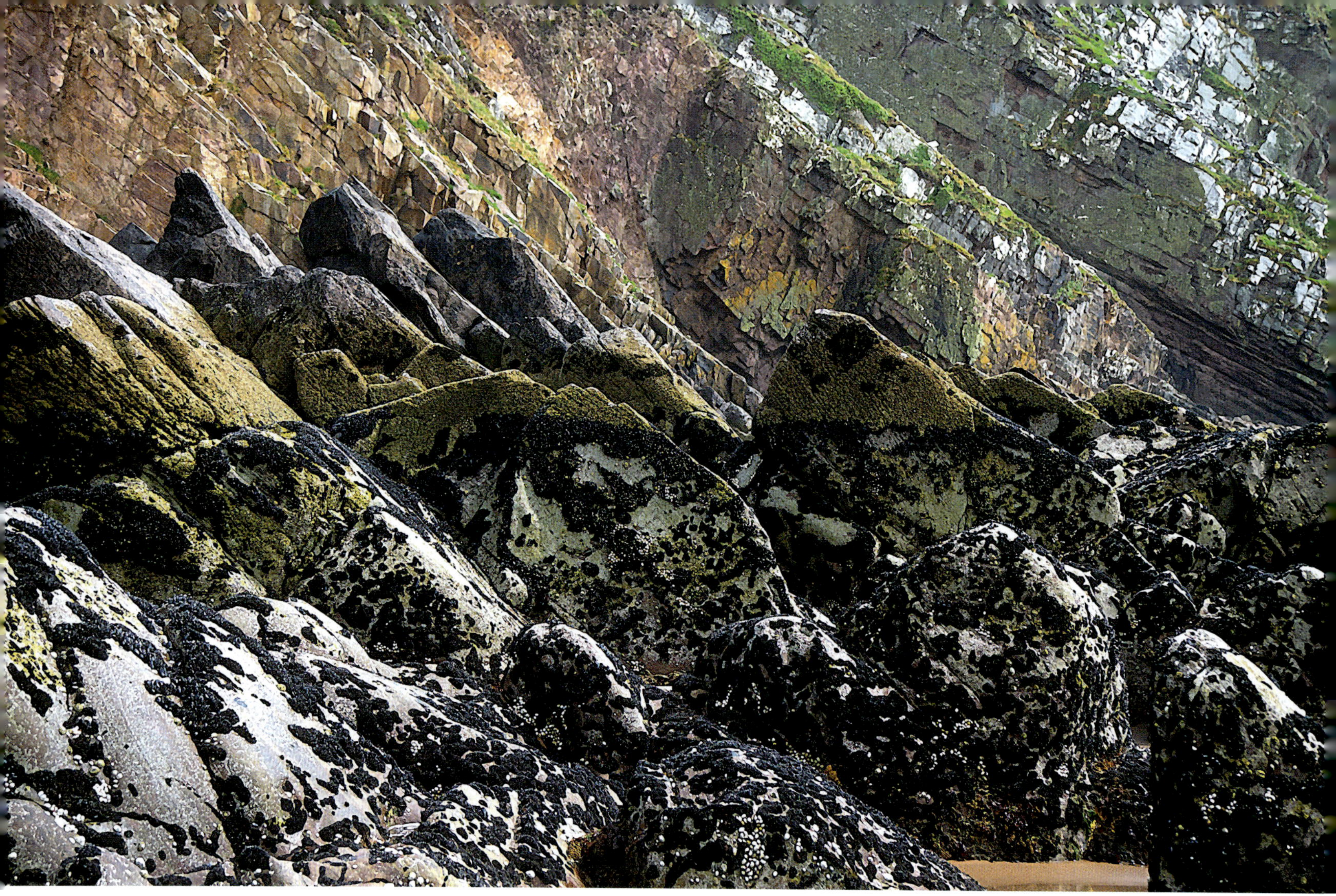

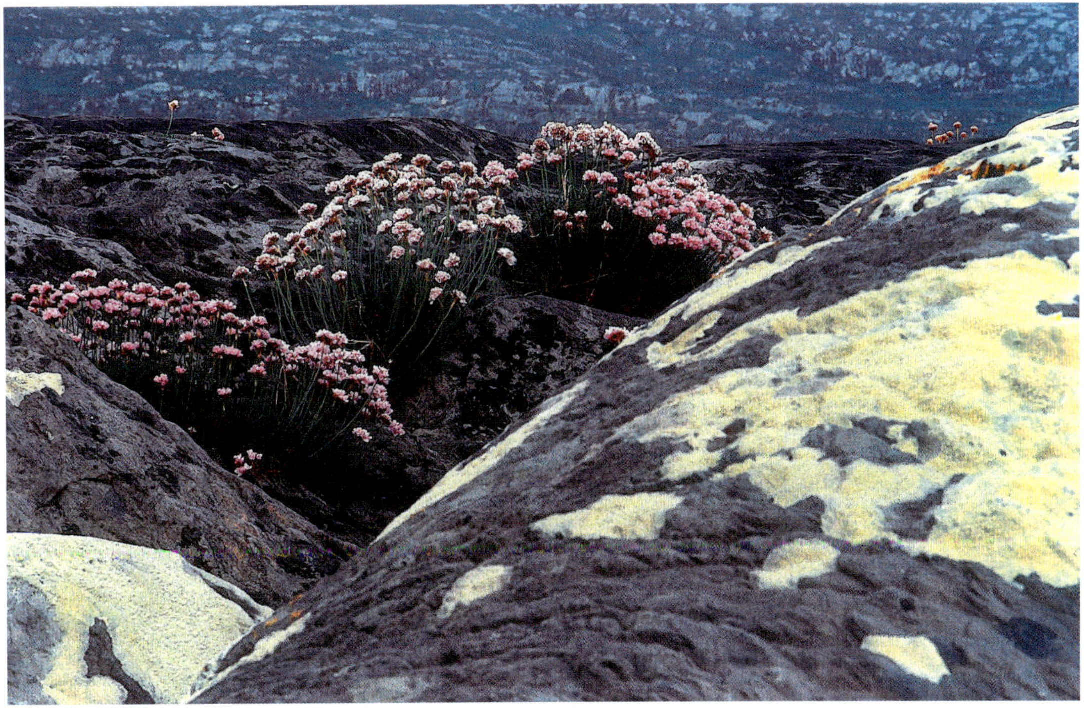

Left page: Acres Point, Dingle Peninsula
Right: Coastal scenery, Dingle Peninsula

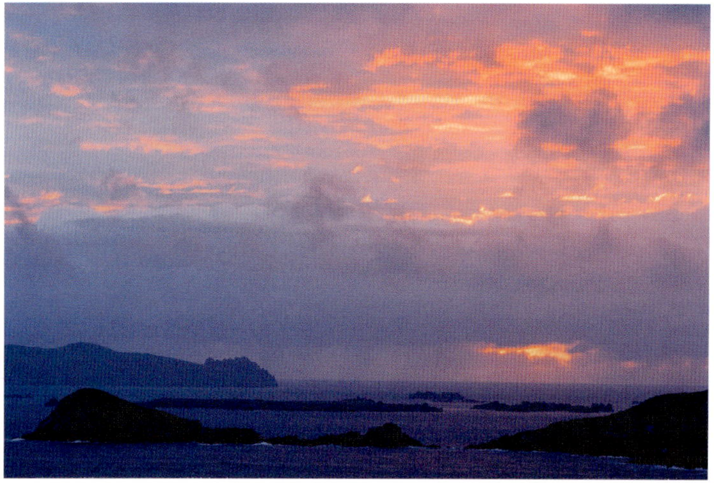

Left: Dingle Peninsula
Right: Skellig Islands

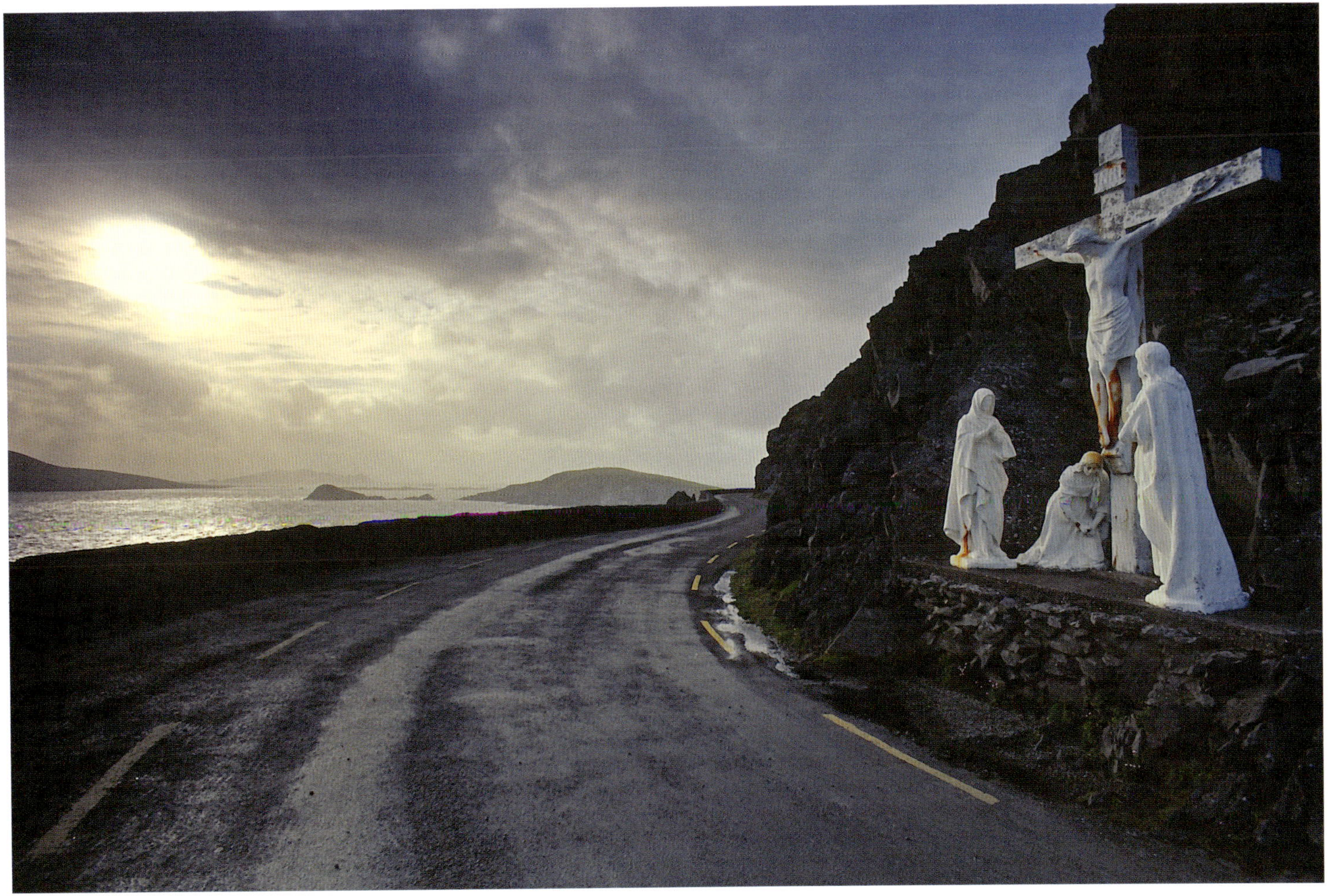

Slea Head

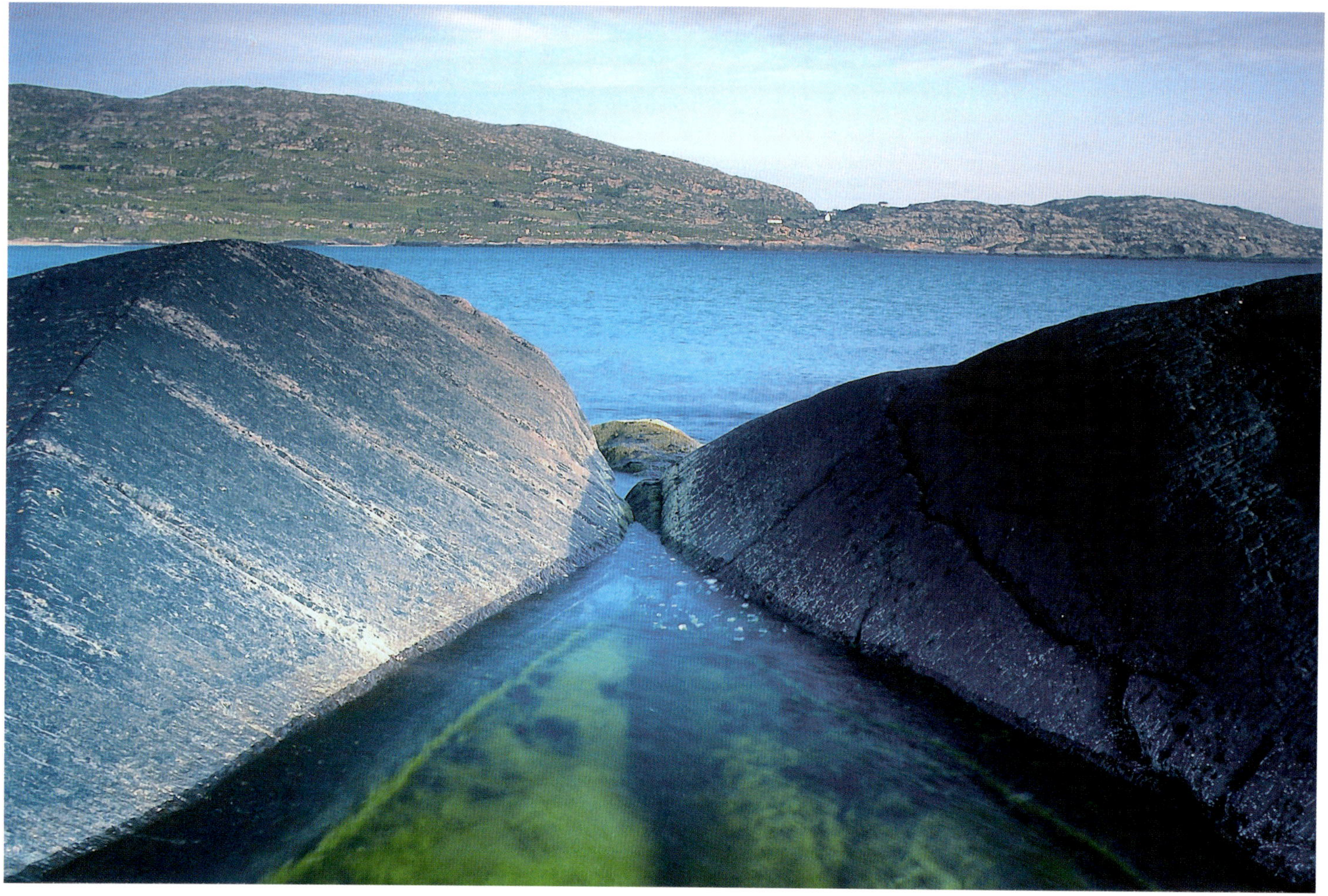

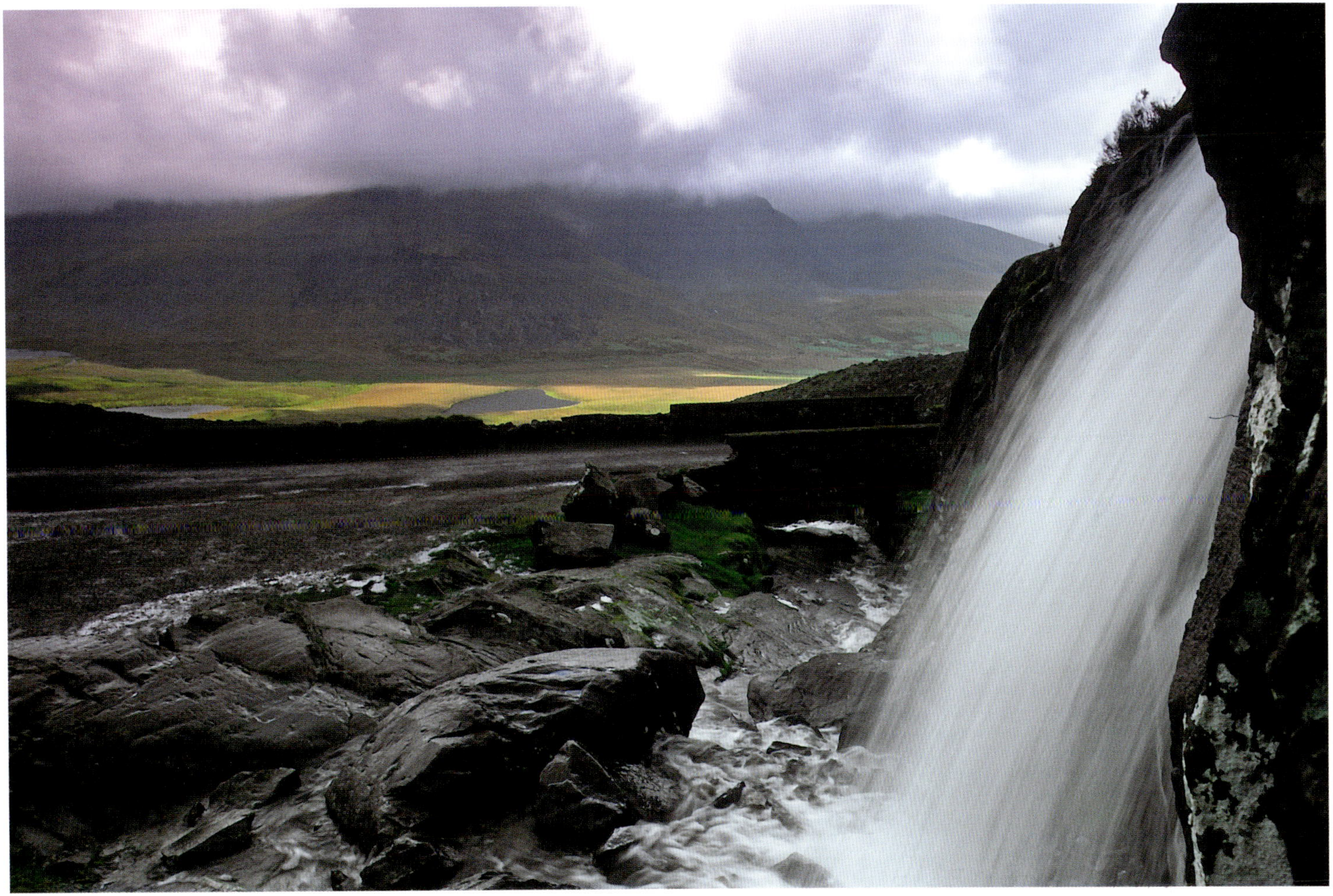

Left page: Derrynane, Ring of Kerry
Right: Conor Pass, Dingle Peninsula

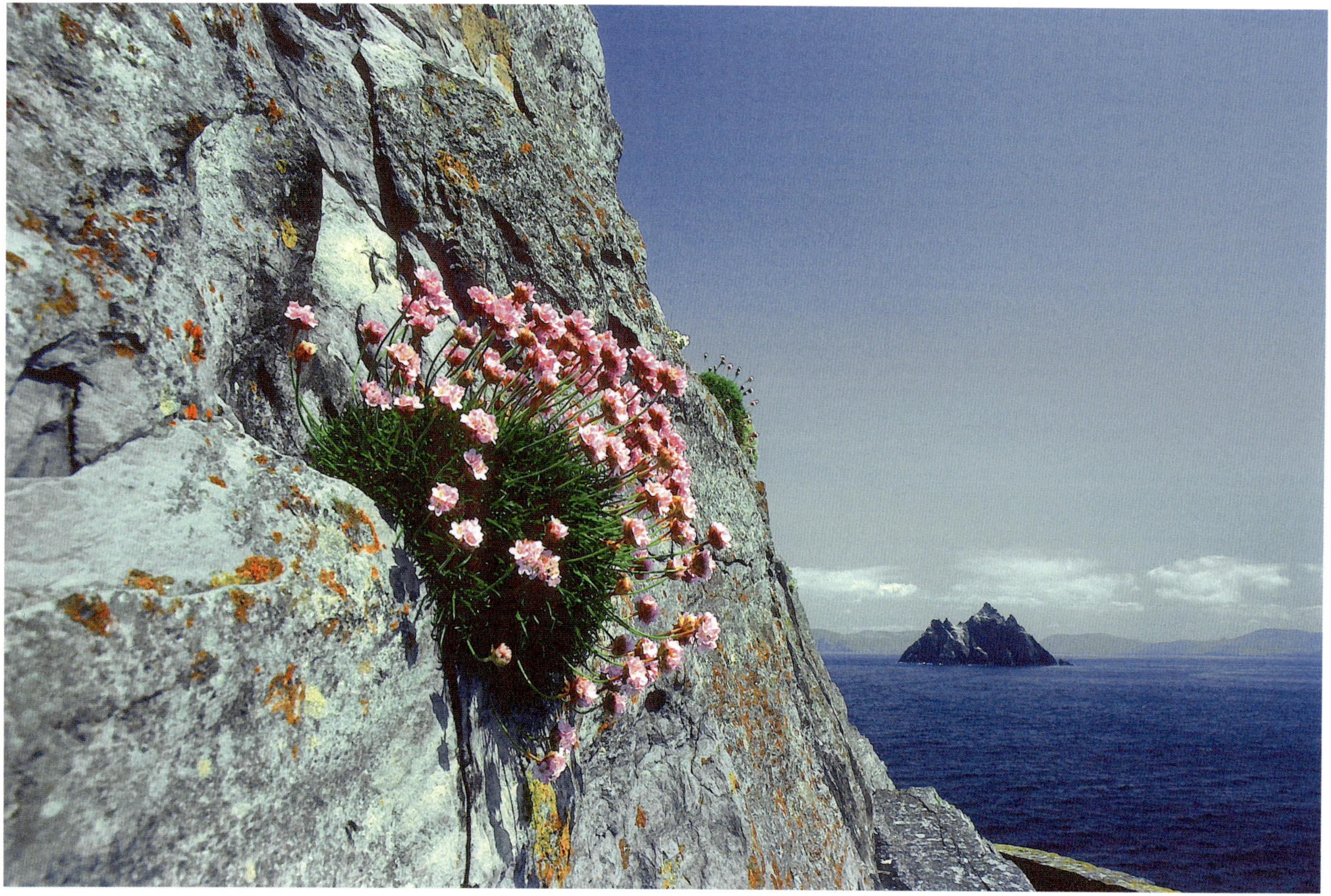

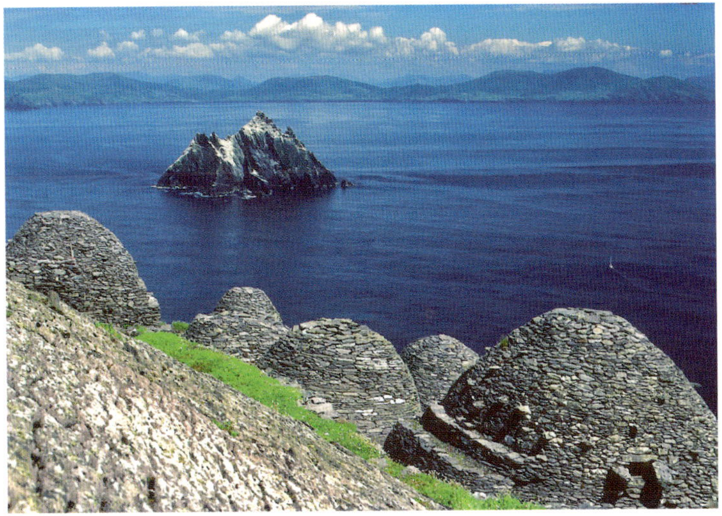

Left page: Great Skellig Island
Left: Beehive dwellings
Right: Great Skellig Island

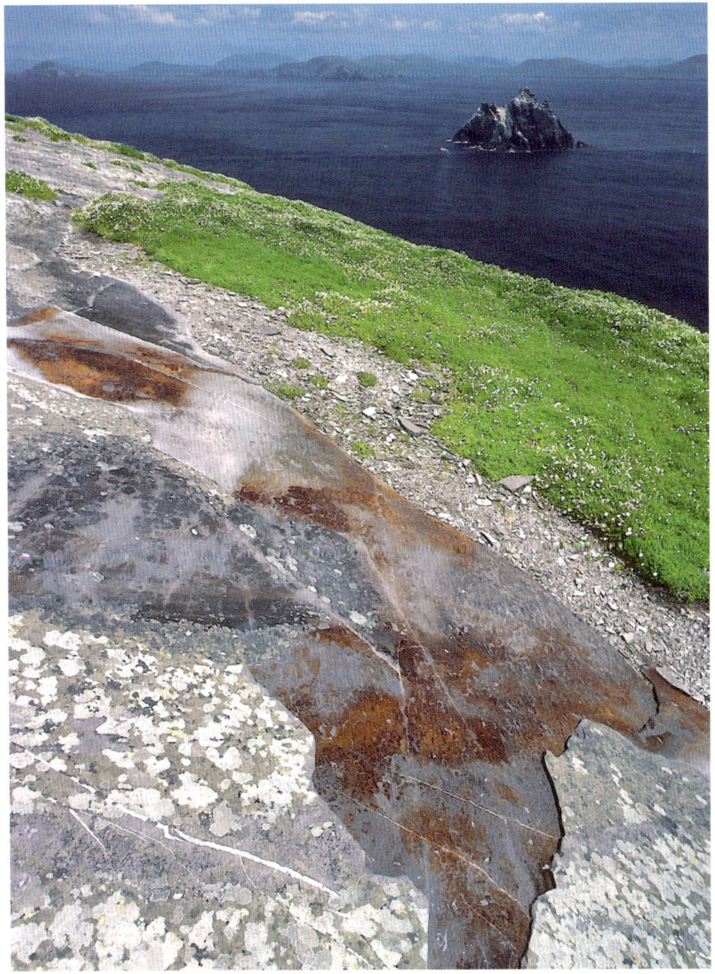

Great Skellig Island

The Prophecy

Ailill and Maeve gathered a great army to march against Ulster. One company wore spotted cloaks and had shaved heads, a second wore dark gray cloaks over skirts embroidered with red and had their hair tied back, and a third wore purple cloaks and had shoulder-length hair. For two weeks, the druids waited for the sign to depart.

"Everyone leaving behind a lover or a friend will curse me today," said Maeve on the day they set out.

Her charioteer turned their chariot to face the sun to bring about a safe return, and there stood a girl with yellow hair in a speckled dress, a red cloak, and golden sandals. Her forehead was broad, her chin slender, her lips blood-red, her brows black as a crow's wings, and her lashes cast shadows on her cheeks. Her eyes had three pupils each.

"What is your name?" Maeve asked her.

"I'm Fedelm, and I am a poet."

"Where do you come from?"

"From Alba, across the sea, where I learned verse and vision."

"Do you have the light of foresight?"

"I have," the girl said proudly.

"Then tell me what you see for my army?" asked Maeve.

"I see scarlet, I see red."

"That cannot be true; Conchobar and his men are writhing in their pangs in Emain Macha."

"I see scarlet, I see red."

"But half the men of Ulster are on our side."

"I see scarlet, I see red."

"Nonsense. Red wounds are nothing unusual when two armies clash. Tell the truth, girl."

Fedelm sighed. "I see a boy with blood at his belt, a hero's hallow around his head, and his brow is full of victories."

"Cú Chulainn," Fergus groaned, "the Hound of Ulster."

"What kind of man is this Hound?" asked Ailill.

"He is just a boy," said Maeve. "And we must go now."

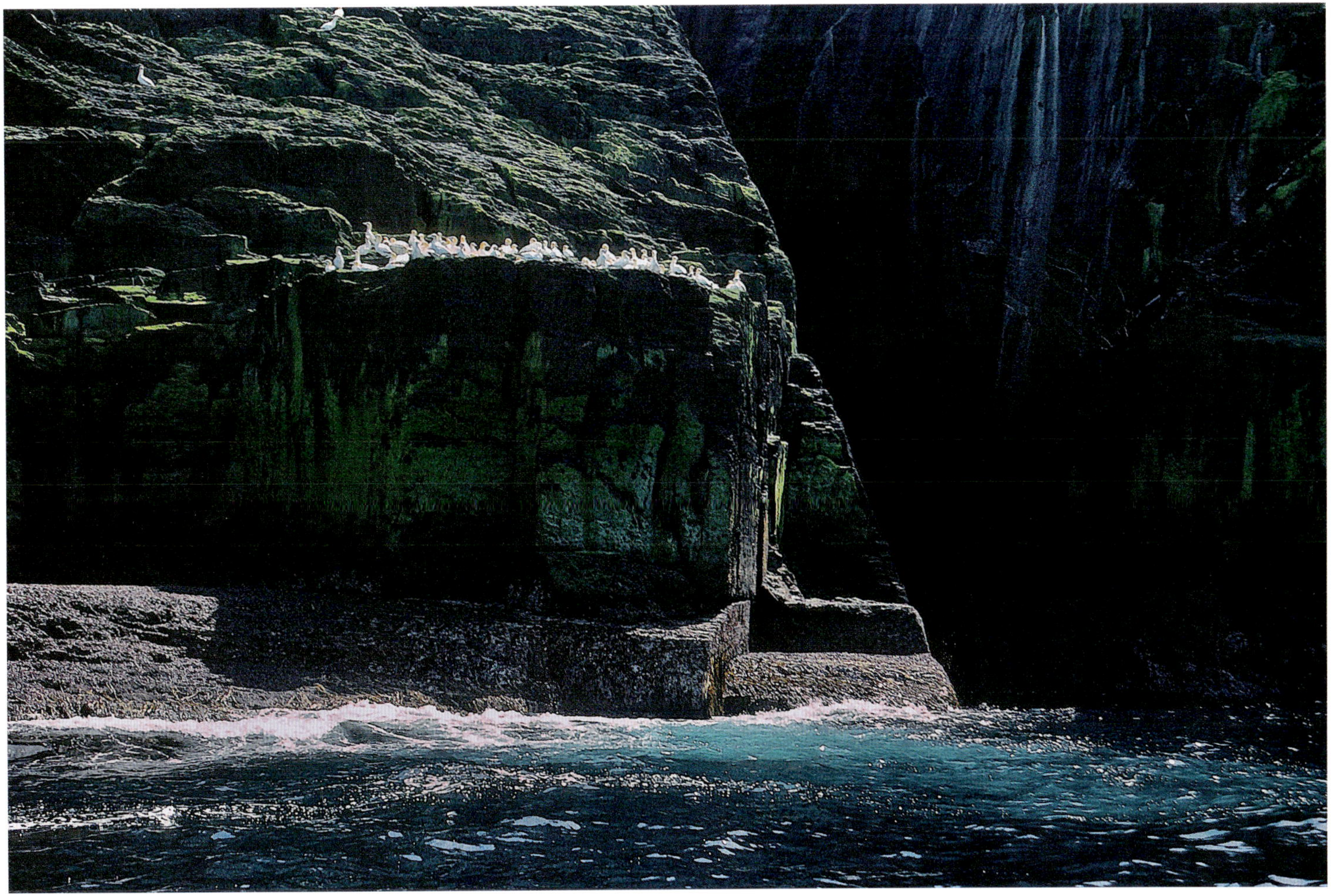

Little Skellig Island

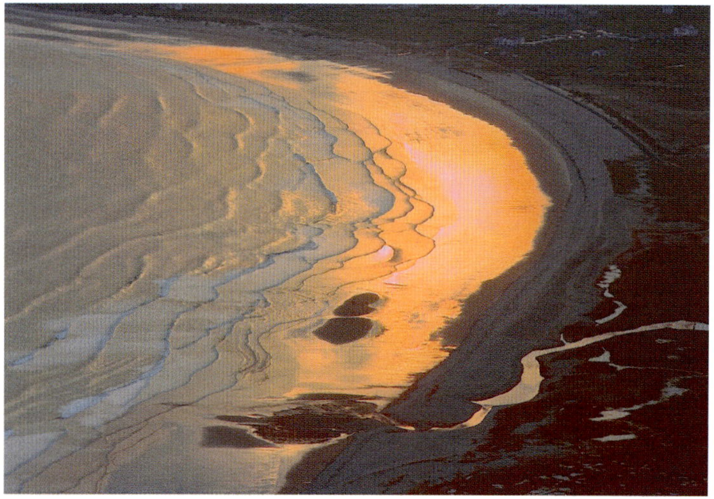

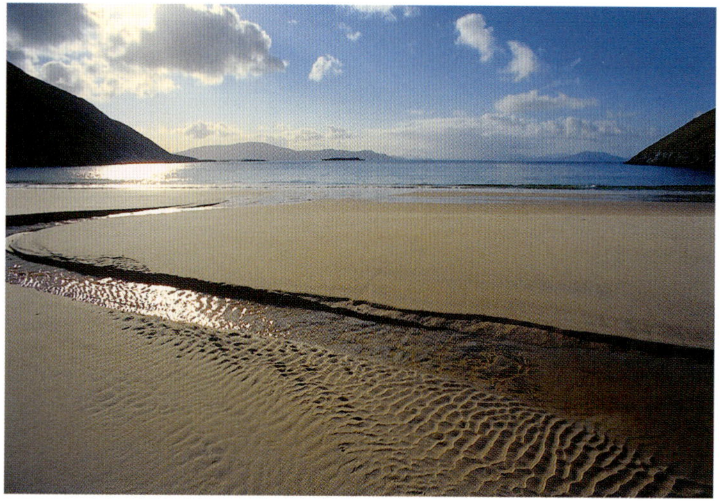

Left and right: Achill Island

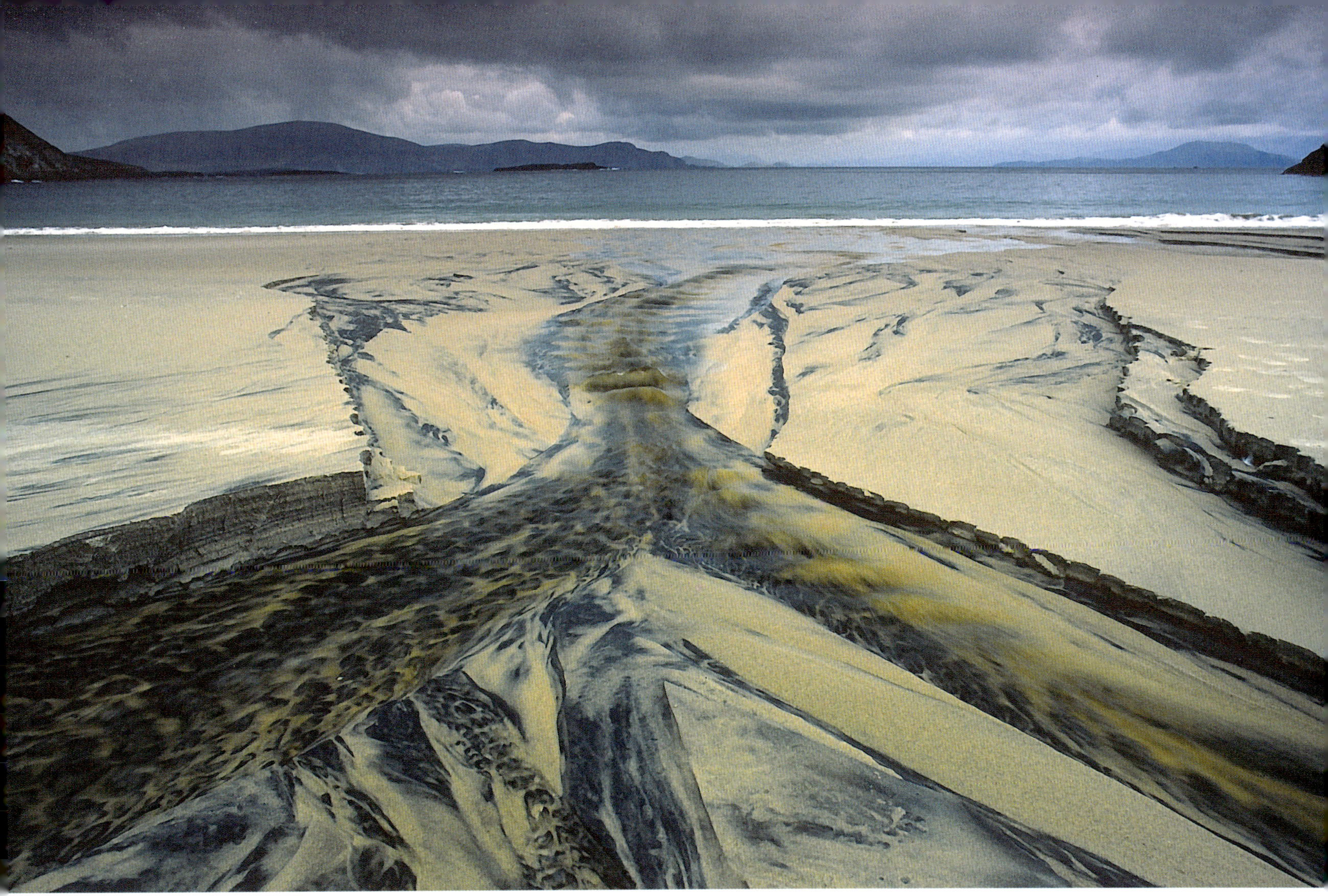

Achill Island, Keem Beach

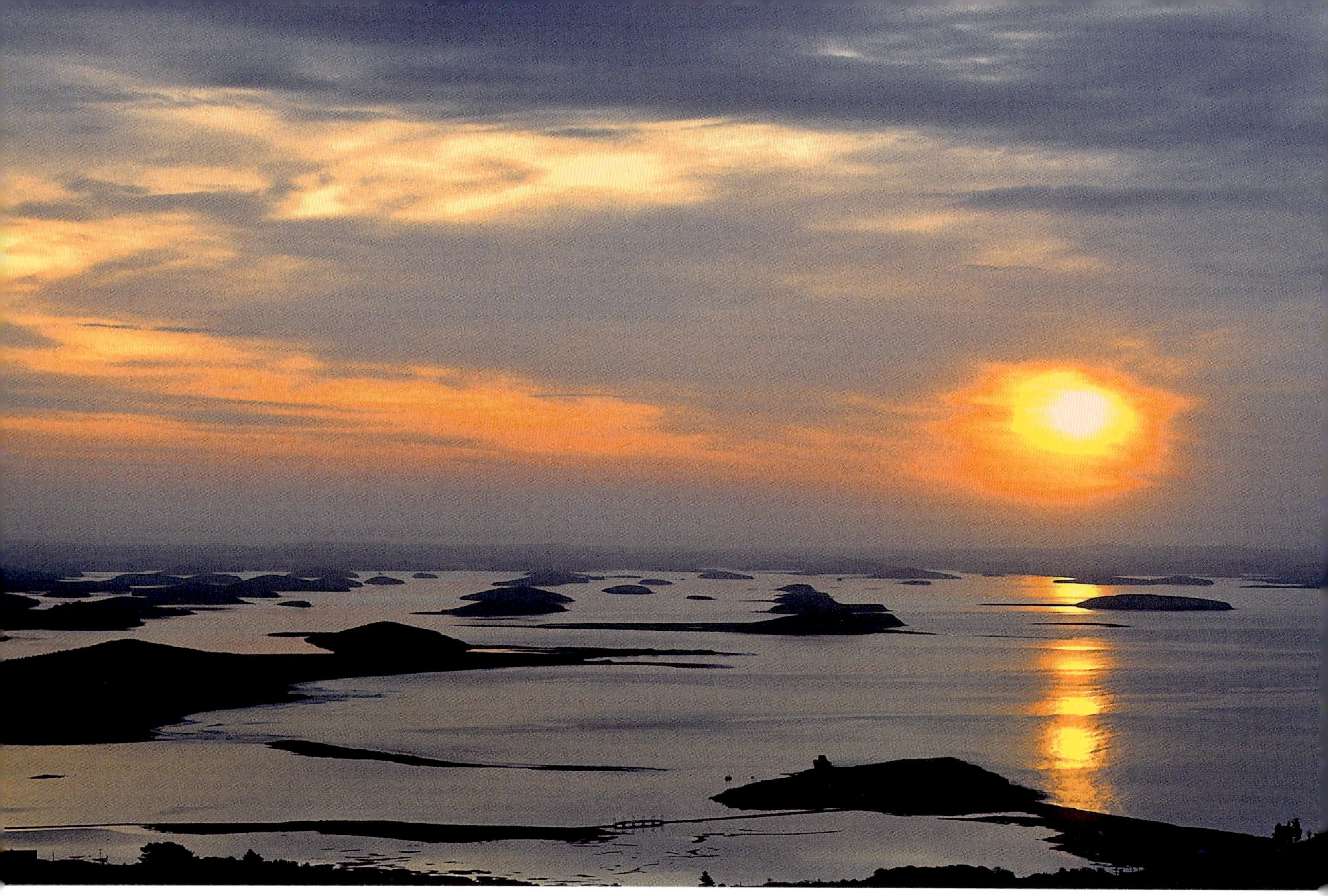

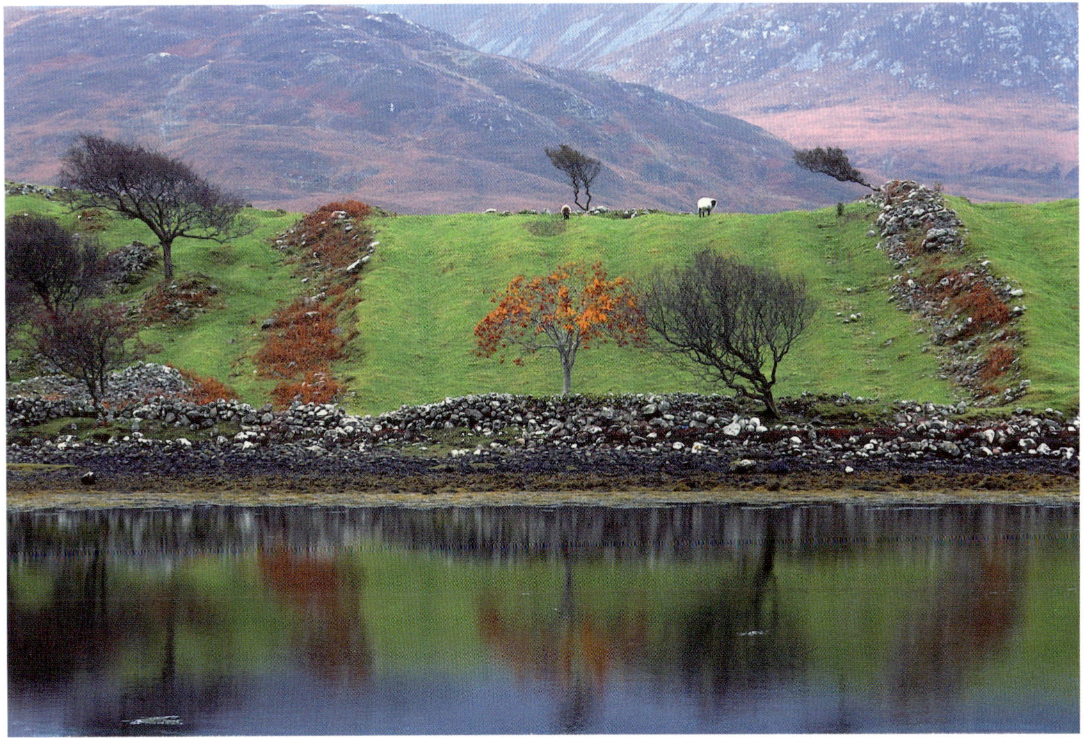

Left page: Drumlins in Clew Bay
Right: Corraun Peninsula

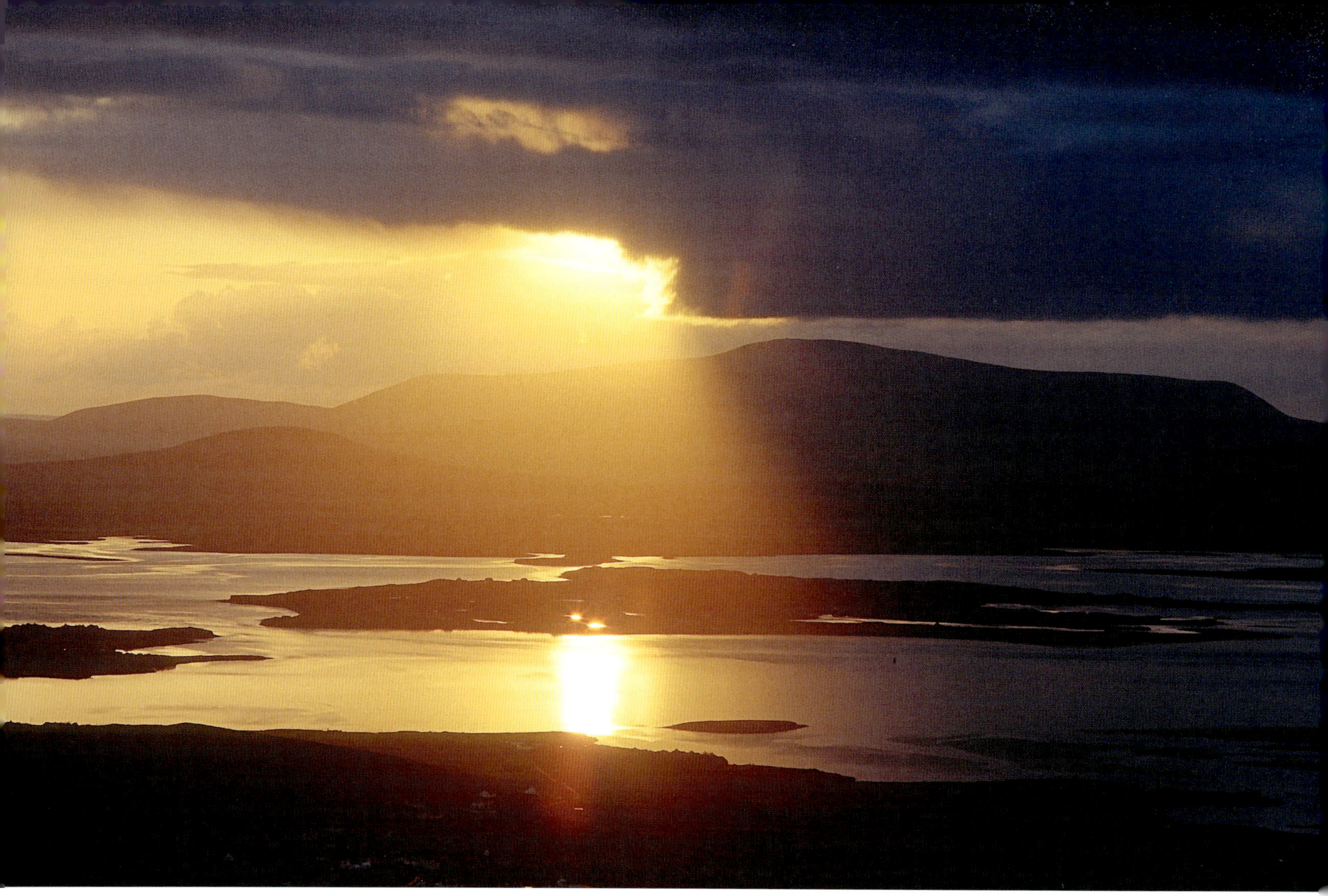

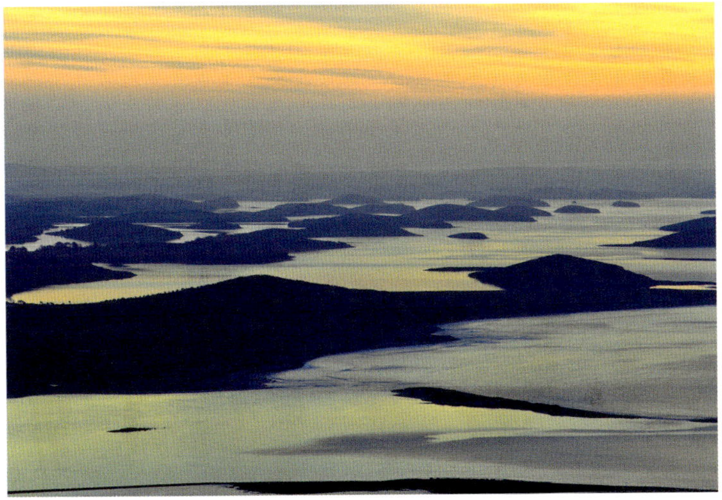

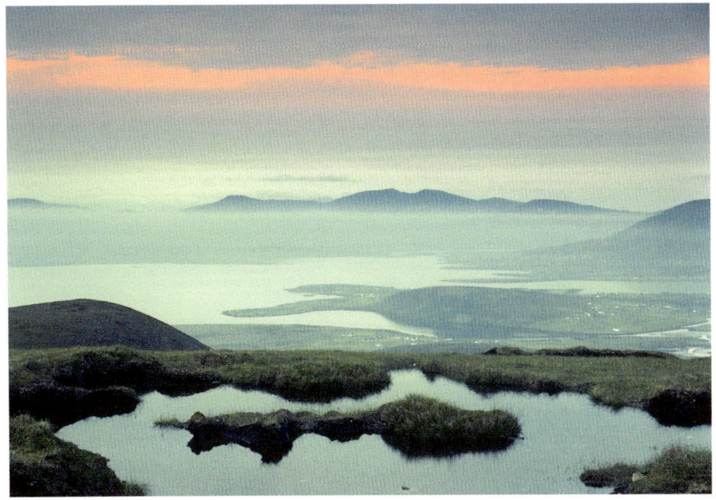

Left page: Achill Sound
Left: Clew Bay
Right: Achill Island

Cú Chulainn's Challenges

Cú Chulainn was seventeen when he faced Maeve's armies, while the men of Ulster lay stricken by their labor pangs. Through forests and rivers, he tracked the troops, hindering them with spells, killing them in single combat or in groups. Again and again, Ailill and Maeve sent warriors out to defeat him, and when their losses became too great, Cú Chulainn agreed to one duel a day and to truces, which no one upheld. The places took their names from his triumphs: the Stream of Blood, the Field of Chariots, the Ford of Foot Fetters. For the grown-up men who refused to fight him, Cú Chulainn glued a beard of moss and lichen to his boyish chin. Then he mounted their heads on stakes and left them in the fords where he had vanquished them.

"It's not as simple as catching a bird," Maeve pondered.

Once, a fair young woman came to Cú Chulainn.

"I bring you my treasures and my cattle, because I love you for all the deeds I've heard of."

"You come on a bad day," he moaned. "The men of Ulster are still in their pangs, and I must face the cattle raiders alone. I have no time for you."

"I could help you."

"I did not take on this fight for the sake of a woman's backside."

"In that case, I will hinder you. As an eel, I will coil around your foot in the ford."

"Then I will catch you with my toes and break your ribs."

"As a gray she-wolf, I will set the wild deer upon you."

"Then I will strike out one of your eyes."

"As a hornless cow, I will drive the cattle into the ford to trample you."

"Then I will break your leg."

And so it happened with the eel, the wolf, and the cattle that trampled through the water until Cú Chulainn cried out: "Alone I stand against these hordes, unable to hold them, unable to let them go. Tell Conchobar to come; I cannot kill all their champions."

Exhausted Cú Chulainn met a squinting old woman crouched by the roadside, milking a cow with three teats, and he asked her for a drink of milk.

"For the giver's health, and may the gods of my people bless you," he said.

The old woman's hump disappeared. She gave him milk from the second teat, and her eye healed; she gave him milk from the third teat, and she no longer limped.

"You said you would never heal me." Morrígu, the goddess of battle and fate, grinned, and then she flew off with the crows.

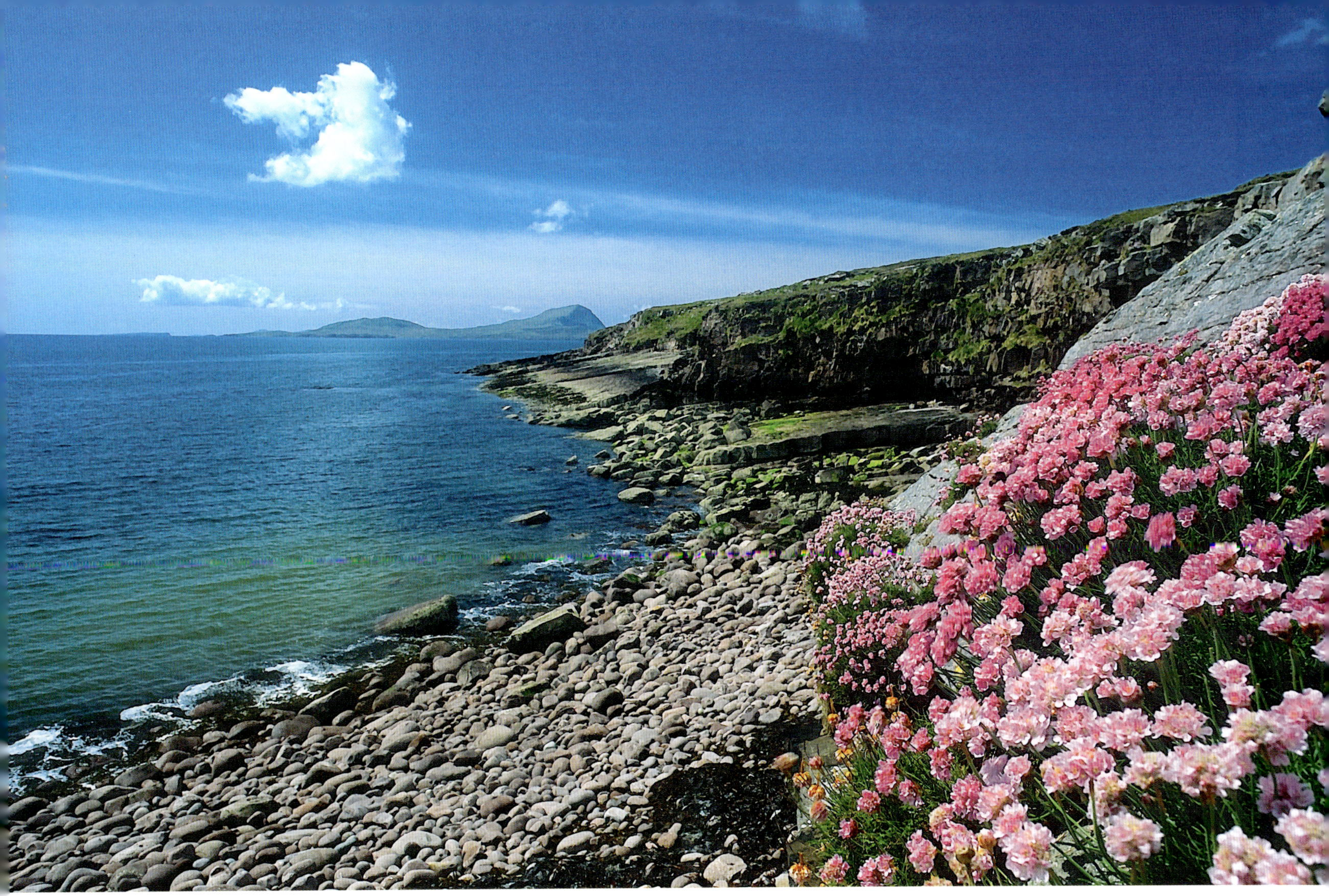

Corraun Peninsula

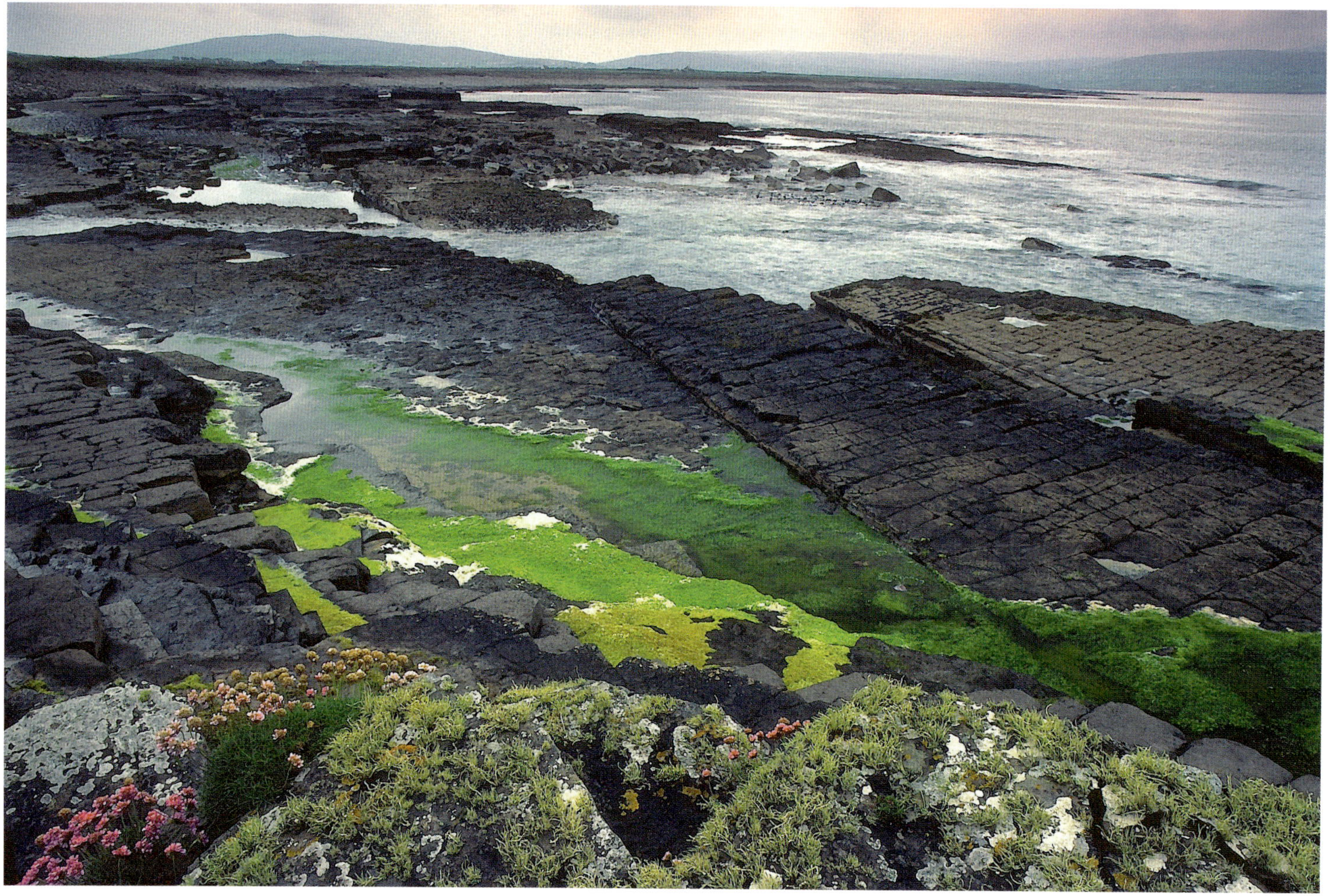

Downpatrick Head

The First Battle

One evening, Laeg, Cú Chulainn's charioteer, saw someone approaching.

"Here comes a man all alone, little Hound," he said.

"What kind of man?" asked Cú Chulainn.

"That's quickly said: a tall, broad, dignified-looking man, with short, blond, curly hair, a green cloak held by a silver brooch, and a knee-length tunic of royal silk embroidered with gold. On his black shield is a golden boss, and he carries a five-pronged spear and a forked javelin. Graceful and unusual, he looks, but no one pays him any attention, as if they couldn't see him."

"They cannot," replied Cú Chulainn. "He is one from the Otherworld, who has pity on me."

It was Lugh the Bright One, Cú Chulainn's fairy father.

"My wounds are grievous," wailed Cú Chulainn.

"Sleep a little," said Lugh, and he sang as men sing for men until Cú Chulainn fell asleep. He slept for three days and three nights, and then Lugh left him, and the Hound of Culann prepared for battle.

Laeg got the sickle chariot ready, donned his armor, and painted the charioteer's mark on his forehead. He took the whip and the goad in his right hand, the reins in his left, and threw the iron armor over the horses, covering them from head to hoof with spearheads, spiked points, blades, and barbs. He protected the chariot with a spell and made it invisible. The hero Cú Chulainn put on his armor—twenty-seven tunics of waxed leather, smoothed and pressed, worn directly on his skin so his rage would not burst them. Over them, hardened battle girdles from his hips to his armpits, then a silk apron, and finally a leather apron. Then the champion took up his weapons and his helmet, from which his war cry echoed like that of a hundred warriors. The cloak of concealment, woven from the fabric his fairy father had brought him from the Land of Promise, was draped over him.

The first spasm that seized Cú Chulainn turned him into a monster, hideous and shapeless. Every bone and joint in him shook like a reed in a stream, and with a furious twist, his body spun inside his skin. His neck swelled, his face turned into a red bowl, one eye disappeared while the other bulged out, his teeth bared, smoke rose from his head, and then black blood spurted forth.

When the spasm had left him, Cú Chulainn climbed into the sickle chariot with Laeg, and they set out. They killed one hundred, then two hundred, then three hundred, then four hundred, and then five hundred. It was the first true battle. Cú Chulainn encircled his enemies. They fell sole to sole, neck to neck, lying six deep, and it was called the Sixfold Slaughter. No man escaped without a wound that marked him for life. Yet Cú Chulainn remained unscathed, losing not a single drop of blood, nor did Laeg or the horses.

As Cú Chulainn felt that his appearance in battle hadn't done him any justice, he revealed himself the following morning to the women and girls, the poets and singers. He was a striking young man, his tri-colored hair styled in three plaits that flowed down his neck, with shimmering strands cascading over his shoulders. He had four dimples on each cheek, seven pupils in each eye, seven toes on each foot, and seven fingers on each hand, with nails like the talons of a hawk or a griffin. That morning, he wore a shimmering garment of purple and silk, a golden sword adorned with an ivory hilt at his side. In one hand, he held the heads of nine men; in the other, ten, shaking them toward his enemies. The women climbed onto the soldiers' shoulders to catch a glimpse of the hero. Only Maeve dared not show her face.

"Dammit, I can't see the boy," she lamented.

"It wouldn't bring you any peace," said Ailill's charioteer.

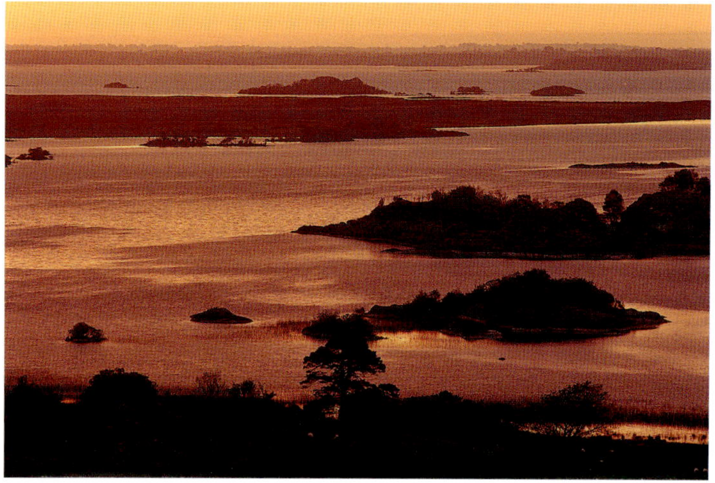

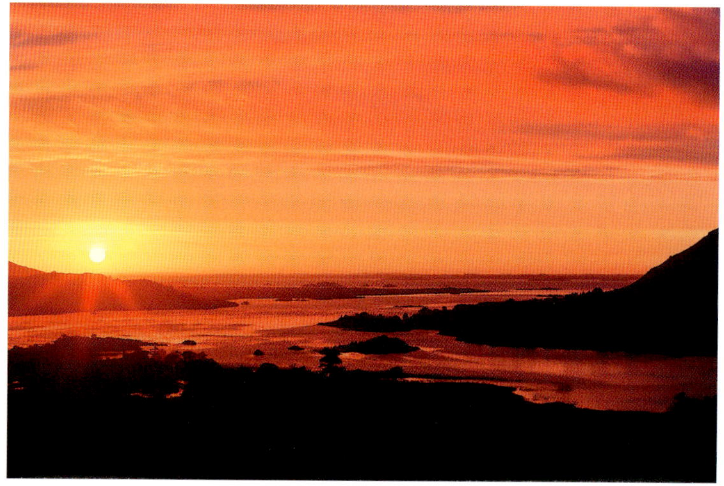

Left and right: Lough Mask

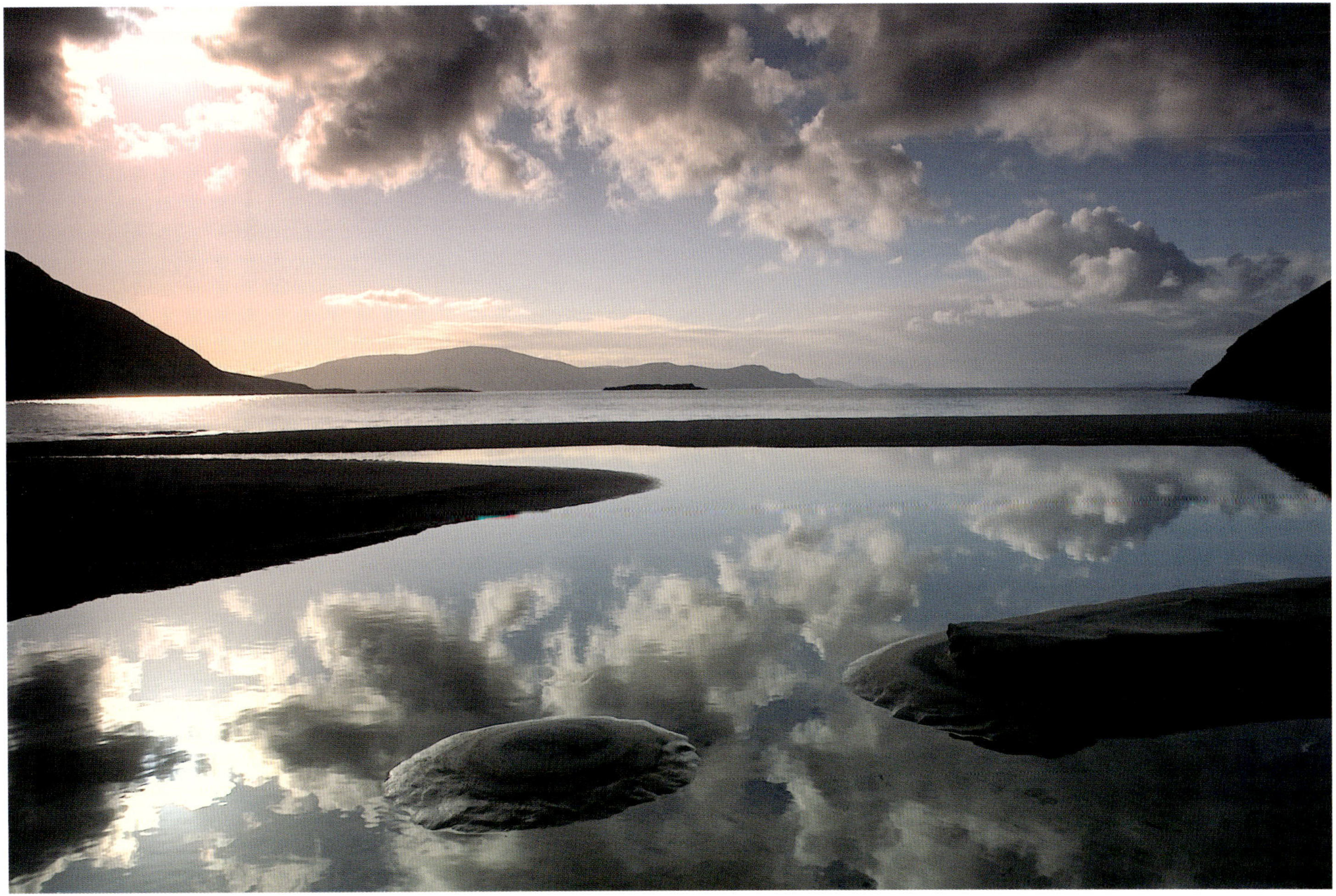

Achill Island

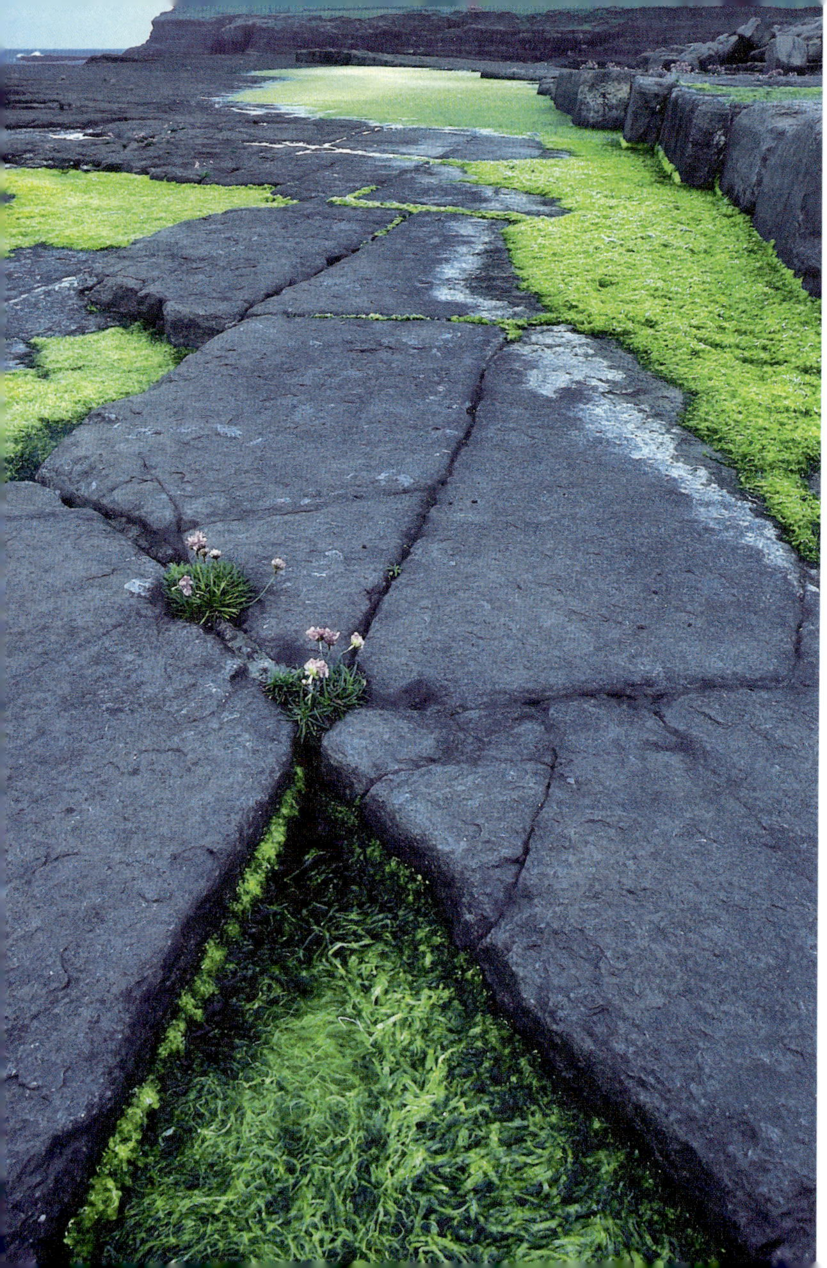

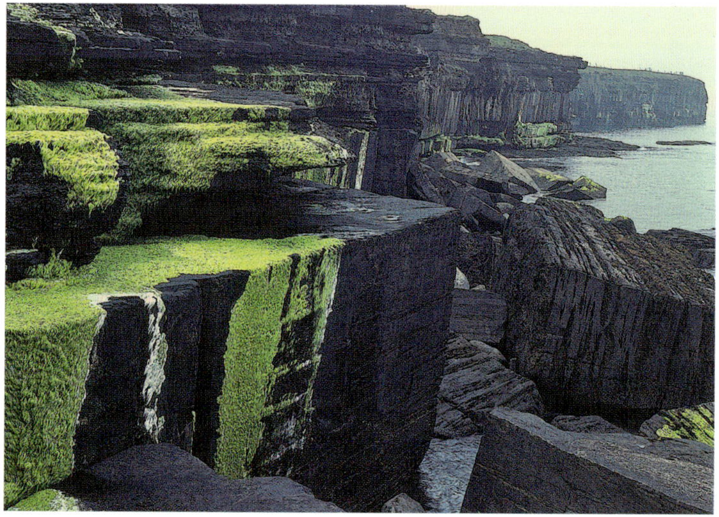

Left and right: Downpatrick Head

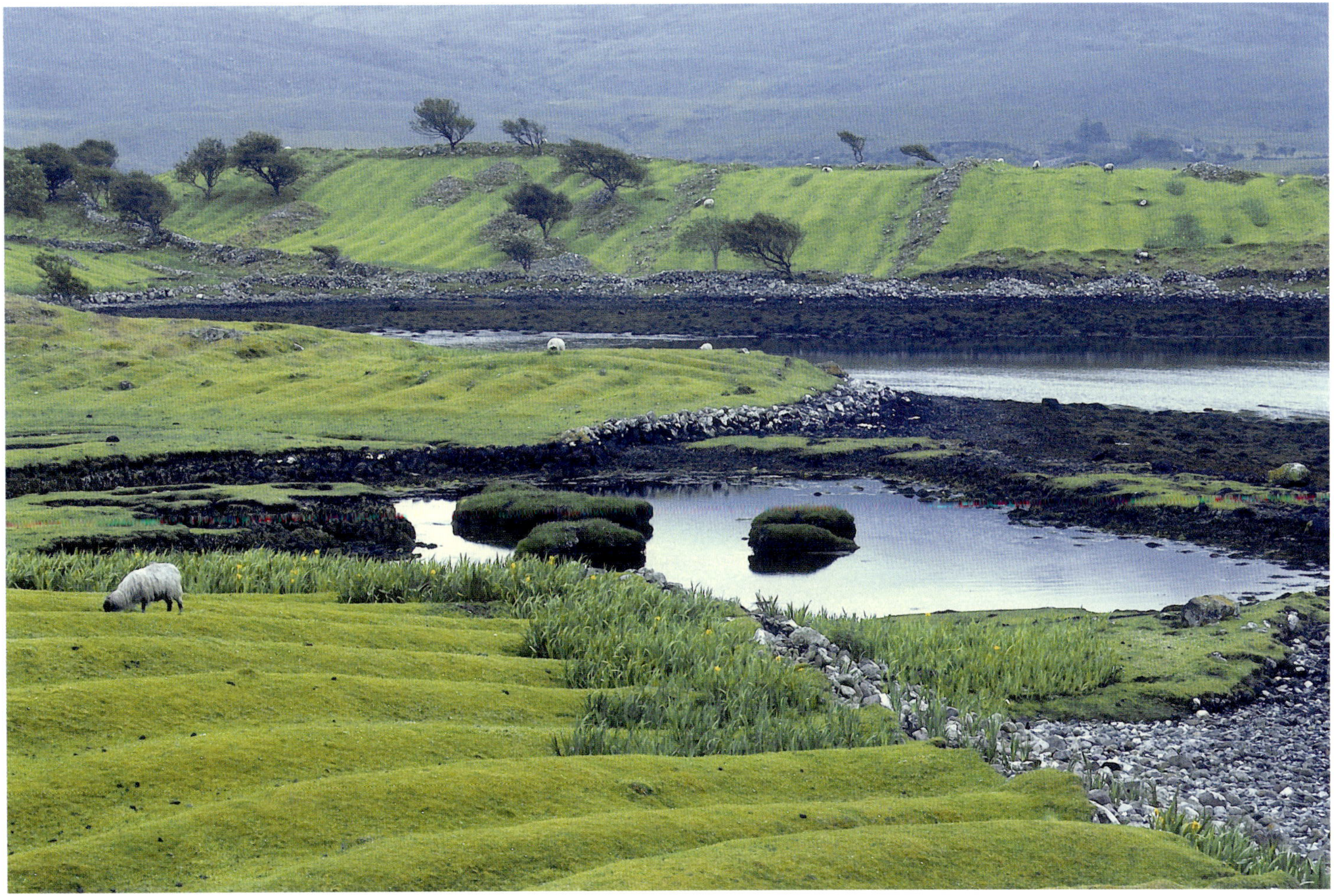

Corraun Peninsula

The Combat of the Brothers

Everybody agreed that Ferdia, Cú Chulainn's foster brother, was the only man who stood a chance against him, and Maeve summoned Ferdia. But he refused to come. So, she sent poets and bards out to mock him until his cheeks burned red and he followed them to Maeve's tent. There, Maeve had him sit beside Finnabair, her daughter, who handed him cups of wine, each with three kisses, and let him pick sweet apples from her cleavage until he felt just great.

"If you defeat the Hound of Ulster, I will give you a chariot worth three times seven bondmaids," began Maeve listing off her rewards: harnesses, a portion of the Plain of Ai, the right to remain forever at her court, wine included, his kith and kin free from tribute and taxes, a leaf-shaped broach cast in gold, Finnabair for his wife. "And you are also welcome between my thighs," she concluded.

"That's all very nice," Ferdia said, "but I'm not going to fight my own foster brother."

Maeve fell silent for a moment. "Then it is true, what Cú Chulainn said."

"What did he say?"

"That it would be no great triumph if his biggest feat was to overcome you."

"He shouldn't have said that," Ferdia howled. "Tomorrow morning, I will fight him."

"You have my blessing," Maeve grinned.

When Cú Chulainn heard that his foster brother would meet him in battle next morning, he returned to Emer and stayed with her for the night. Ferdia, meanwhile, could not sleep, and his charioteer reminded him of all the times Cú Chulainn had stood by his side, saving him from death and shame. "You should have told me that before," Ferdia said, "I wouldn't have come looking for this fight but let me sleep now."

The two brothers fought in the ford for three days, their swords screaming like demons, and the river diverted its course. On the fourth day, Cú Chulainn could bear it no longer, and he reached for the Gae Bolga and drove it through Ferdia's armor. The spear unfurled within him, releasing a thousand spikes.

"Hound of great deeds, you have slain me with treachery," Ferdia cried. "Your guilt clings to me, my blood to your hands. My bones are broken, my heart is blood. I fought poorly, Hound; I die."

"Ferdia, my brother, slain by treachery, how I mourn our final battle. As fair as Finnabair may be, she is but a hollow trinket. You are dead now, and I must live and miss you forever."

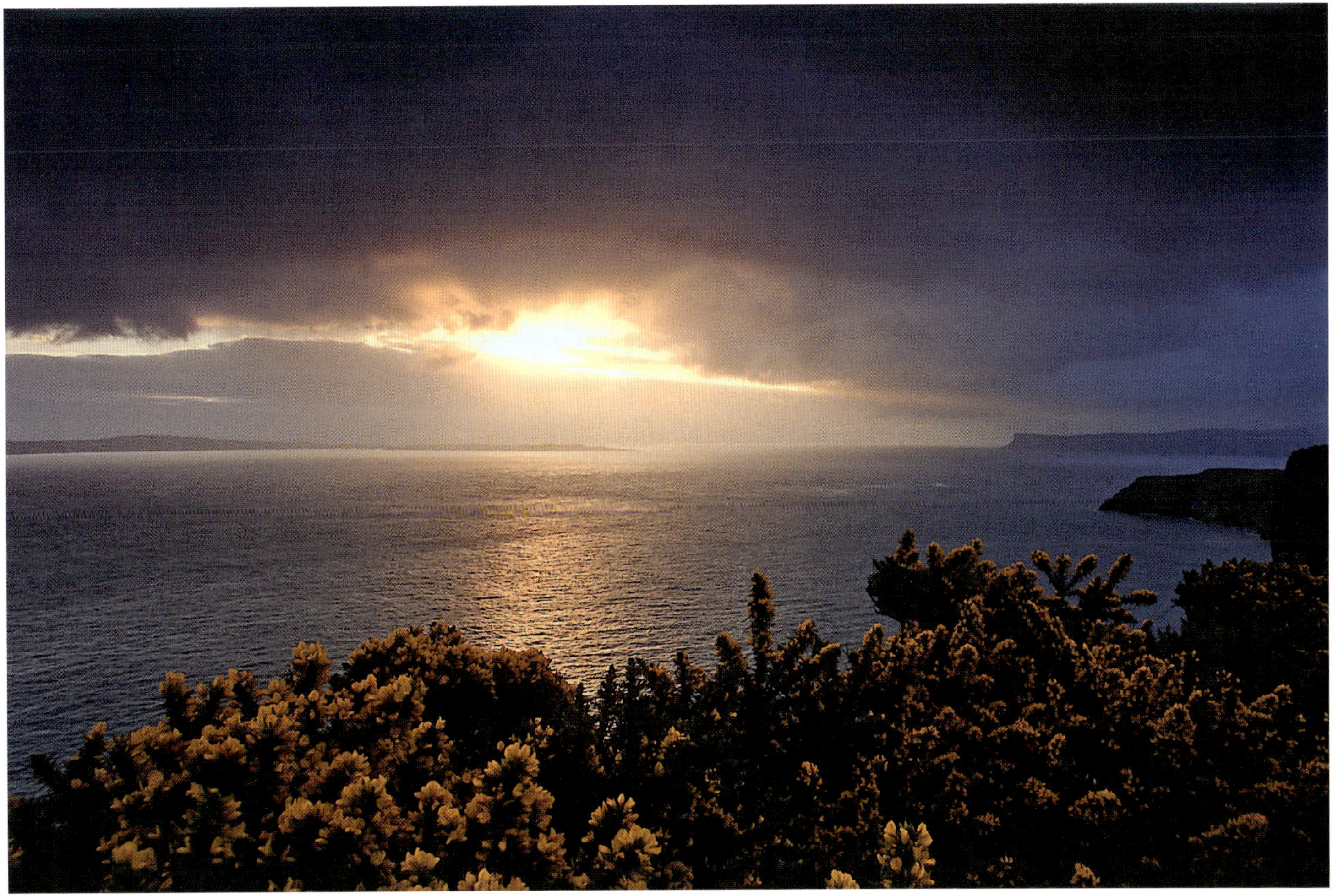

Rathlin Island

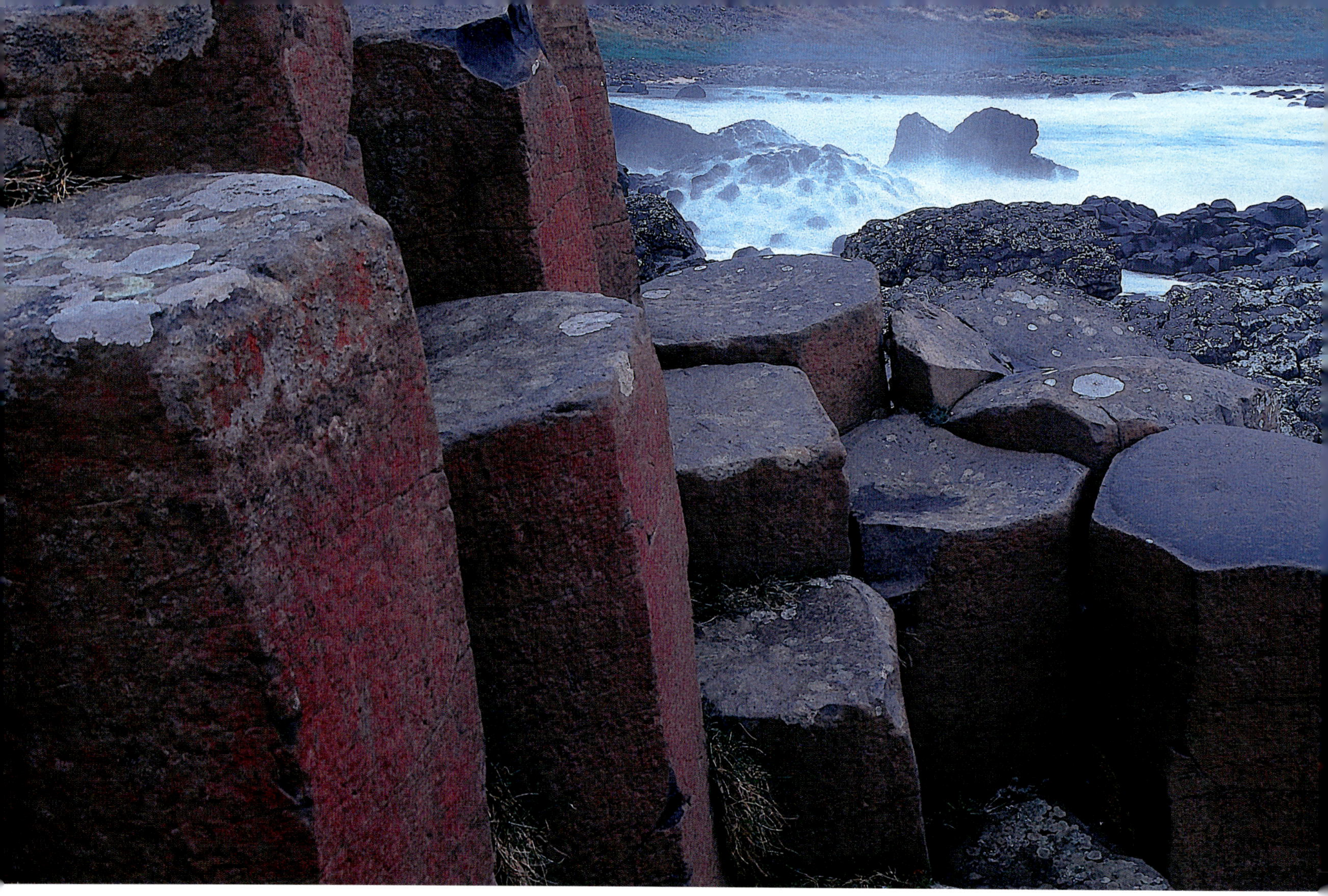

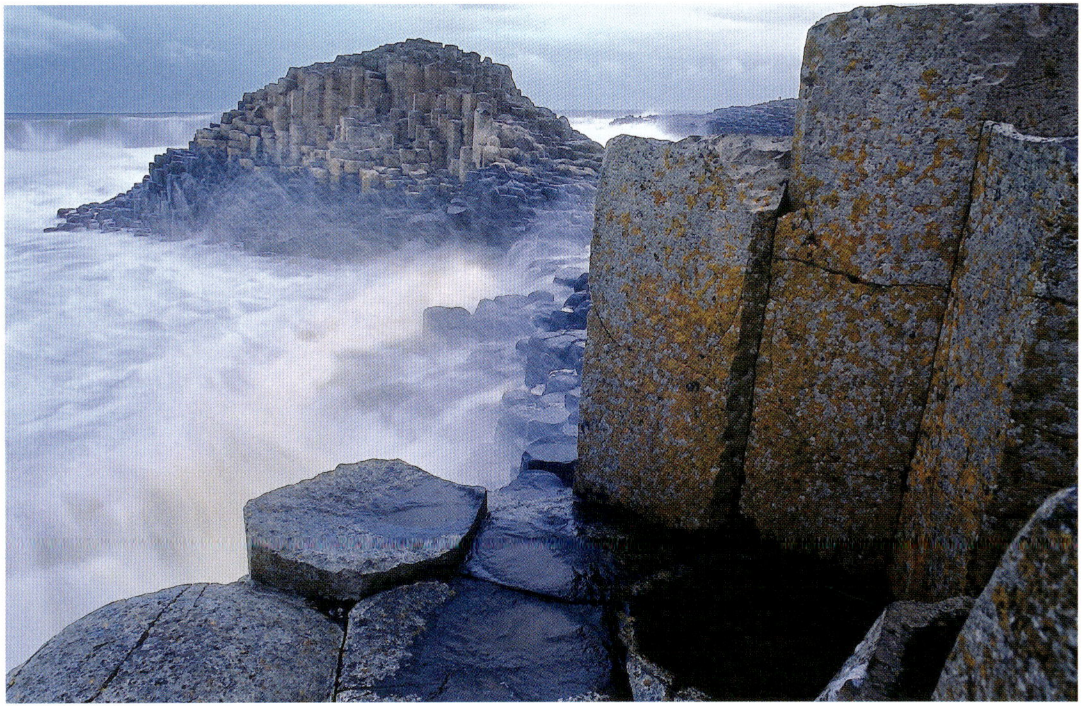

Left page and right: Giant's Causeway

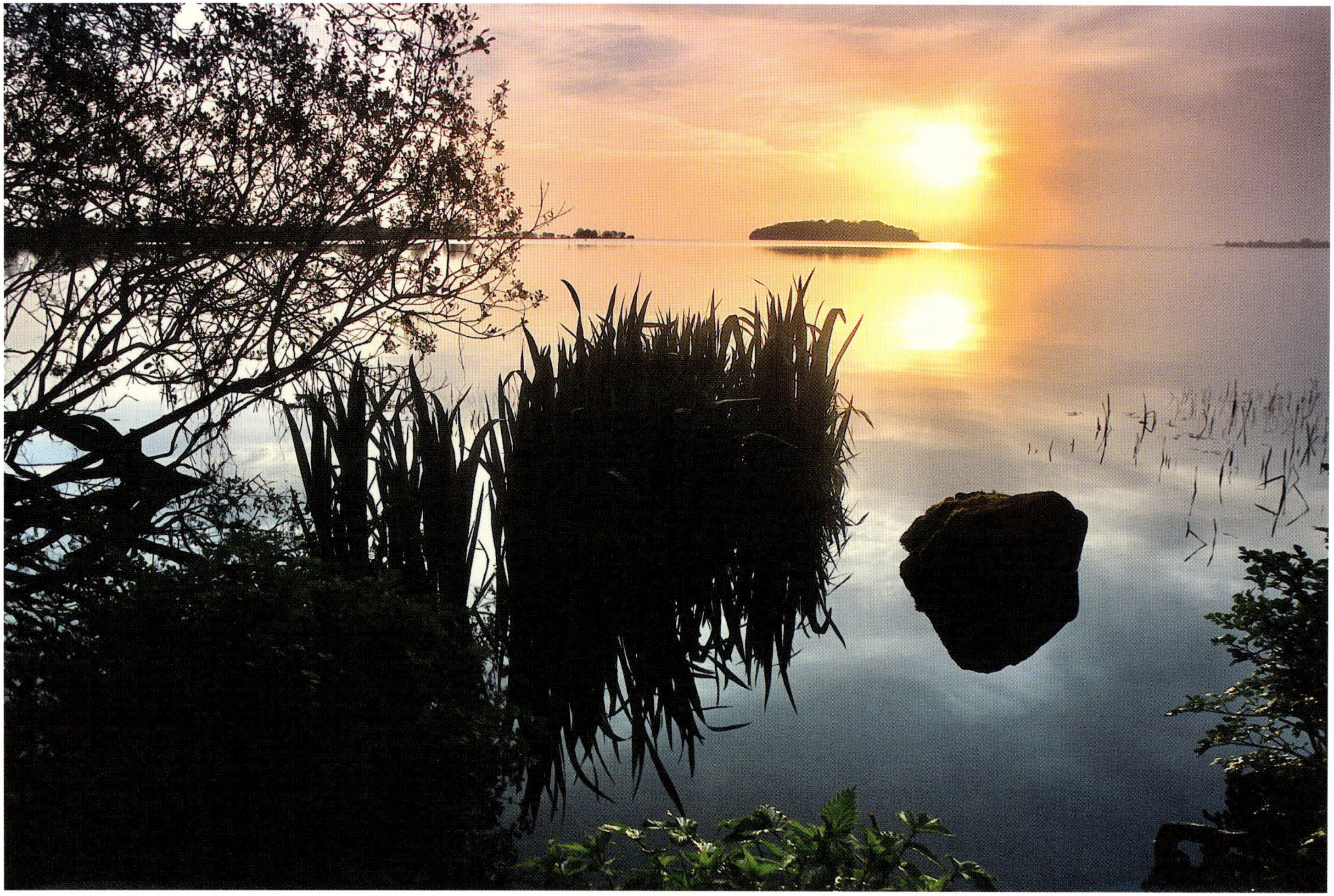

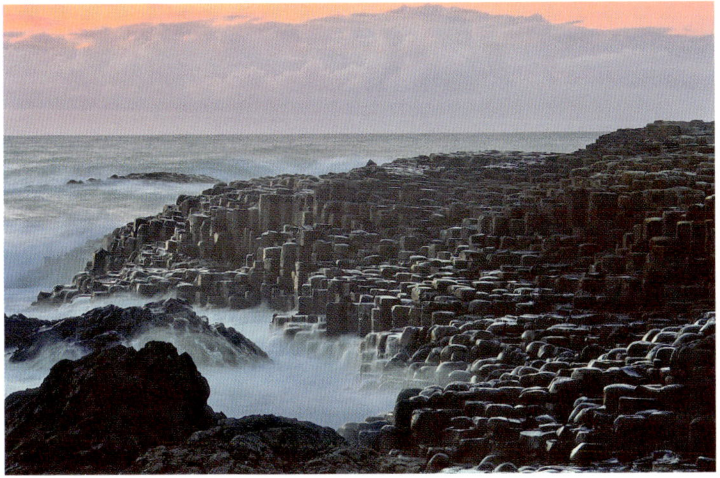

Left page: Lough Neagh
Left and right: Giant's Causeway

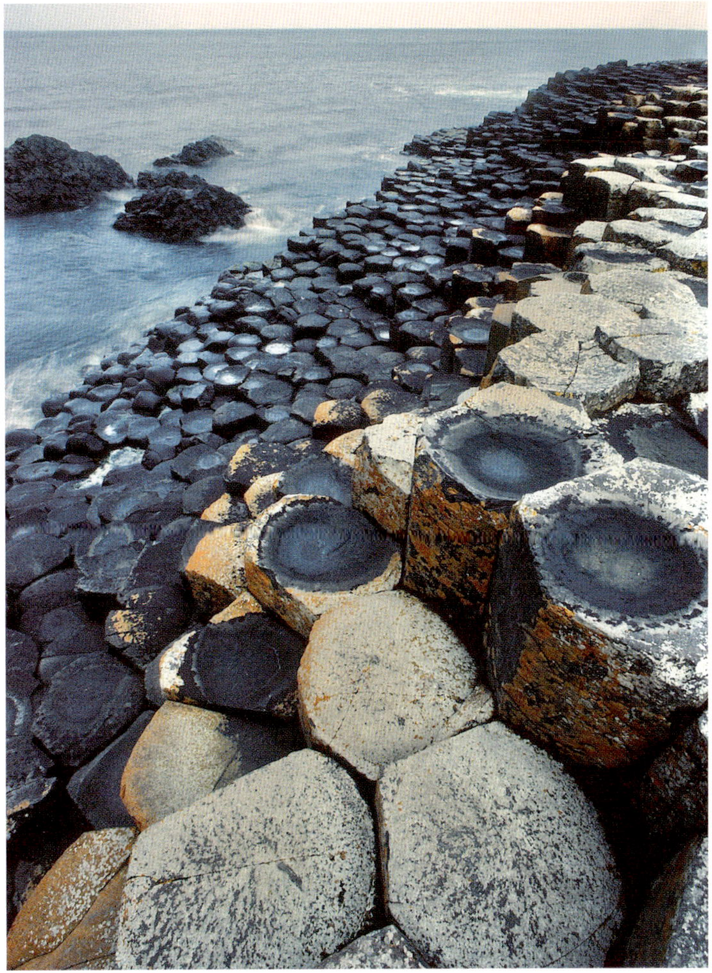

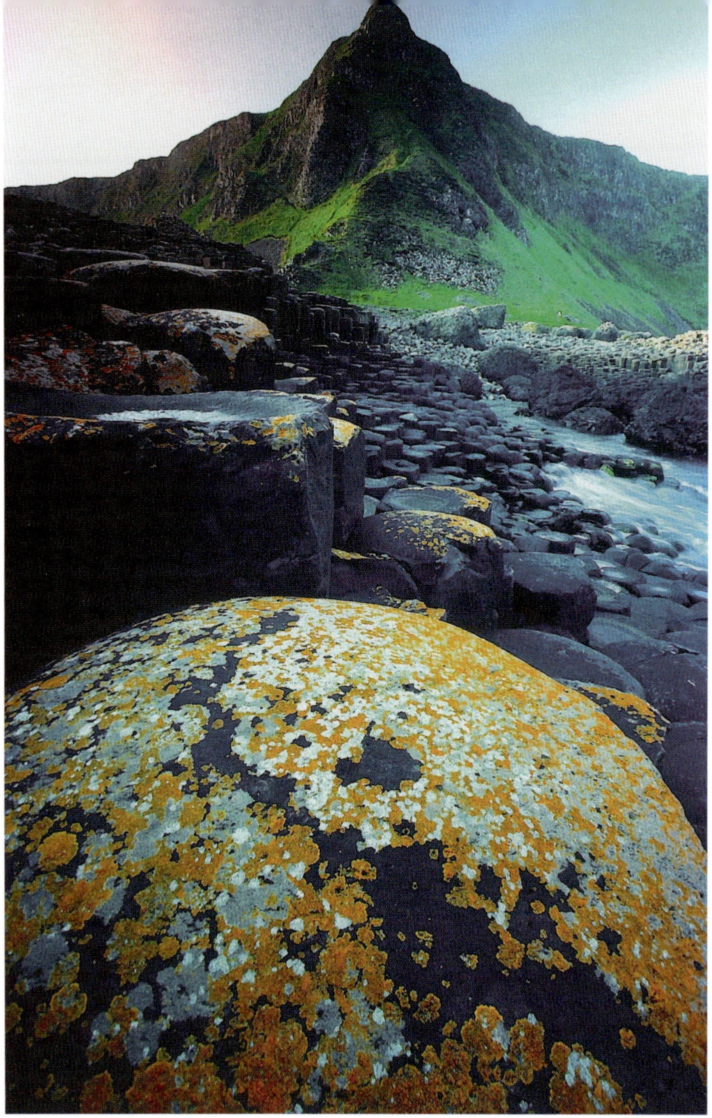

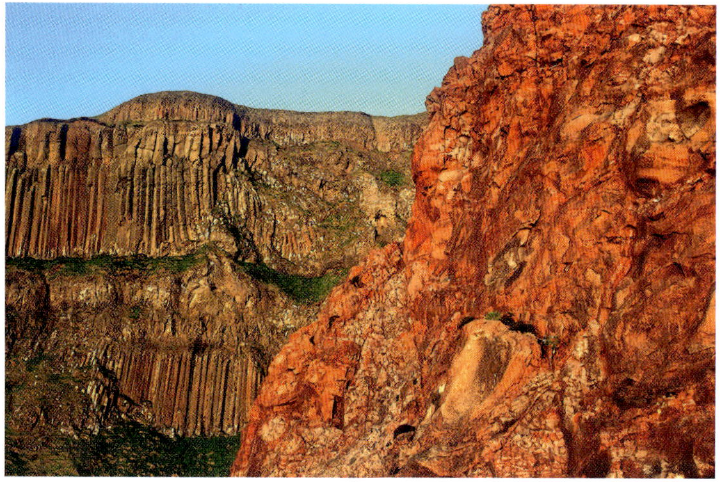

Left and right: Giant's Causeway

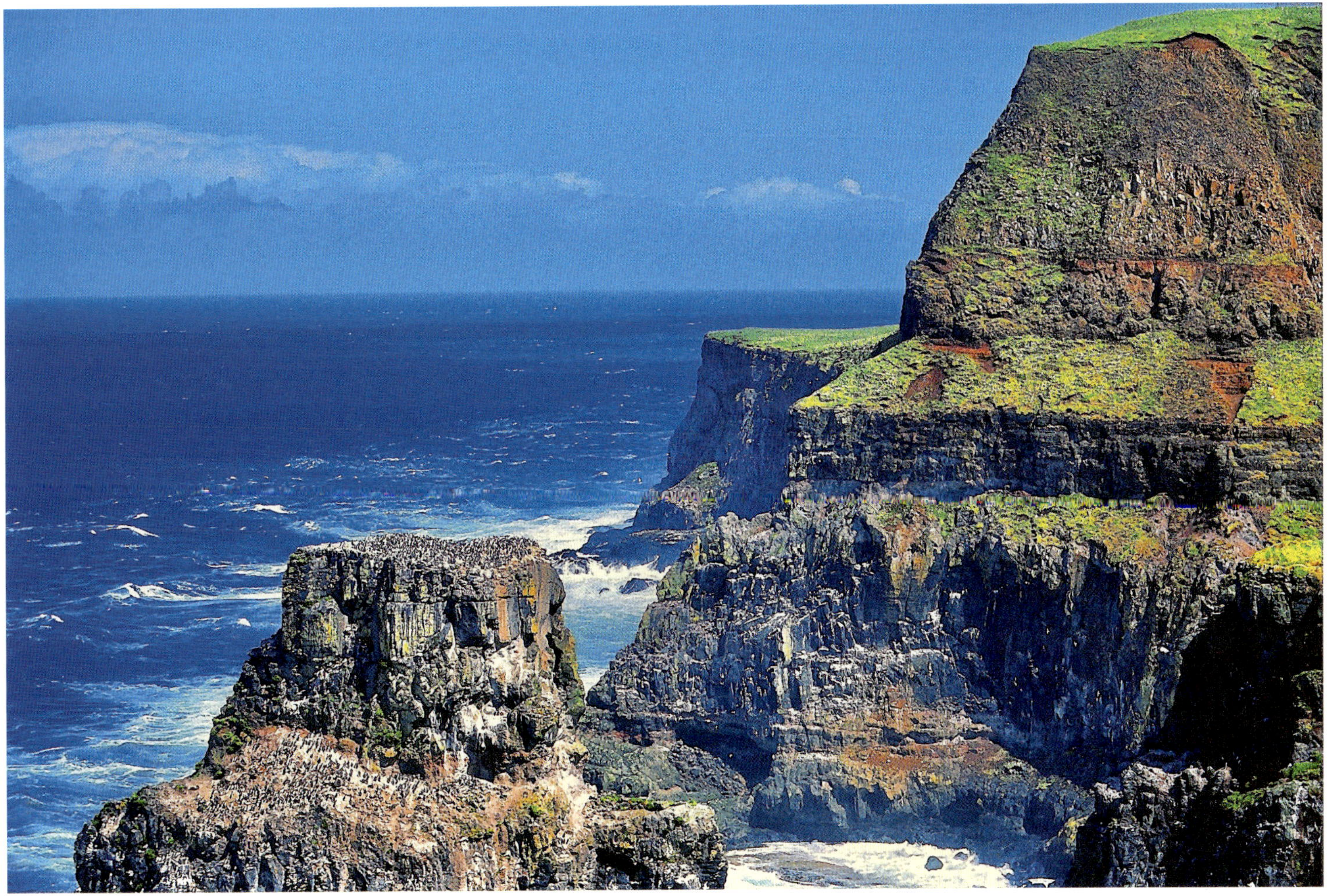

Rathlin Island

The Cattle Raid—how it ended

The men of Ulster rose from their pangs and marched against Ailill and Maeve. When Cú Chulainn joined the battle, it was already noon, and he smashed their last company. This time, nothing was left of his chariots but a handful of ribs from the frame and a handful of spokes from the wheels.

Maeve had set up a shelter of shields to protect the rear of her army. There she got her gush of blood. “Fergus,” she called, “you have to take over while I relieve myself.”

“You have picked a bad time for that, woman.”

“I can’t help it.”

When Maeve relieved herself, it dug three great channels, each one big enough to sweep away an entire house, and to this day the spot is called Maeve’s Foul Place. Cú Chulainn found her there. “I should kill you,” he said, but he was not a killer of women.

“We had shame and shambles here today,” Maeve said to Fergus when she returned.

“That happens,” he answered, “when a herd is led by a mare.”

On the Plain of Ai, the Brown Bull of Cuailnge met the white-horned Finnbenach. That night, the bulls circled the island, and in the morning, the men of Ireland saw the Brown Bull in the West with the White on its horns. Ailill and Maeve made peace with the men of Ulster, who returned to Emain Macha. Finnabair, their daughter, stayed with Cú Chulainn. When he died in his thirty-third year, Morrigú, the crow, perched on his shoulder.

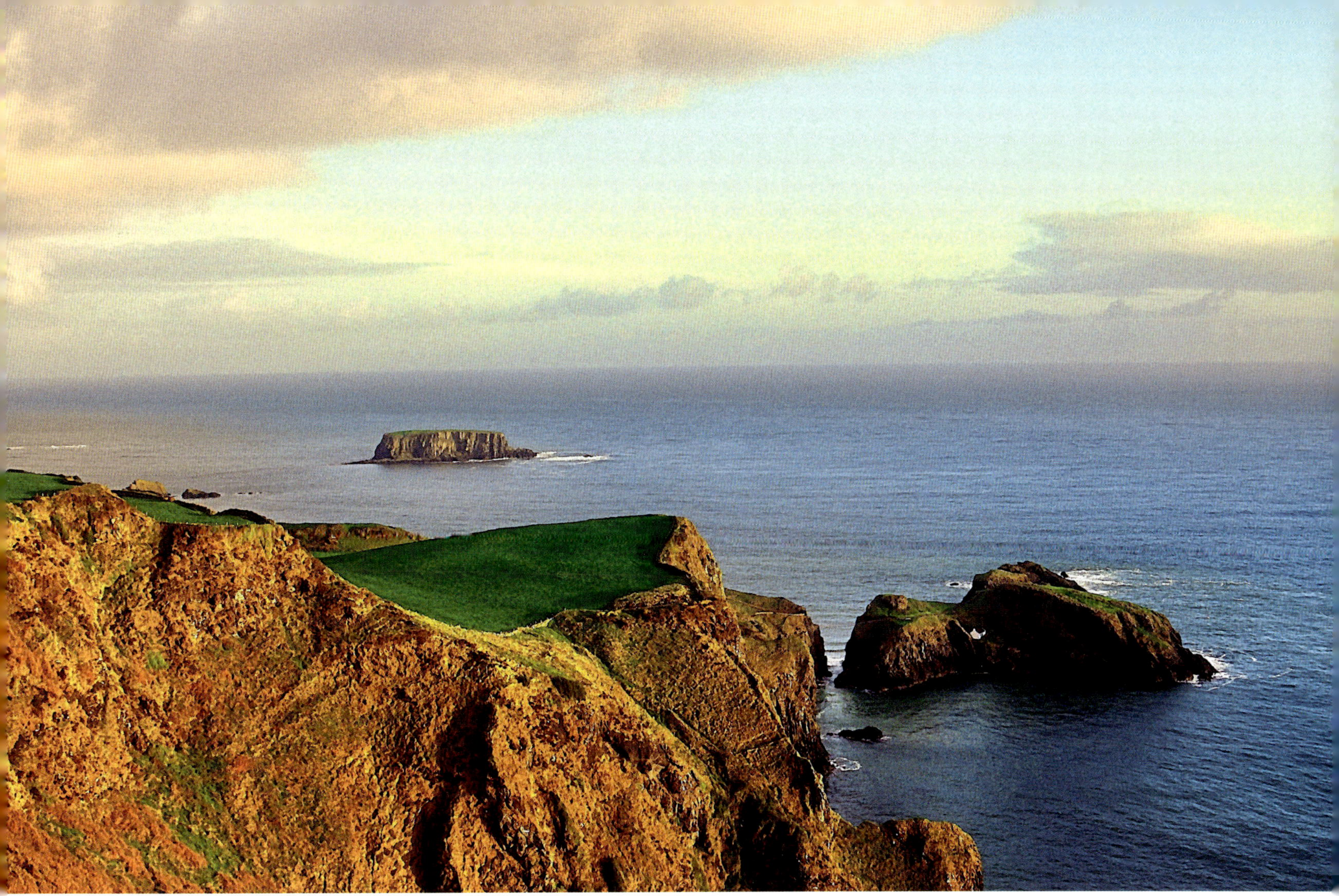

Antrim Coast

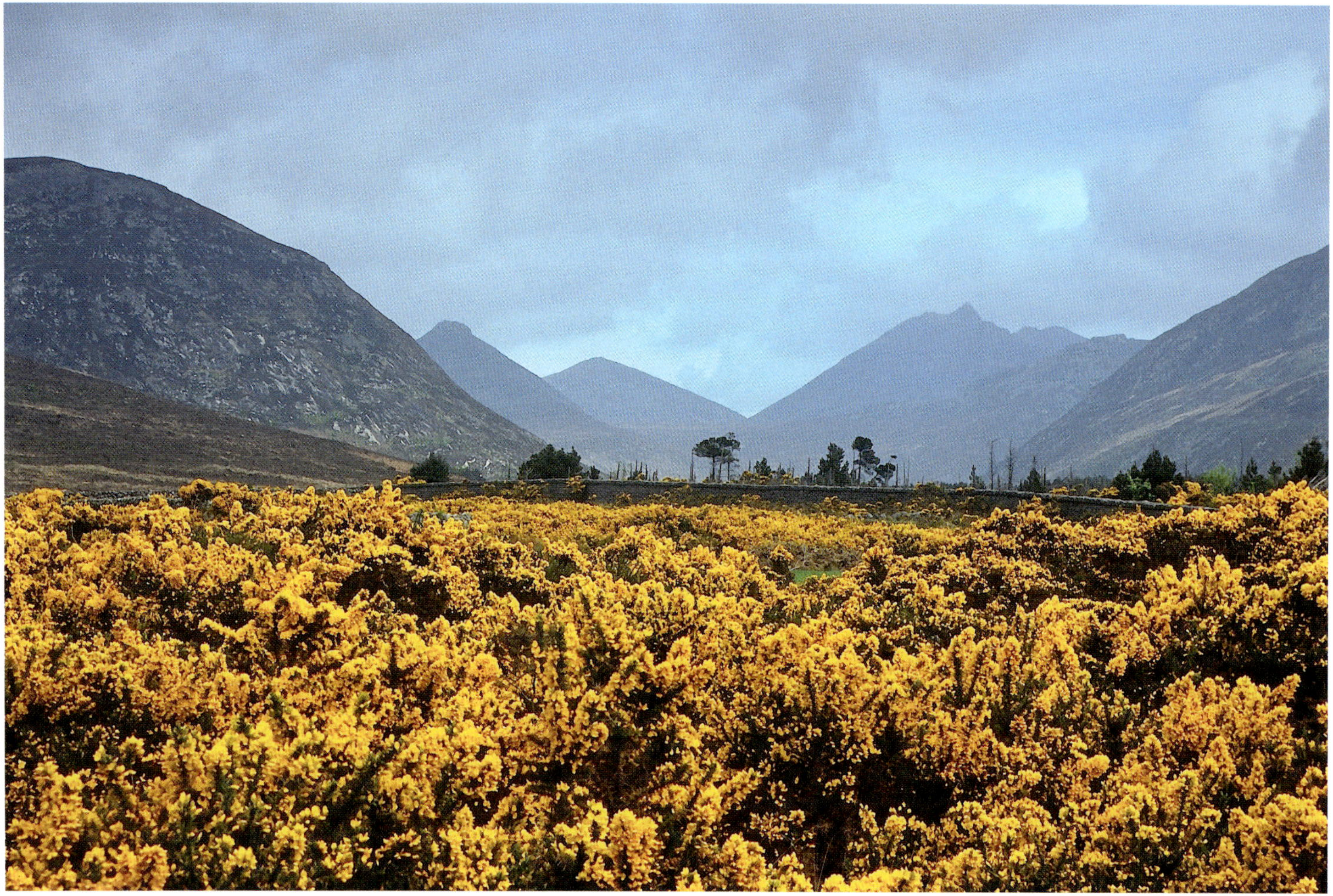

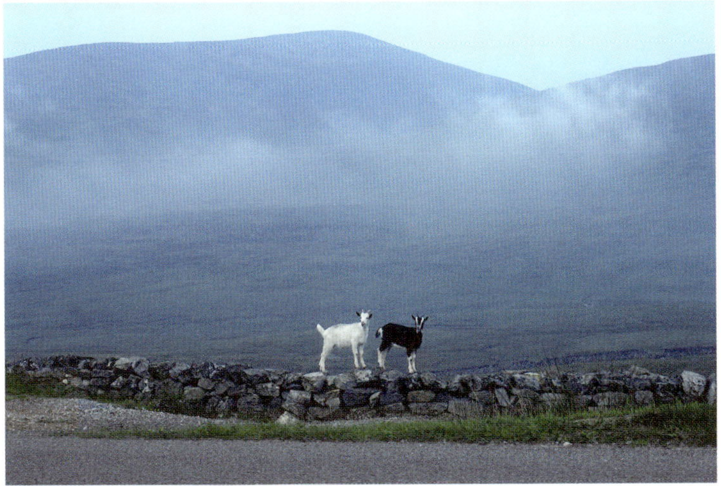

Left page and left: Mourne Mountains
Right: Carrick-a-Rede

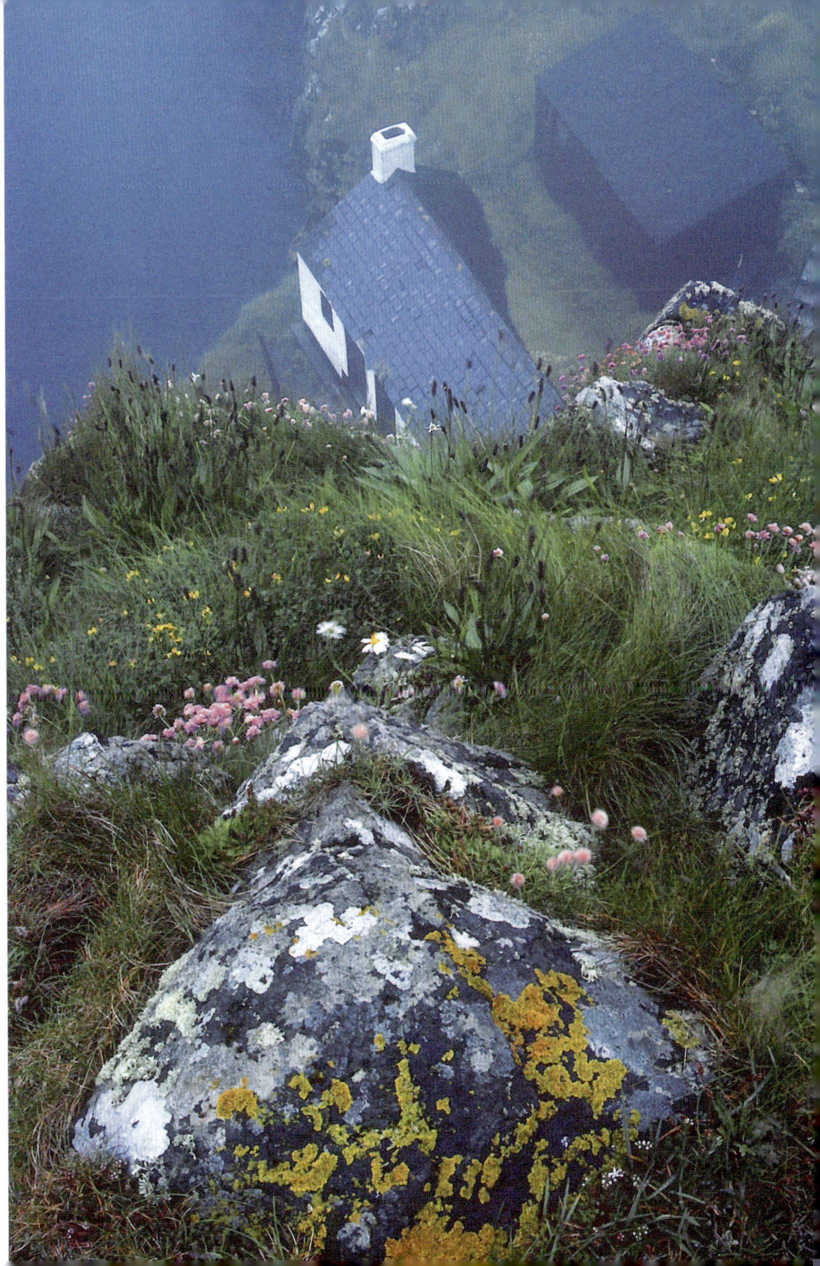

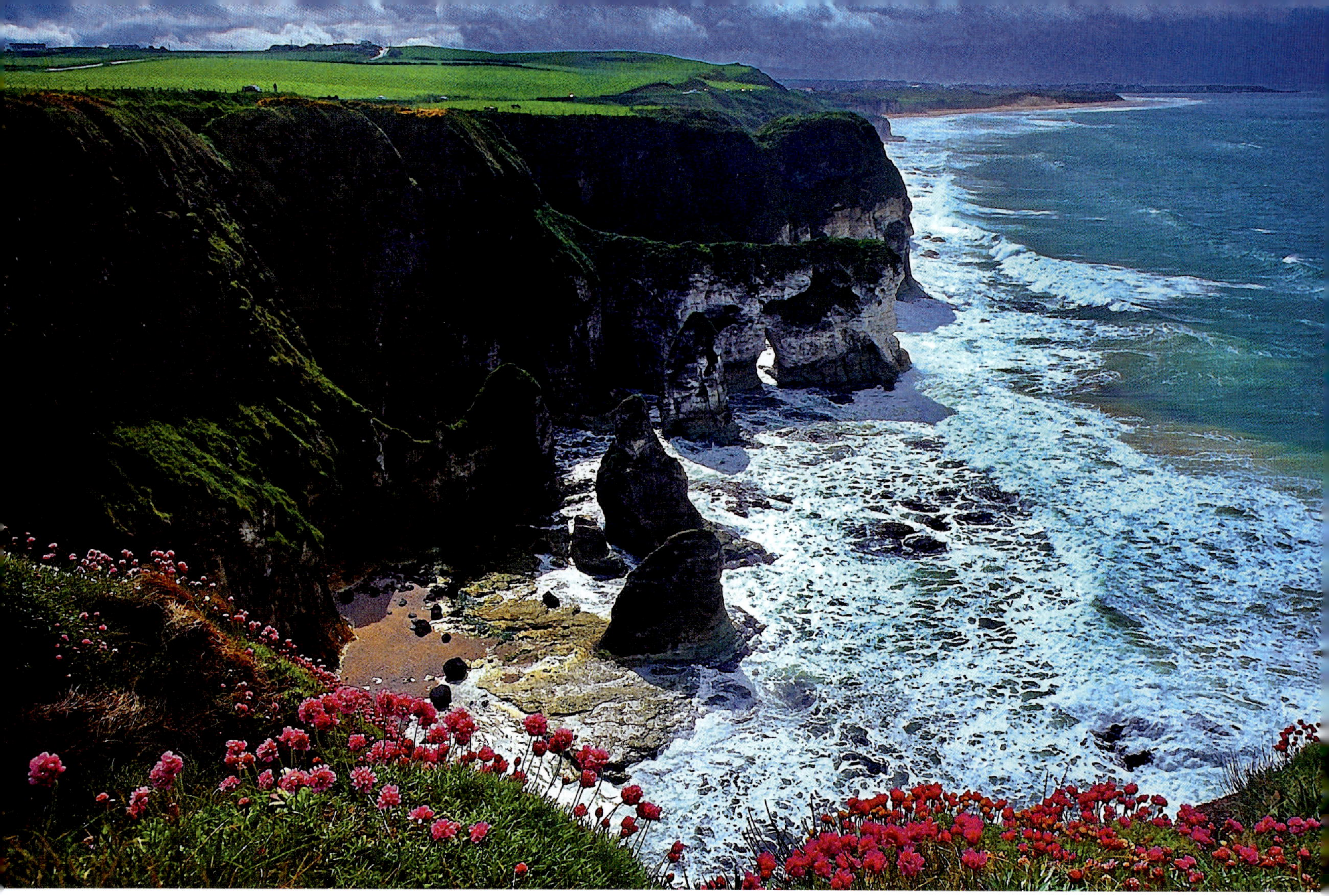

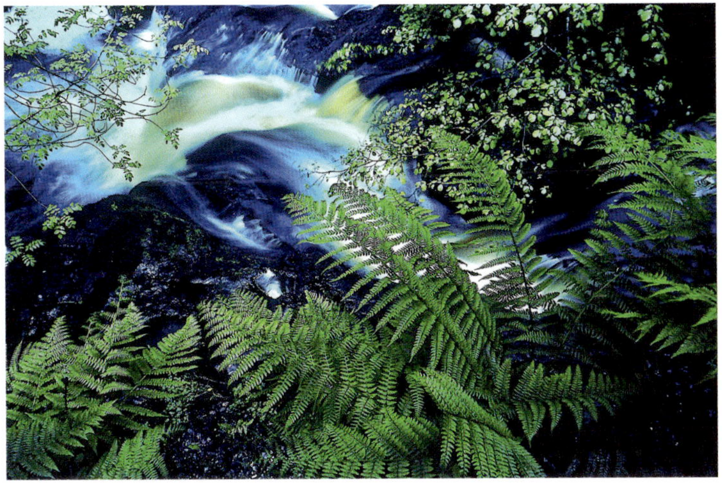

Left page: Antrim Coast
Left and right: Valley of the waterfalls

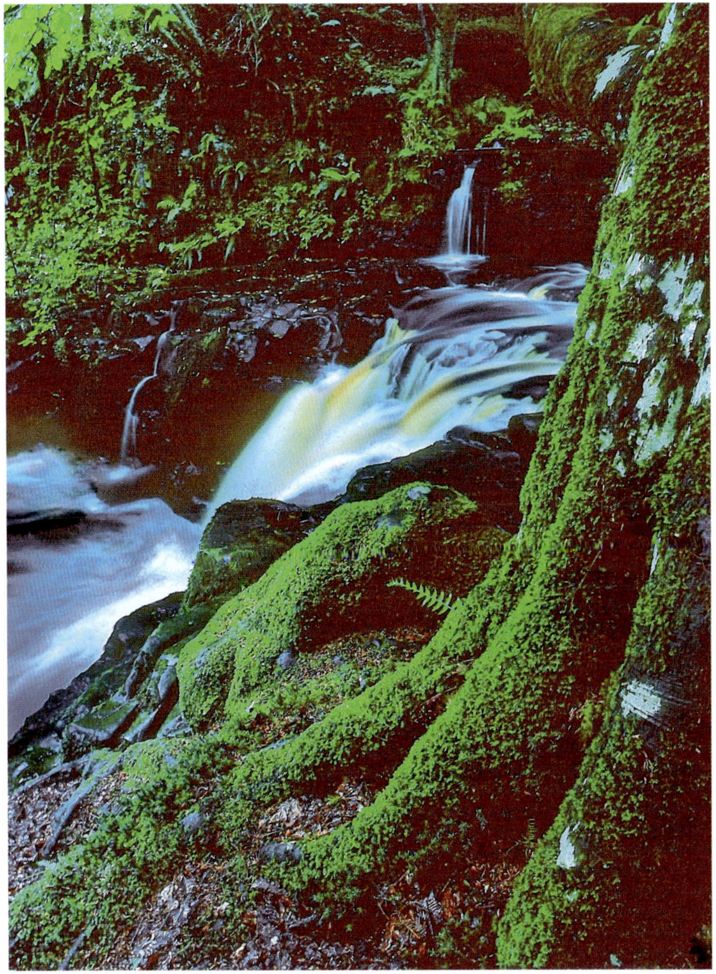

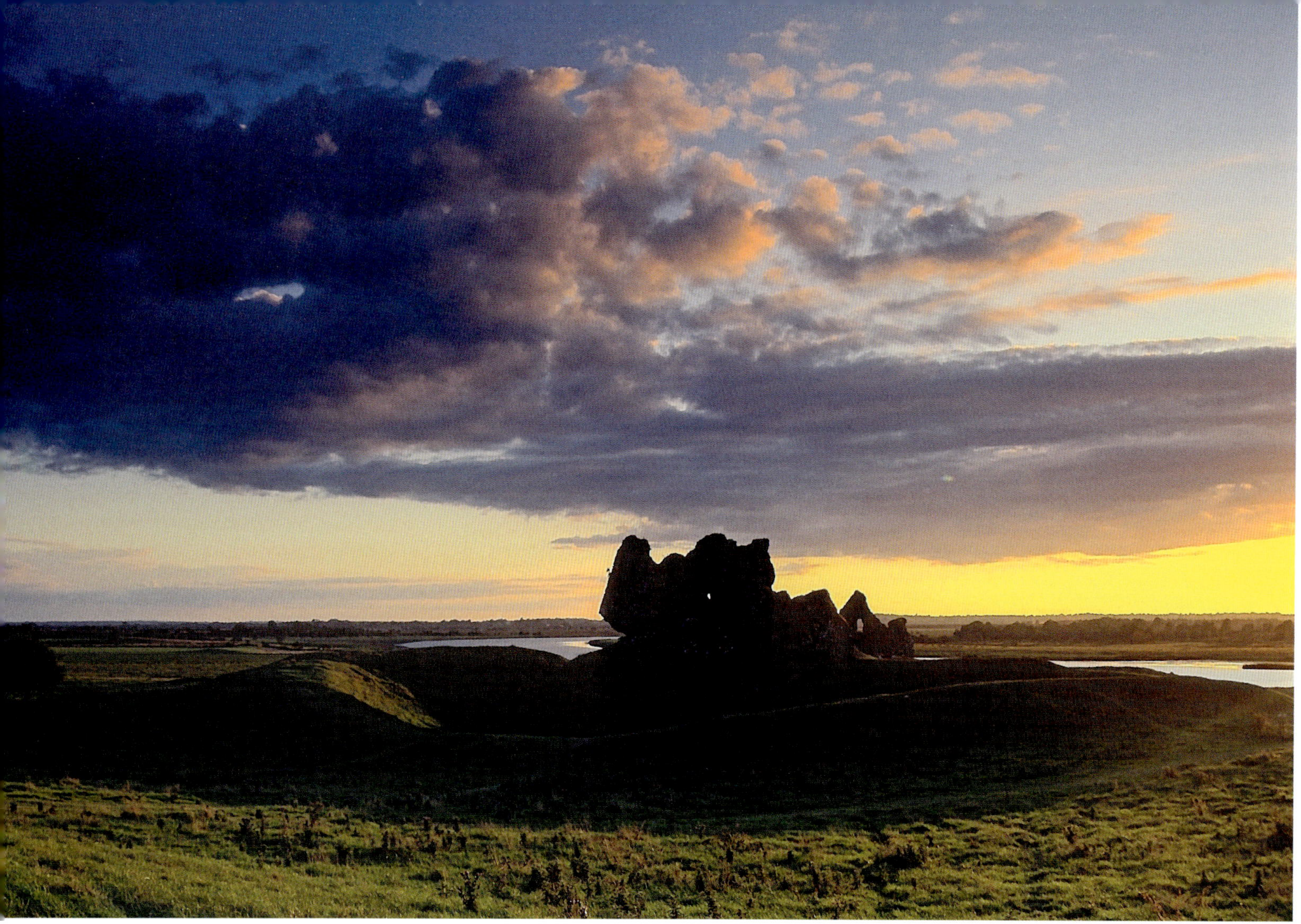

Clonmacnoise

The Stepmother

Aoife looked up to her older sister, Aobh, like any second-born girl would do. When Bodb, their father, was elected king of the Tuatha Dé Danann he gave his eldest daughter to Lir in marriage to gain his support. Aobh made quite a success of it. Bodb was pleased, and Aoife could see how happy the couple was. They had four kids, Fionnuala first, and then three boys. But Aobh died, and for Bodb—still in need of Lir's backing—it must have been obvious that his younger daughter should now take her place. Thus, from one day to the next, Aoife found herself with a husband and four small kids, and like her big sister, she wanted to make a success of it.

But in all fairness, this wasn't easy. The four children were missing their mother, and her new husband mourned his late wife. Aoife tried to get some stability back into the lives of the children, she made rules; and she tried to earn Lir's attention with her skills, her compassion, and her looks. But he had eyes only for his offspring, doting on his kids, letting them get away with anything. After Aobh's passing, he had them sleep in his bedroom so he could watch them last before he went to bed and first when he woke up. Now, this was Aoife's bedroom too, but even at the smallest noise she made, the brats started to cry, and Lir got angry. "It's only a matter of time," Aoife told herself. She needed to be patient. And in all fairness, she was. She kept training the children, taught them to sing and to swim, she learned cooking, stitching, and playing cards to please Lir. She made sure she always looked her best. Months passed, years passed. One night, she woke to find the marital bed beside her empty. There was a moaning in the room coming from Fionnuala's corner or perhaps from her dreams. A surge of disgust flooded her—she couldn't take this any longer.

The next morning, she rallied the servants she thought were loyal to her and ordered them to take the children away. They refused even when offered money. So, Aoife went to the armory, picked up a sword, but she couldn't raise it against the kids. Eventually, she took the children swimming to a remote lake, and there, the moment they went into the water, she turned them into four beautiful swans.

Right away, Fionnuala started to complain, begging for mercy. Suddenly, she reminded Aoife of her dead sister, and she felt ashamed. But she could not revoke the spell. "It will be only a matter of time," she heard herself saying, "until a woman from the South marries a man from the North."

Fionnuala opened her beak and let out a hiss that went right through Aoife.

"And you may keep your human voices and thoughts," she conceded.

Three times three hundred years, the four swans spent on different lakes, until they heard the tolling of a bell, got christened by a compassionate monk, and regained their human form just before they died. The people who, over the years, had listened to their singing felt joy and sadness at the same time, and to this day every child in Ireland knows their story.

Only a few wonder what happened to Aoife. Surely, it did not take long until the deed of the evil stepmother was revealed, and some say, Bodb, her own father, turned her into a demon and left her to the winds for all time. Others say Aoife was turned into a crane that had to stay in the air until she died. Only then Manannán mac Lir, the son of the sea, took notice of her and made a bag out of her plumage, in which he kept all that was precious to him: his knife, his shirt, the king of Scotland's shears, the king of Lochlainn's helmet, the bones of Assal's swine, and the girdle of the great whale's back. At high tide, the treasures were visible in the sea, but at ebb tide they vanished. Later, some said the bag also contained the letters of the Ogham alphabet that look a bit like the legs of a crane and were used for writing before Christian times. In any case, the bag lent influence and strength to its owner, and for a time it also belonged to Fionn mac Cumhaill.

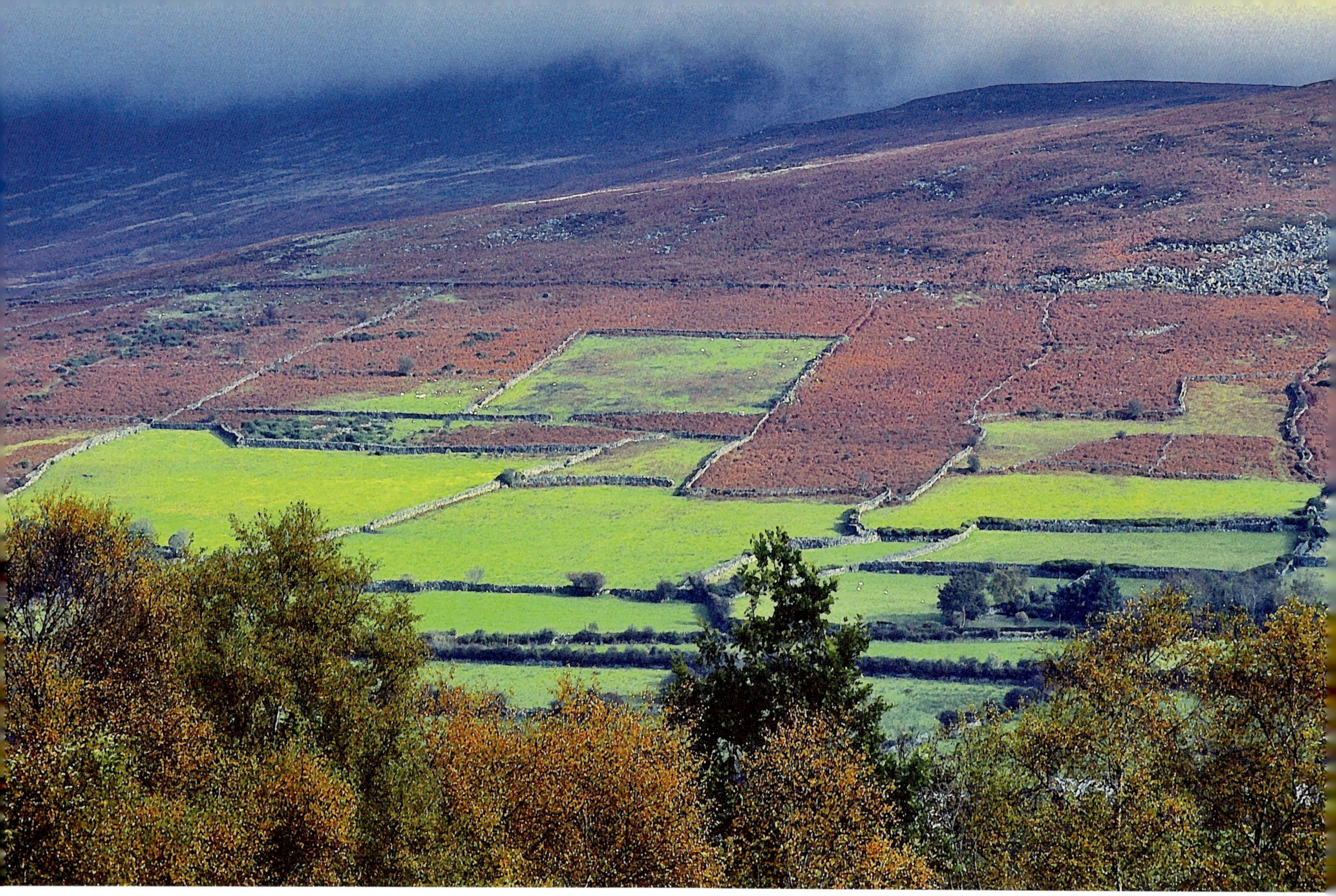

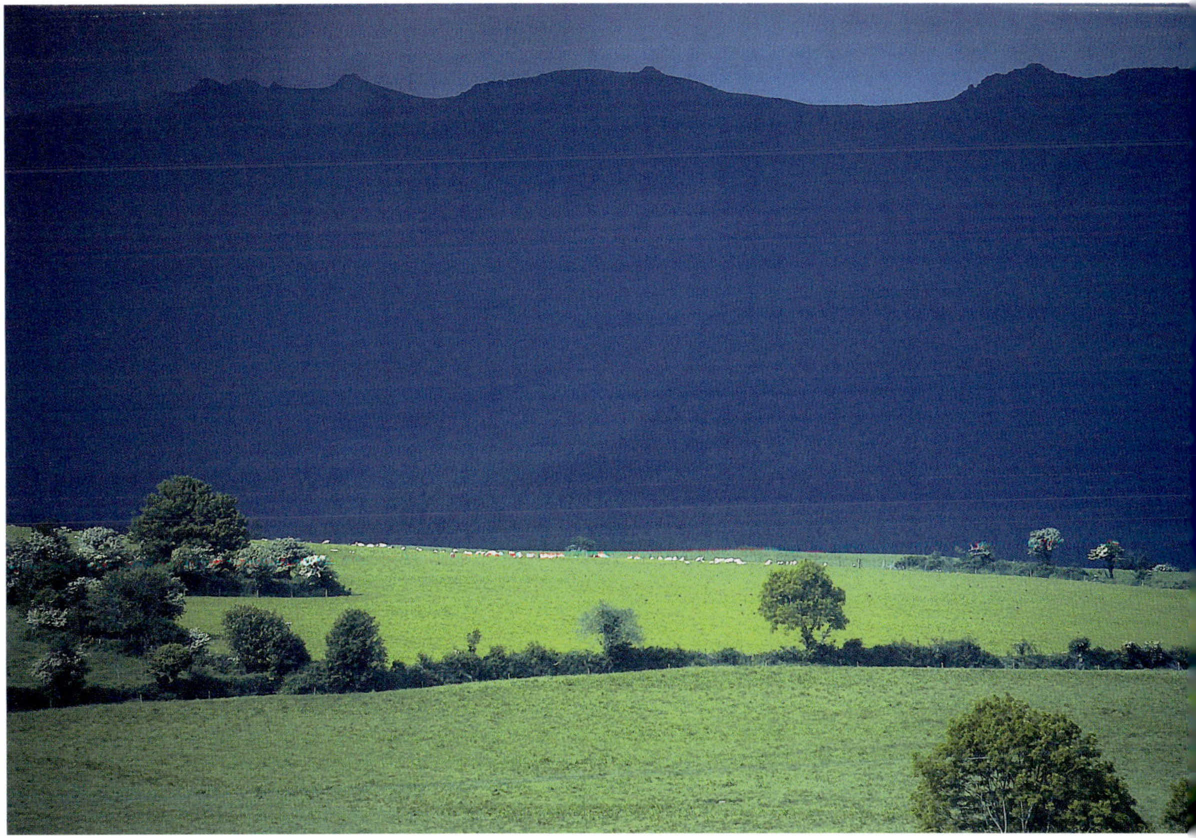

Left page: Blackstairs Mountains
Right: Comeragh Mountains

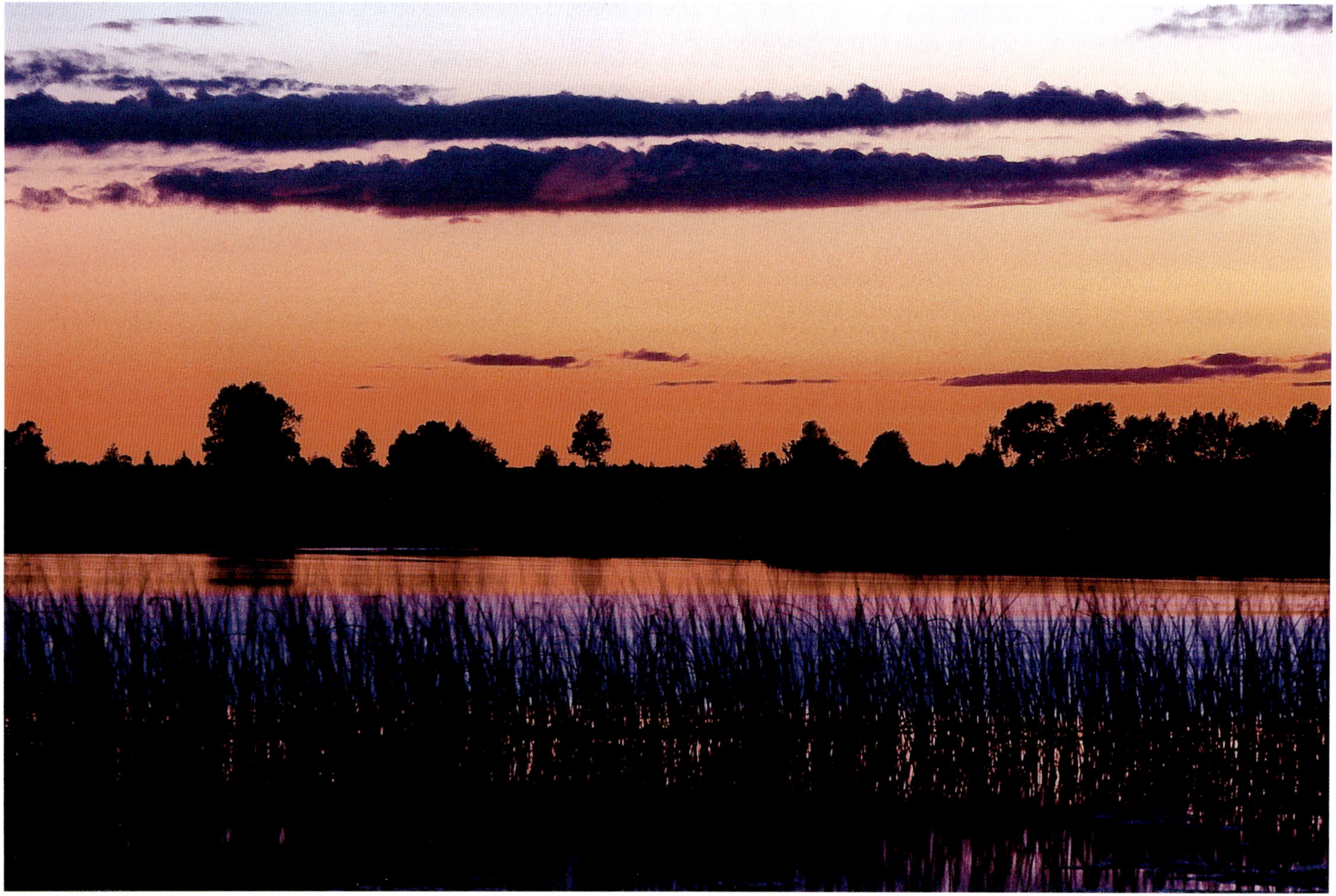

Left page: River Shannon

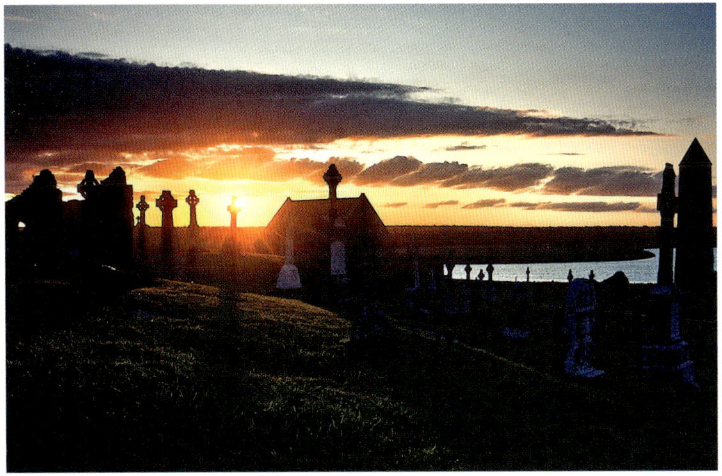

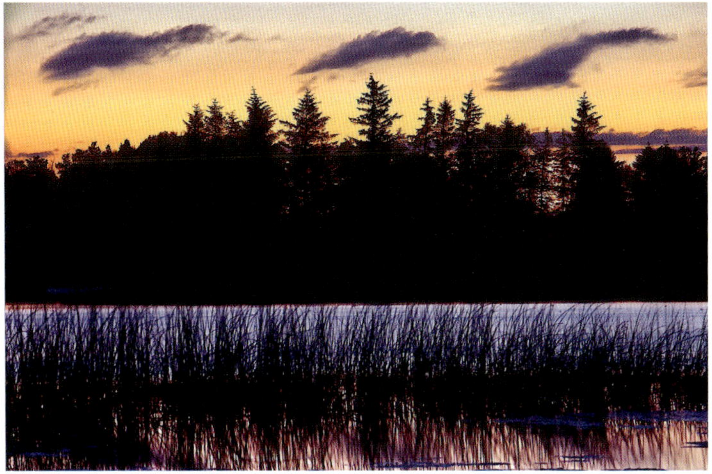

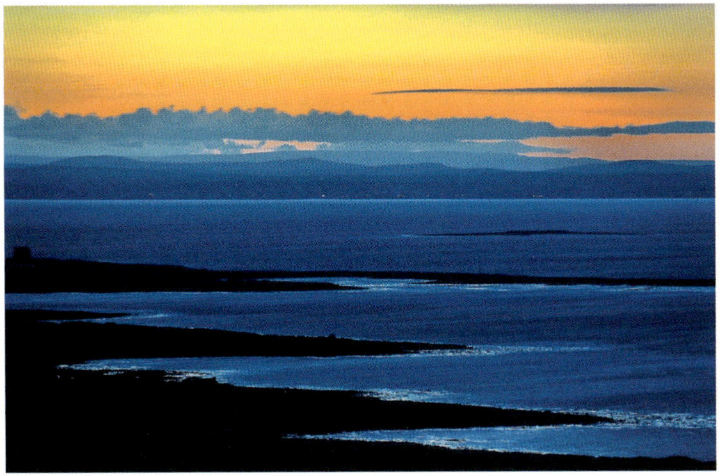

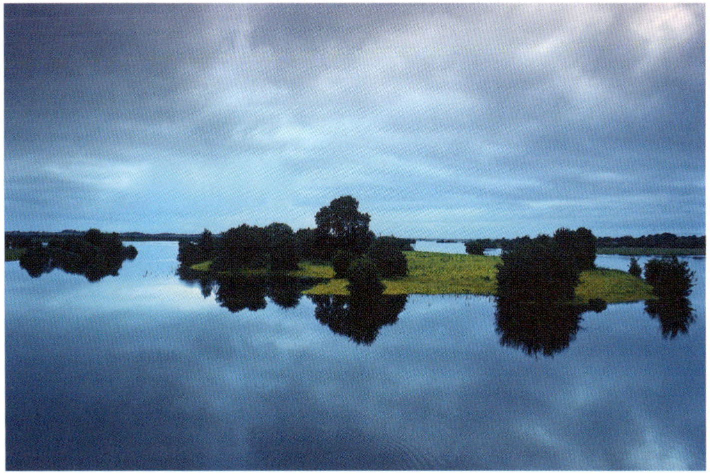

Above: Clonmacnoise
Below: River Shannon near Limerick

Above and below: River Shannon

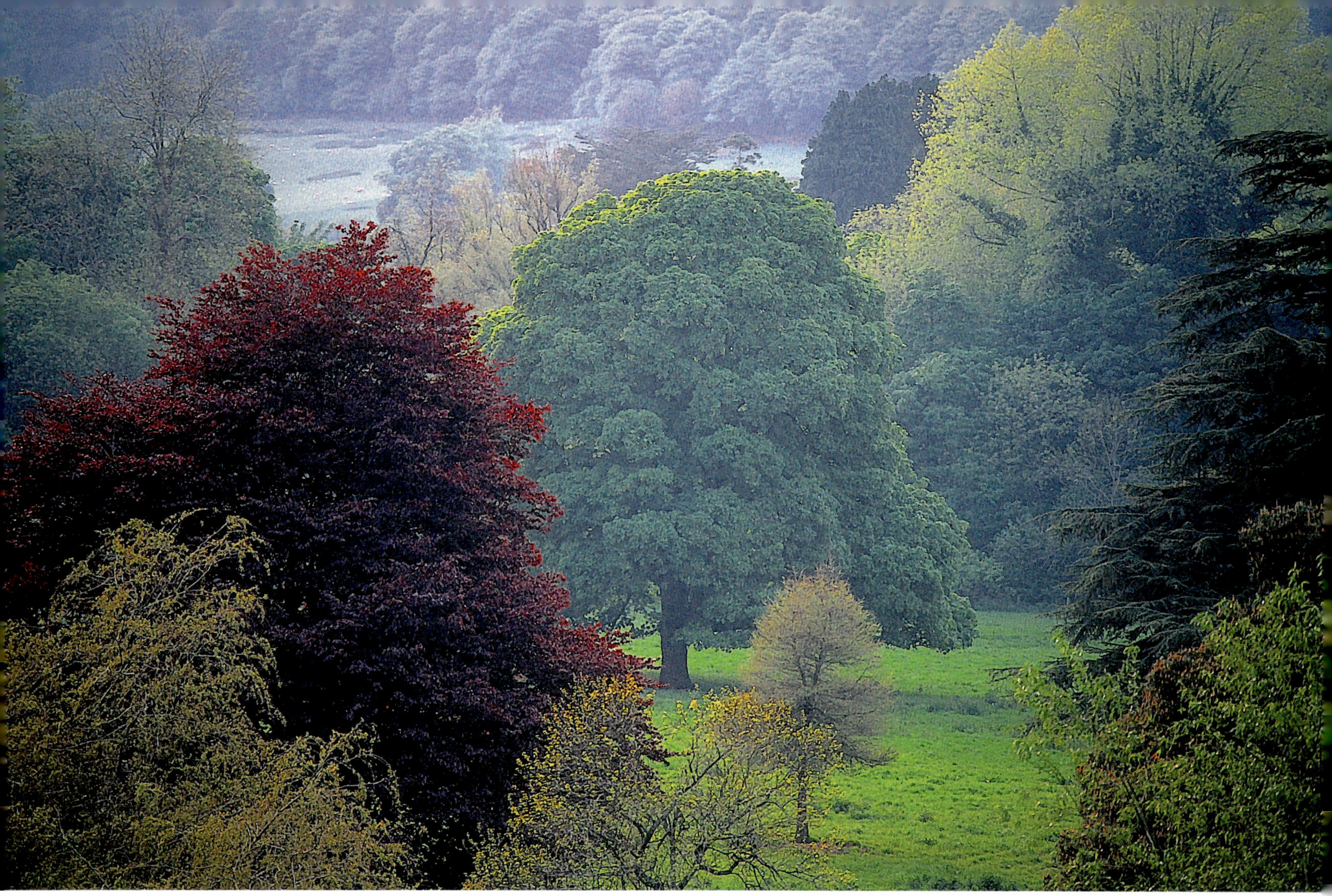

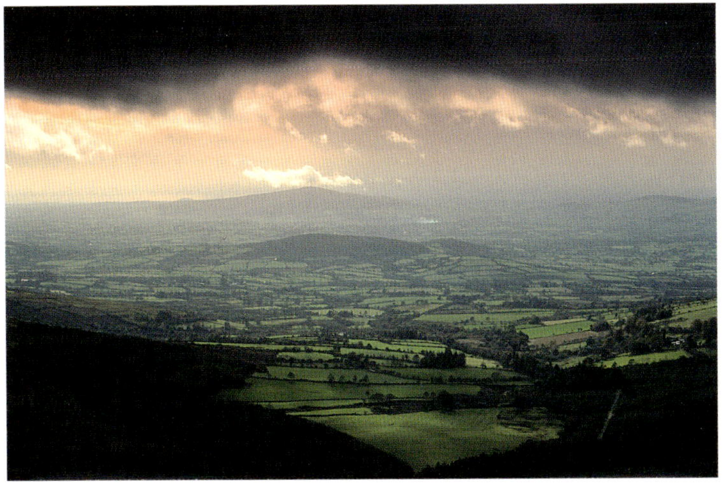

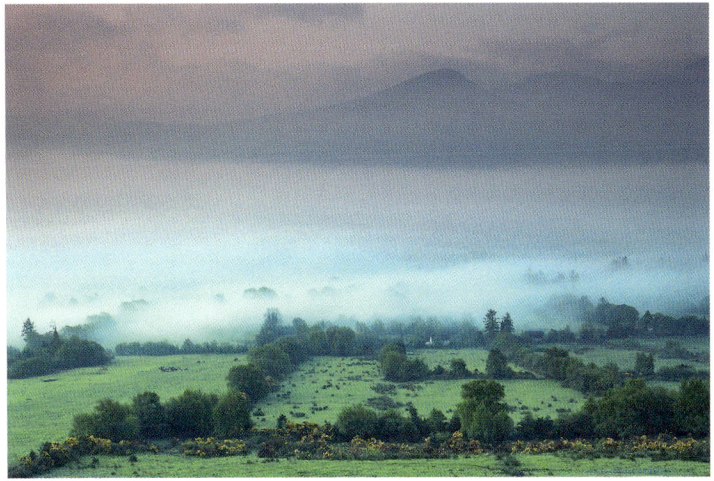

Left page: Lismore
Left: Blackstairs Mountains
Right: Galtee Mountains

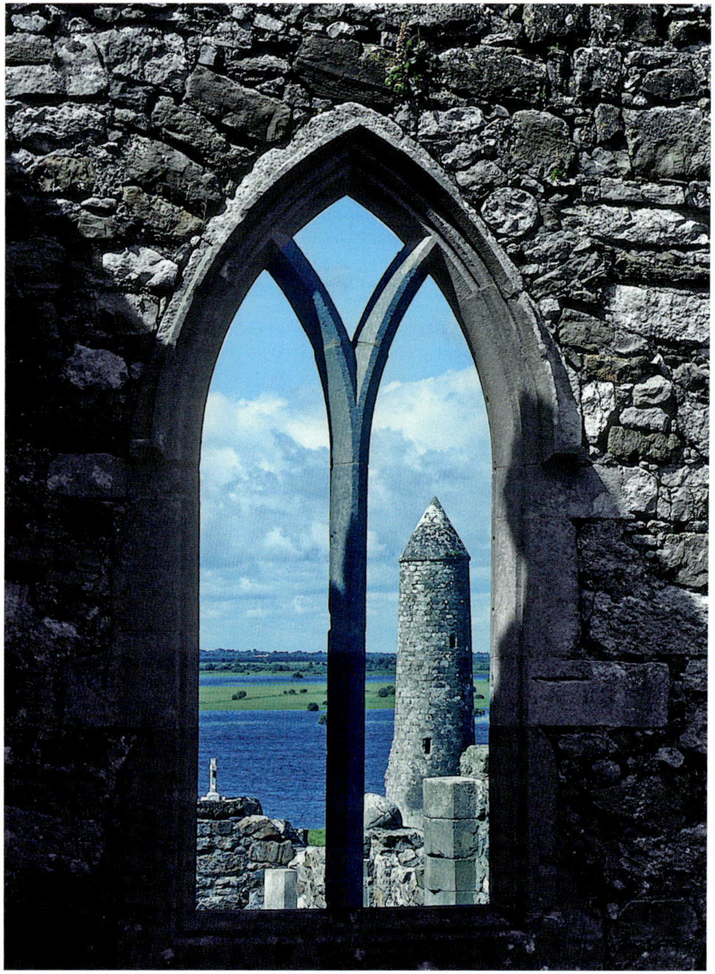

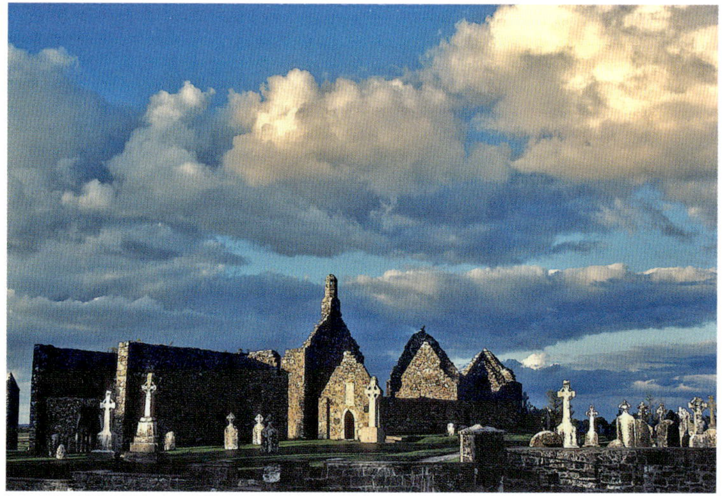

Left: Clonmacnoise, River Shannon
Right: Clonmacnoise

The Salmon of Wisdom

The salmon was the wisest of all creatures, for it had swallowed the nine nuts that had fallen from the hazel bushes into the well of wisdom. Only Nechtan and his three cup-bearers were allowed to come close to this well, and when Boann approached it, but this story has been told already. Now the salmon swam in a pool in the river Boyne, glistening in all the colors of the rainbow, and it was said that whoever ate the fish would gain its wisdom. For seven years, the druid Finegas waited by the riverbank until the clever salmon finally swam into his net. Then things probably got a bit hectic. Finegas lit a fire and started to roast his catch. The fish was big; he needed more firewood, or maybe he was just bored by the mundane task of grilling it. In any case, he asked Demne, his pupil, to watch over the sizzling fish.

Demne was the son of Cumhaill, leader of the Fianna, a band of warriors who lived in the wild, hunting, raiding cattle and fighting for whoever paid them best. His mother was Muirne with the Lovely Neck, whom Cumhaill abducted after her father refused to give her to him in marriage. She was already pregnant when Cumhaill was killed in the battle that followed the disagreement, and when the boy was born, she called him Demne, meaning "certainty."

Now, Demne was the pupil of Finegas and roasted the salmon of wisdom for him. However, he was not a very skilled chef, and promptly burned his thumb on the fish. As anyone would do, he stuck the hurting finger into his mouth, and thus it came to be that he—not Finegas, the druid—received all the wisdom from the salmon. When Finegas saw what had happened, he gave Demne the name "Fionn", which means the bright one, the fair one, the one that is blessed. From now on, whenever Fionn mac Cumhaill put his thumb in his mouth, the knowledge he needed at that very moment was revealed to him.

The Causeway

At the time when Fionn was a giant, he lived in a cave on the coast of Antrim, alone or with some woman, and Benandonner, also a giant, lived just across the Irish Sea on the coast of Scotland. Fionn broke some chunks of stone from the cliffs and built a pathway across the water in order to meet him. Did they have a disagreement, a fight, or did Fionn just turn back when he saw the size of his neighbor? In any case, Benandonner went after him. Fionn ran as fast as he could, and by the time he reached his cave, he was exhausted and frantic. But Oonagh, the woman he stayed with, kept cool. She put a baby bonnet over his head, pushed him into a pram and pulled a Mickey Mouse blanket up to his chin. Then she started to sing a little lullaby.

Benandonner got to the cave, huffing and puffing. Wistfully, he looked at the homely scene. "Whose baby is this?" he wanted to know.

Oonagh smiled. "This is the newborn son of Fionn mac Cumhaill."

Benandonner needed a moment to take this in. The baby was huge, the rattle in its hand looked like a mace.

"Fionn will be back in a moment," Oonagh said.

Benandonner still stared at the baby. How large would the father be when this was his newborn son?

"Feel his first teeth," Ooangh said and opened the baby's mouth.

Benandonner put his finger in the jaw of the child, and in this moment, the boy snapped at him. The giant howled. Clearly, it wasn't worth his while to wait for Fionn, and Benandonner turned back. He ran as fast as he could, and in the process, he destroyed the causeway Fionn had built.

However, some say it wasn't Benandonner at all; Fionn wanted to meet across the water, but the giant's wife. This went on for some time, until one day the cuckold caught the lovers in the act. Fionn had to make a run for it, and it was then that the Giant's Causeway collapsed. Today, there are a few steps of it left on the coast of Antrim, a few on the coast of Scotland, and two tales you may choose from.

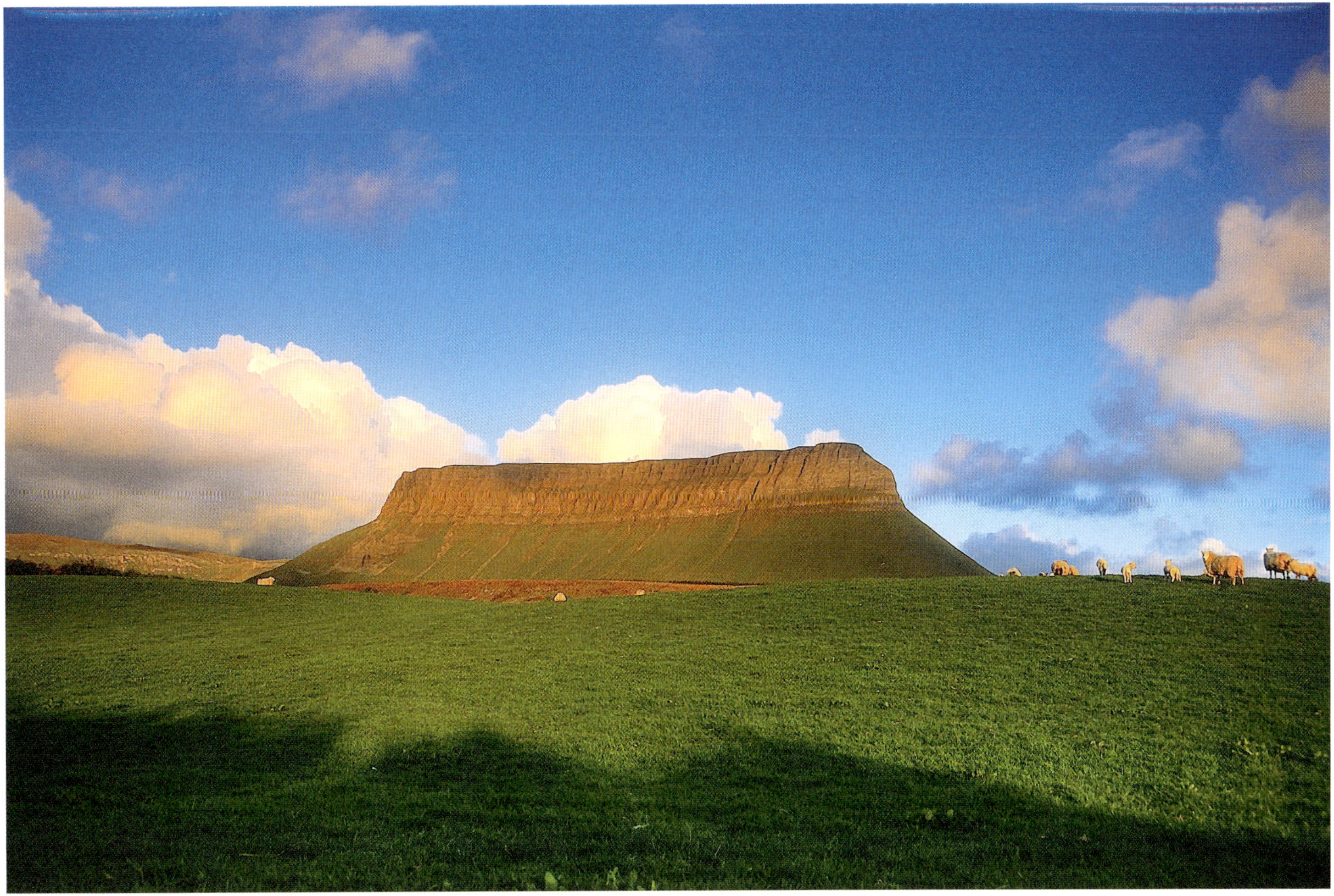

Mt. Benbulbin

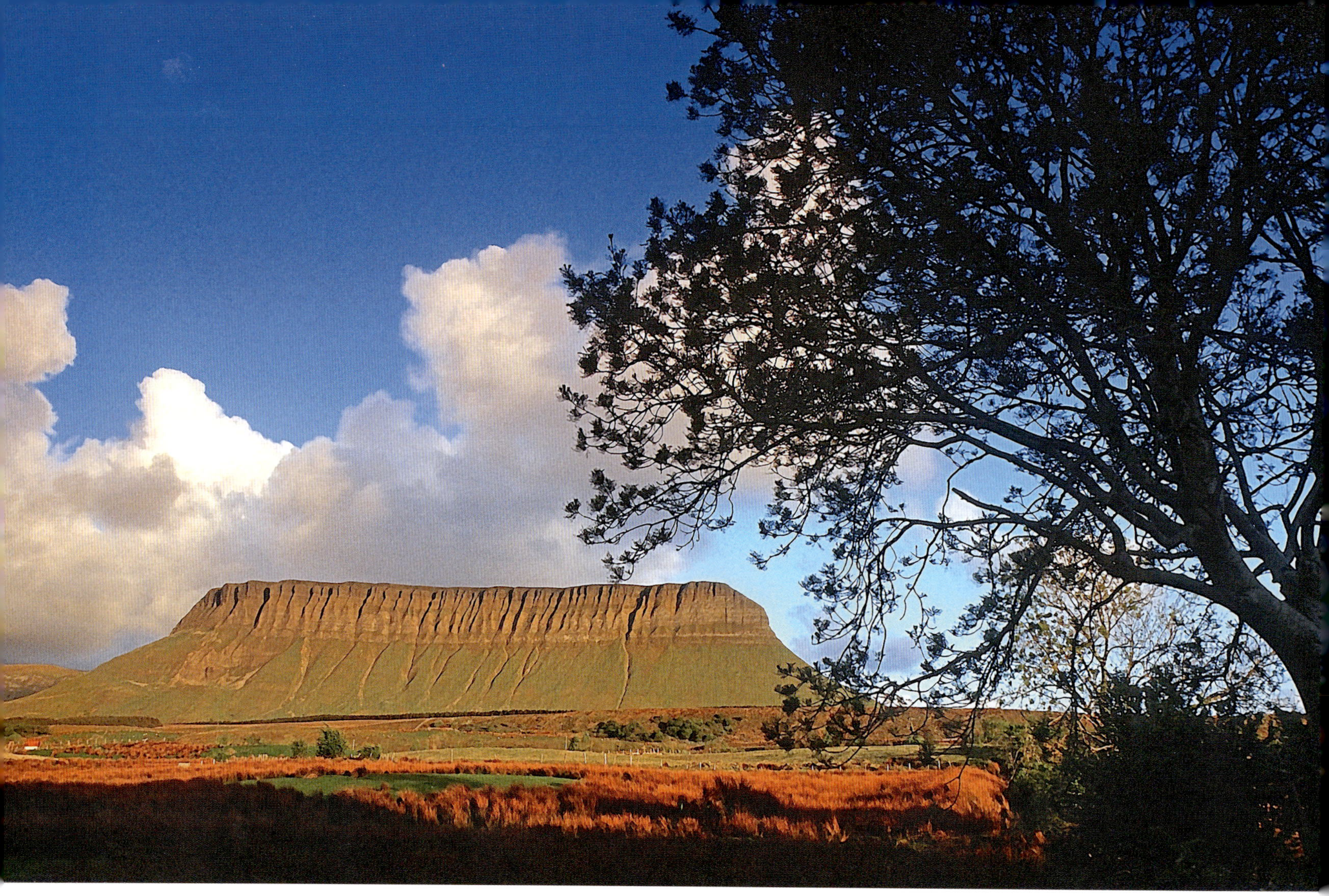

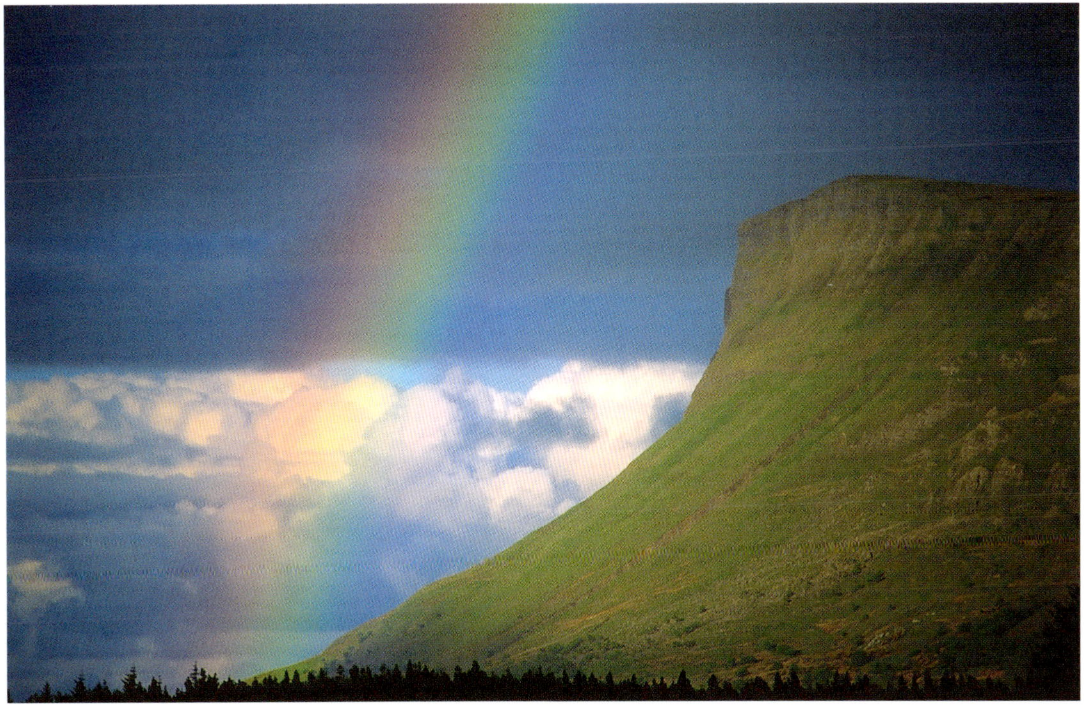

Left page: Mt. Benbulbin
Right: Dartry Mountains

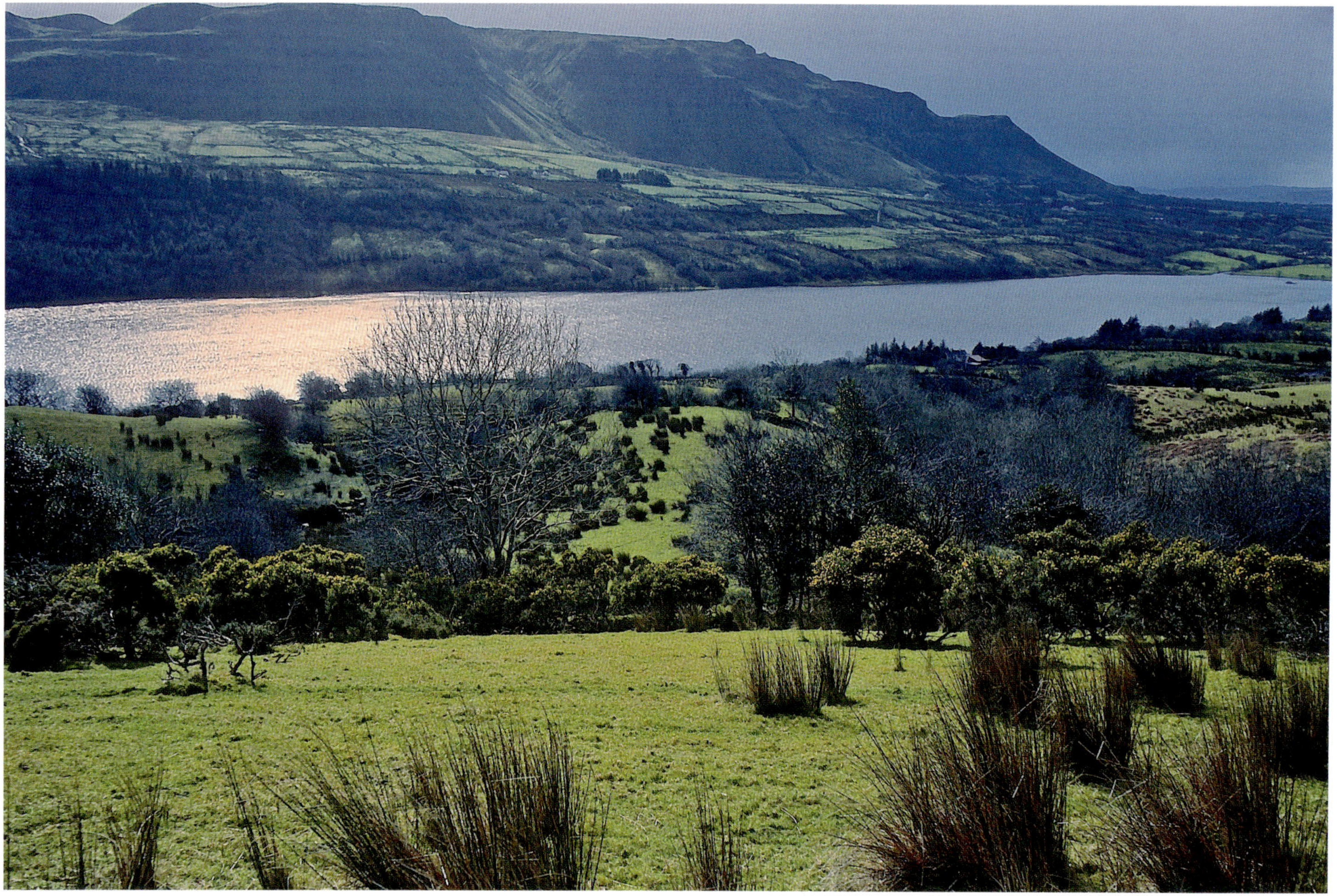

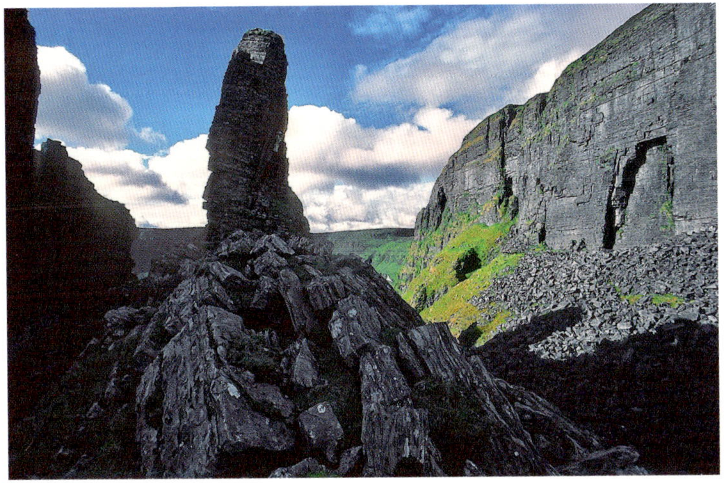

Left page: Lake Glencar
Left: Dartry Mountains
Right: Glencar Falls

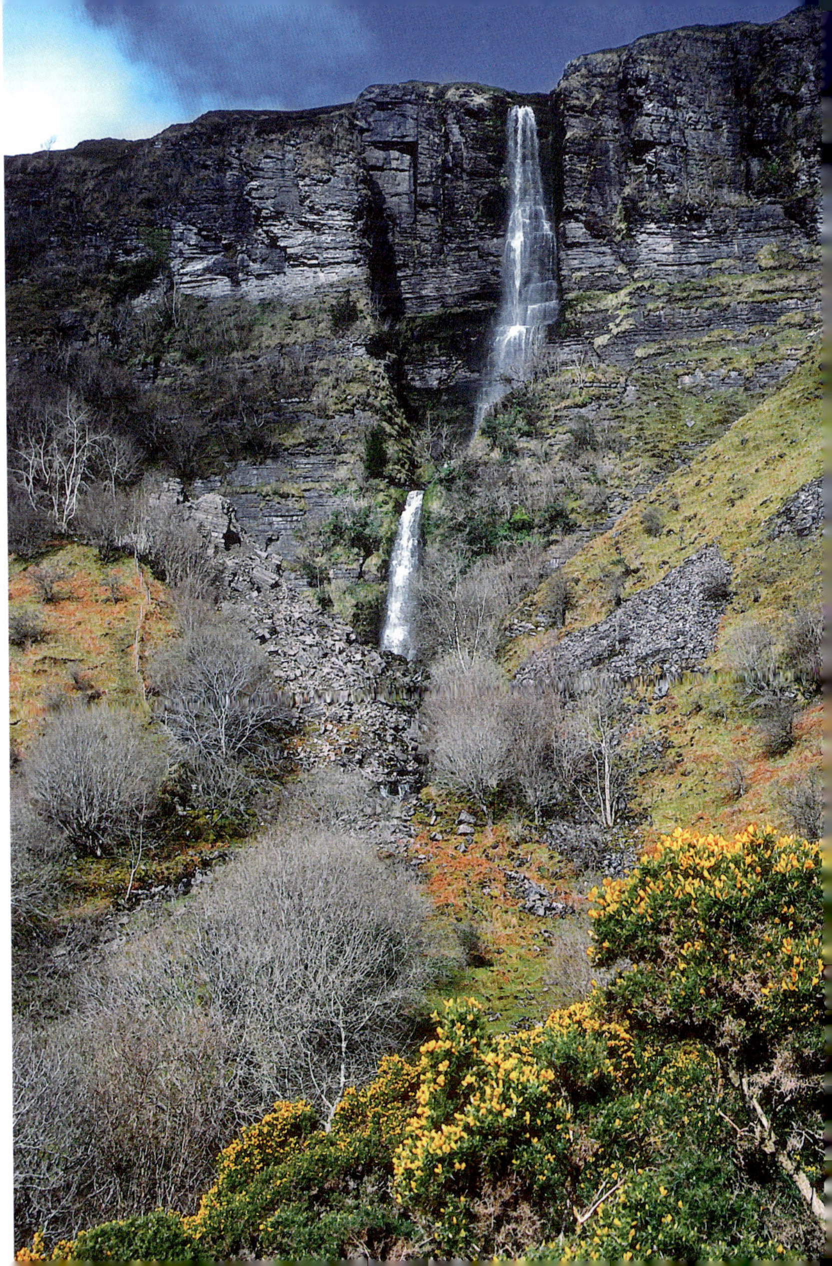

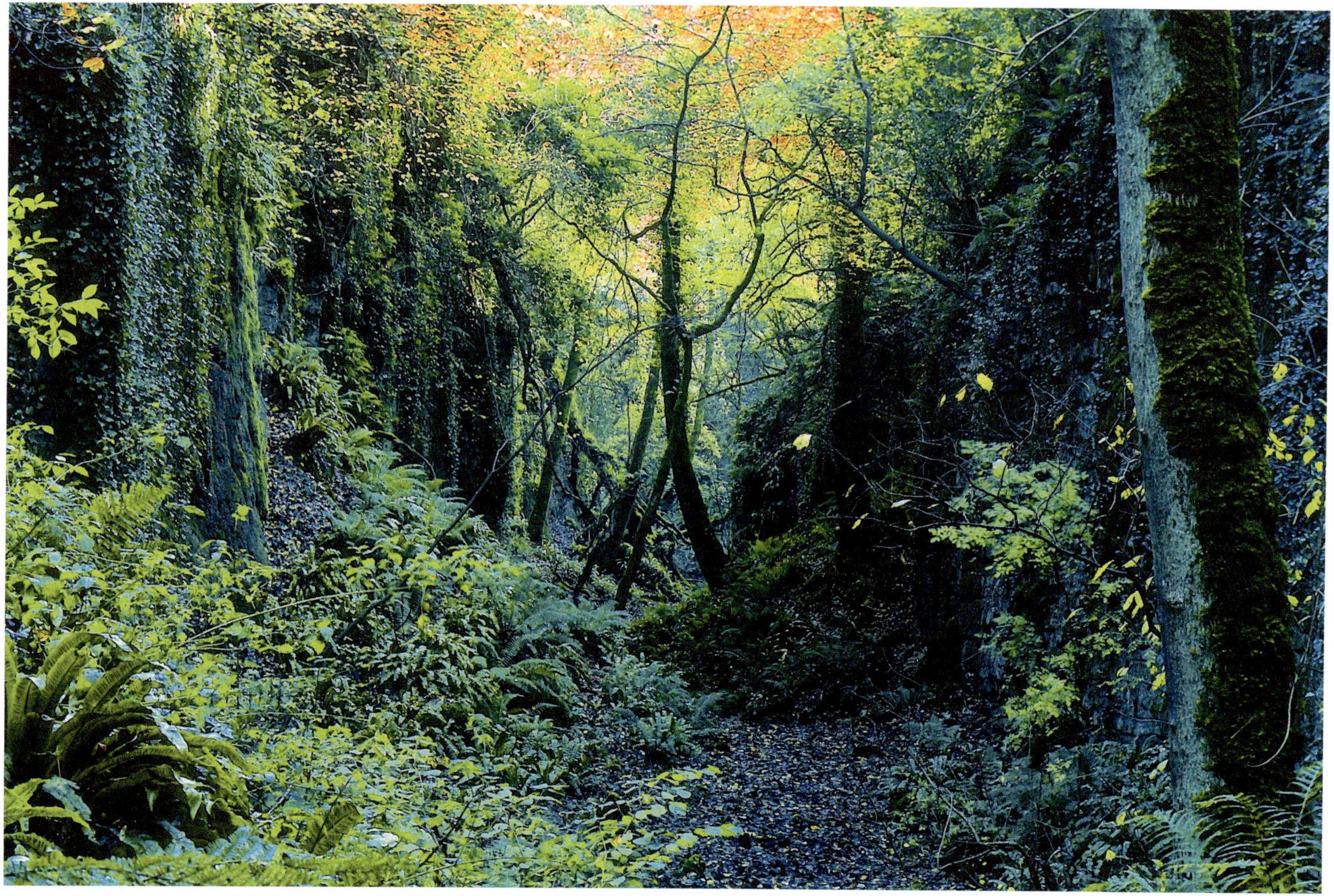

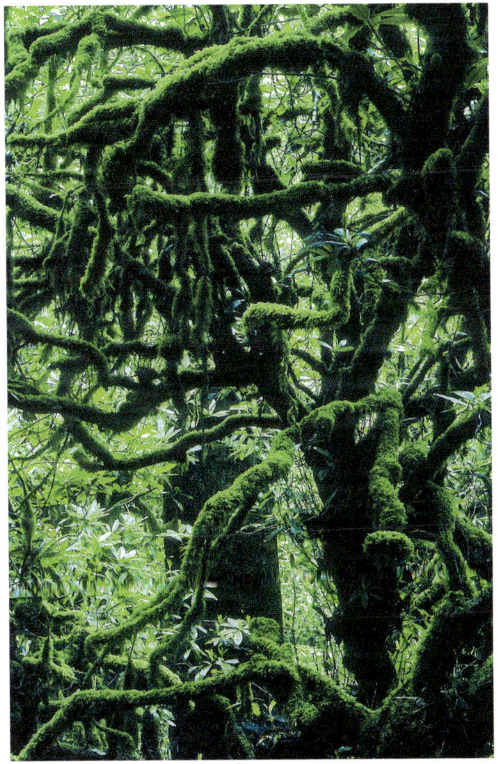

Left page: The Fairy Glen
Left: Oakforest
Right: The Fairy Glen

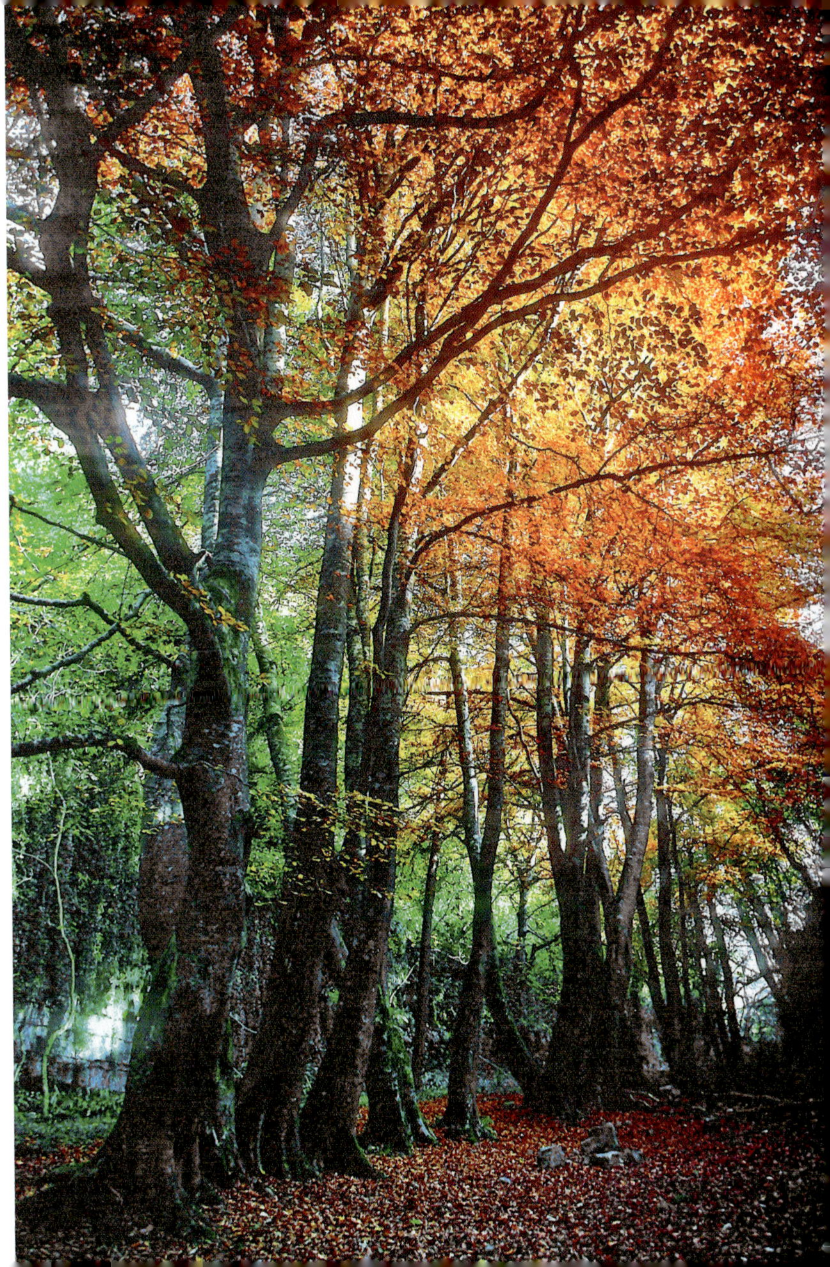

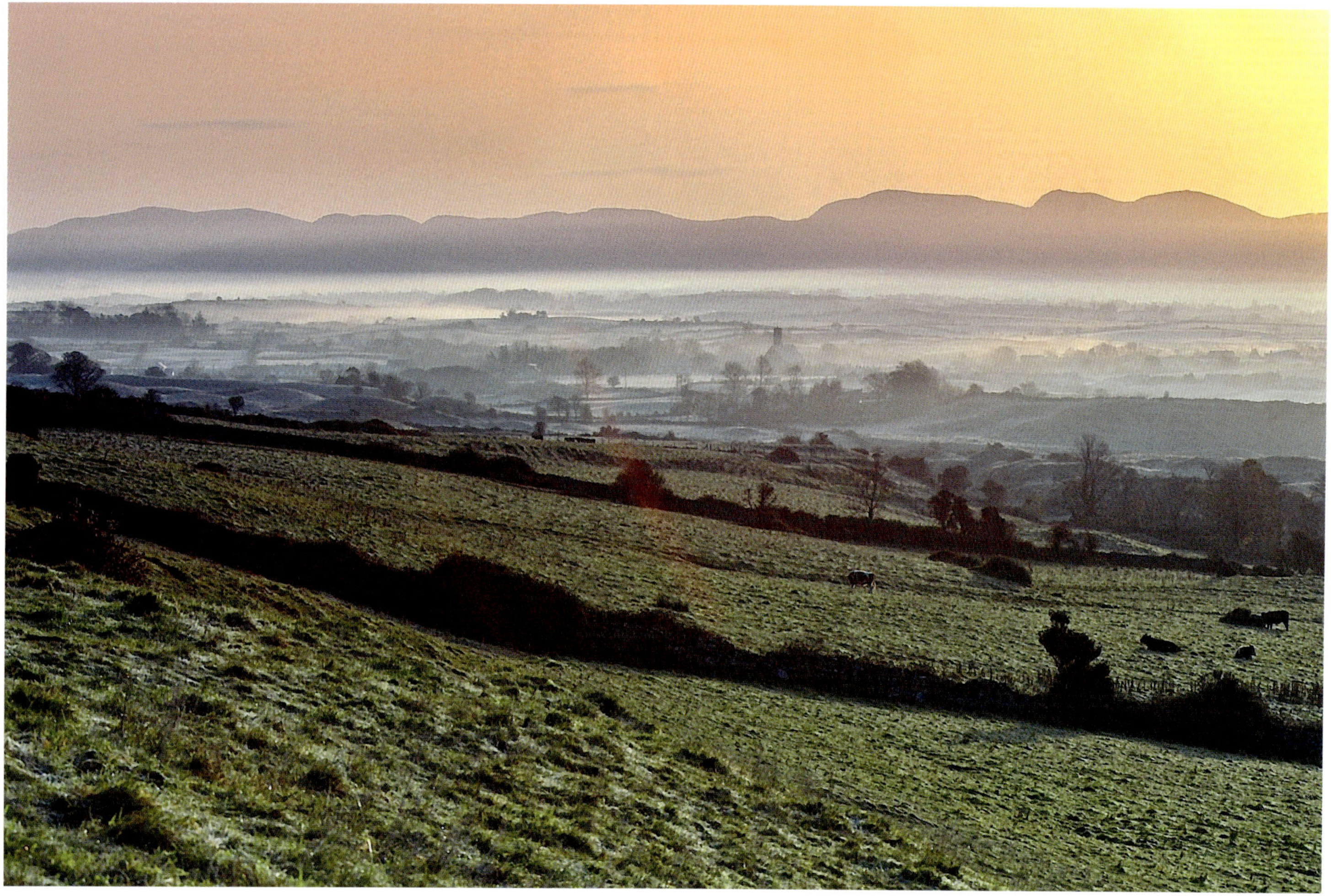

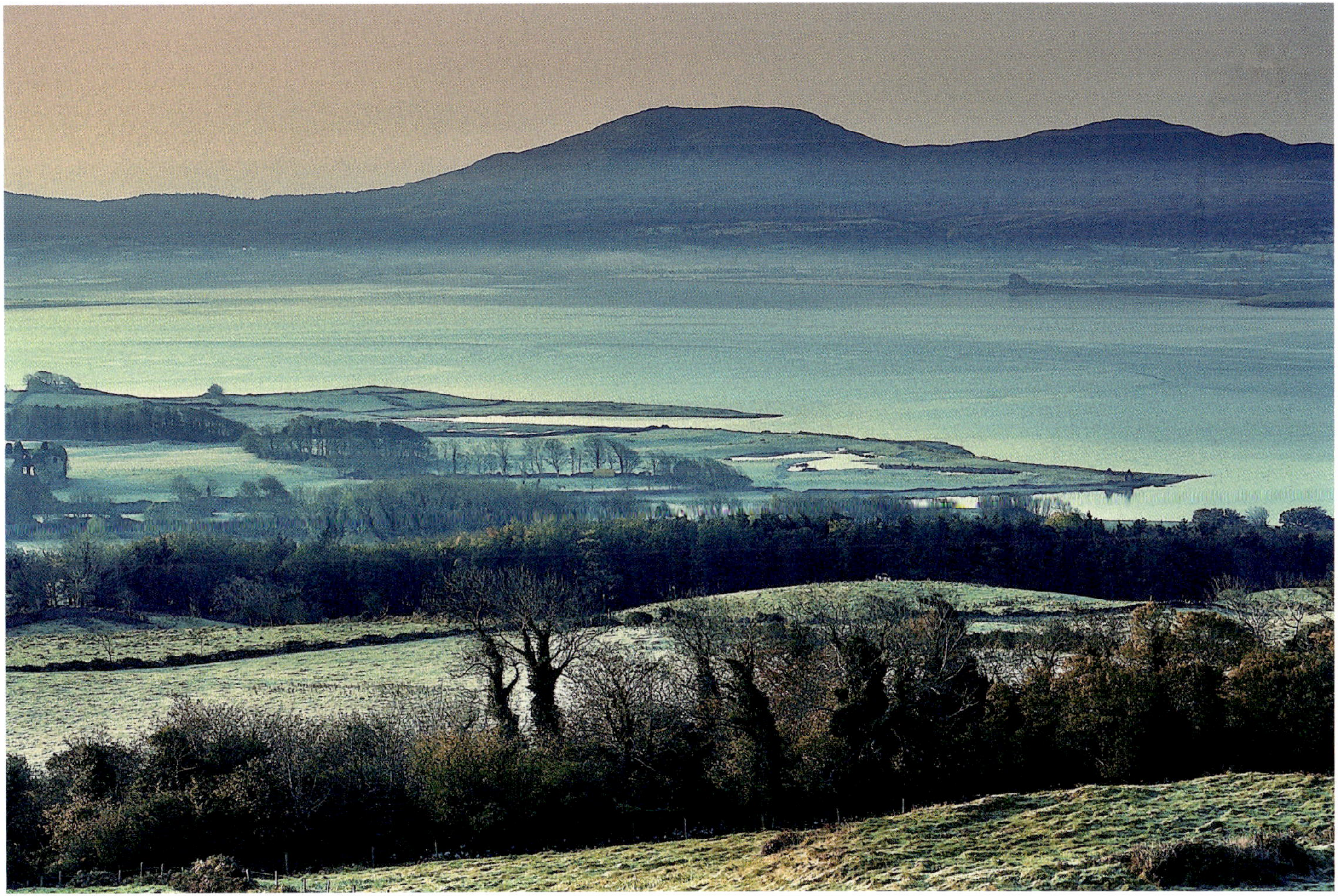

Left page: Morning light over Sligo county
Right: Scenery at Sligo coast

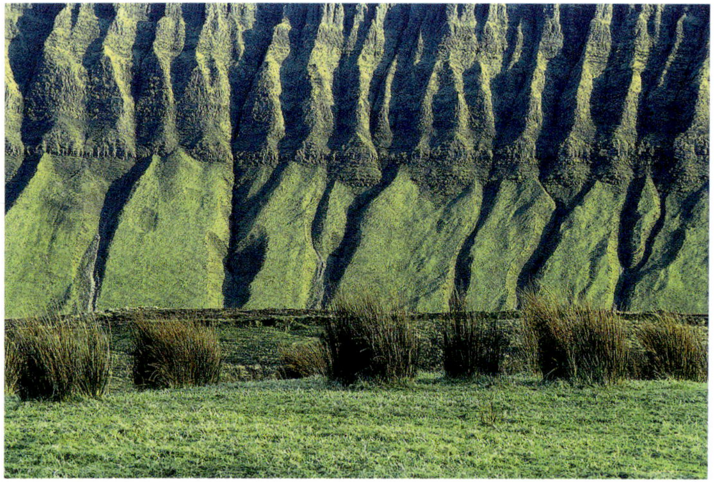

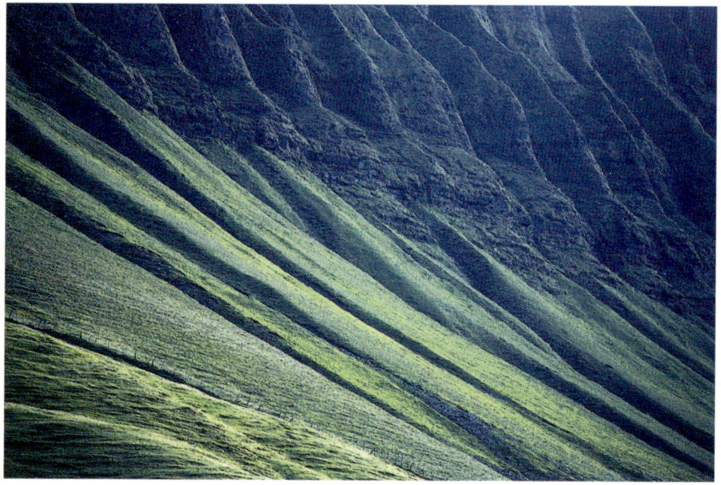

Left and right: Slope patterns at Mt. Benbulbin

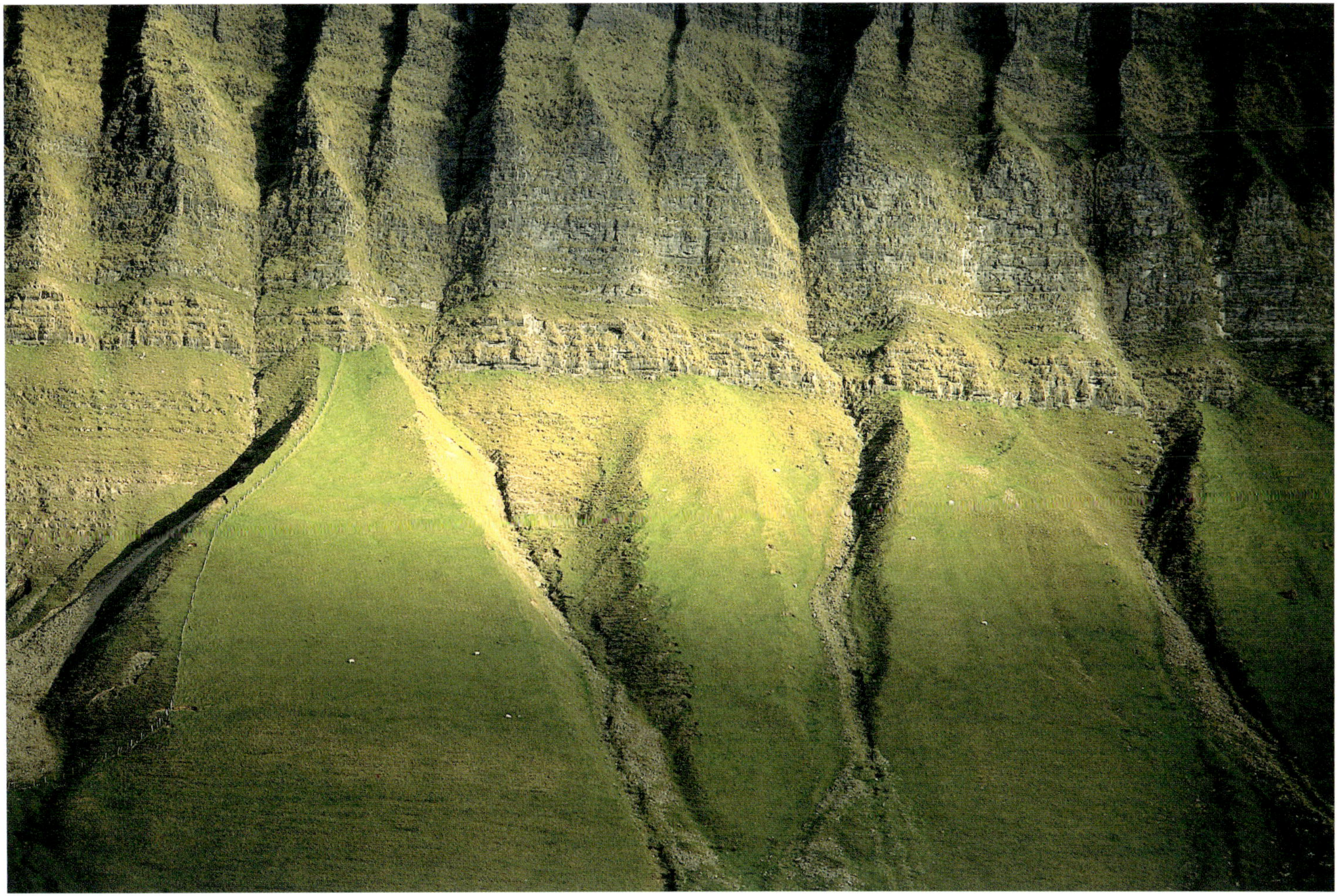

Slope patterns at Mt. Benbulbin

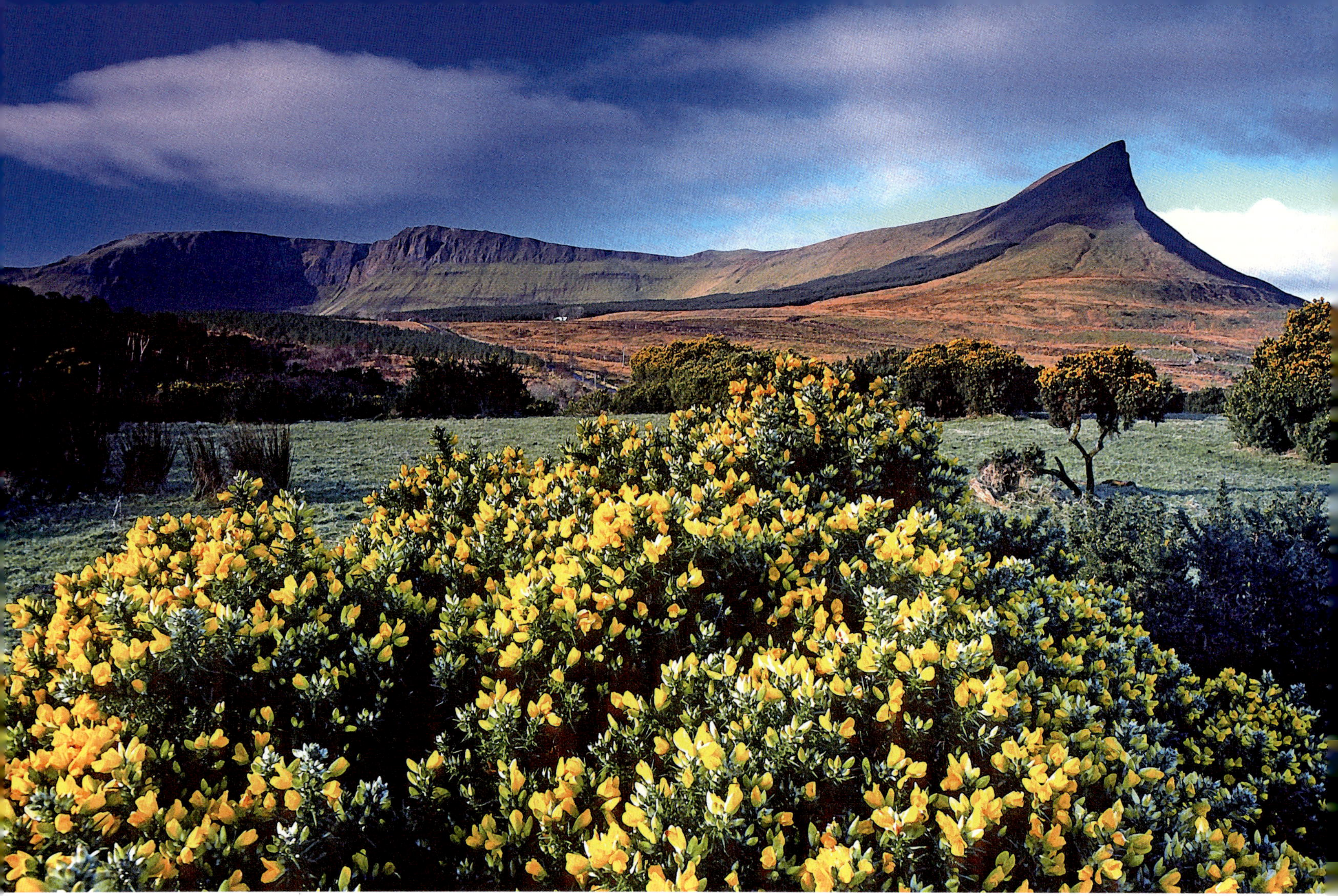

The Runaway Bride

Fionn was stricken with grief after losing Maigneis, another one of his wives, and his men worried about him. In a joint effort, they talked him into marrying again, Gráinne this time, the daughter of Cormac mac Airt, the High King of Ireland. She was young and headstrong as princesses are, and Fionn, who was old, sent his son Oisín to win her over. Shrewd as this may have been, it led to a bit of confusion, and only at the wedding feast did the young bride realize that Oisín had not courted her for himself but for his old man. In a fury, she put a spell on the guests to fall asleep except for Diarmuid, with the love bite, whom no woman could resist.

"You will abduct me tonight," Gráinne said to the handsome young warrior.

"I will not," Diarmuid replied; he was loyal to Fionn.

"Then I will put a geis on you that you will never ..."

Diarmuid sighed. He didn't need to know what handicap the spoiled princess fancied for him. Her geis would lead to disaster one way or the other, and by the time the wedding guests woke again, Dairmuid and Gráinne were gone.

They hid in the woods across the river Shannon, and some say that at first Dairmuid didn't touch Gráinne at all out of respect for Fionn. "The water leaping up my legs is braver than you", she teased him, and eventually she got pregnant. Fionn chased the couple. They evaded him several times, once with the help of Aengus, who was Dairmuid's foster father. The god of love covered Gráinne with his cloak of invisibility, while Dairmuid jumped over the pursuers' heads. After sixteen years, Aengus convinced Fionn to leave the pair alone. But he could not forgive Diarmuid and led him into a trap. As Diarmuid lay dying, injured by a magic boar, he asked Fionn for a saving drink.

"No," the jealous codger said, and by the time Oisín forced his old man to show mercy, Diarmuid had died.

Aengus took his dead foster son with him to Brú na Bóinne, and whenever he wanted to talk with him, he brought him back to life. Fionn, however, spoke so long and so sweetly to Gráinne that she married him after all; and Oisín, who was a great poet, eventually followed Niamh, the daughter of Manannán mac Lir, to the island under the water. But this is another story.

Left page: Dartry Mountains

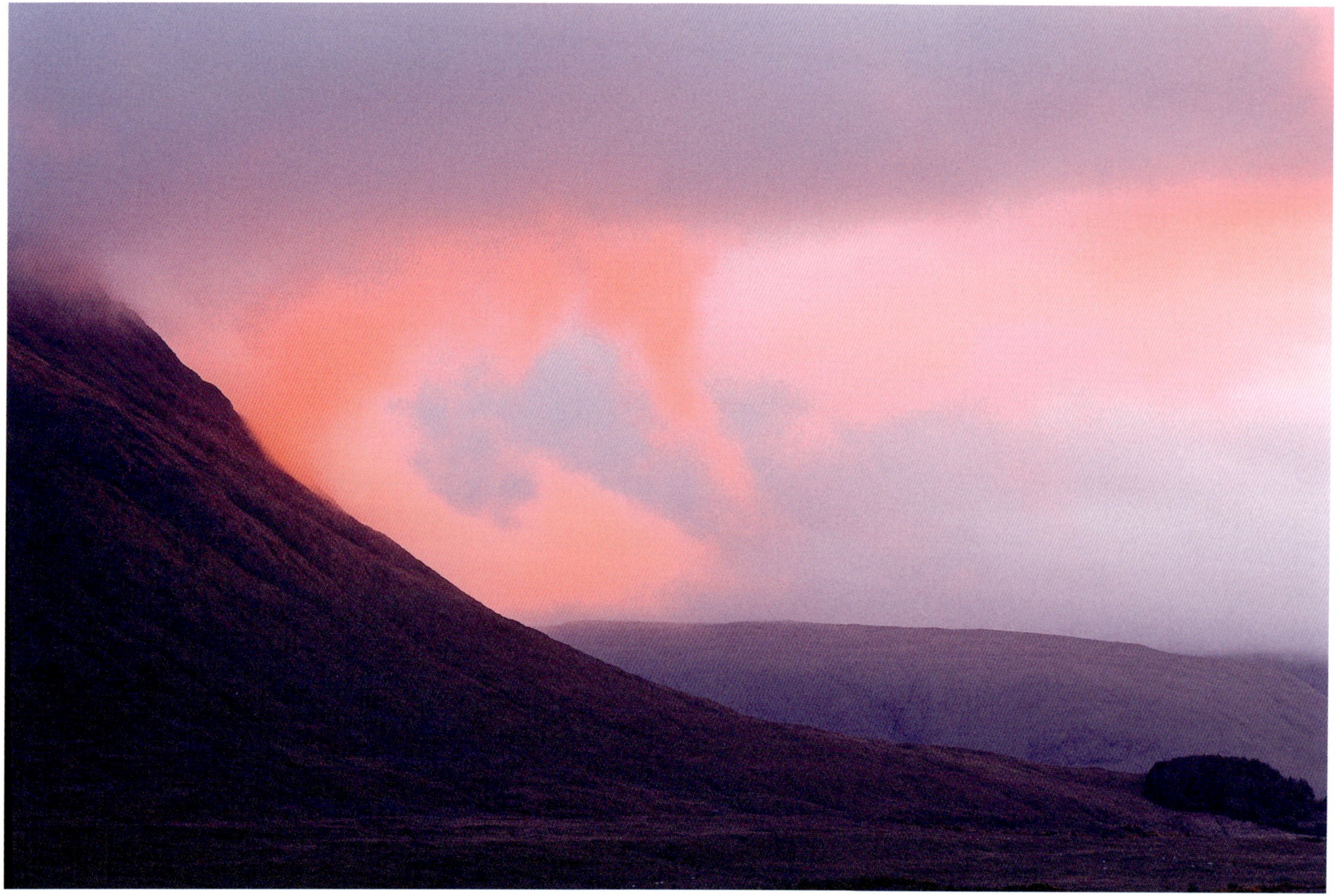

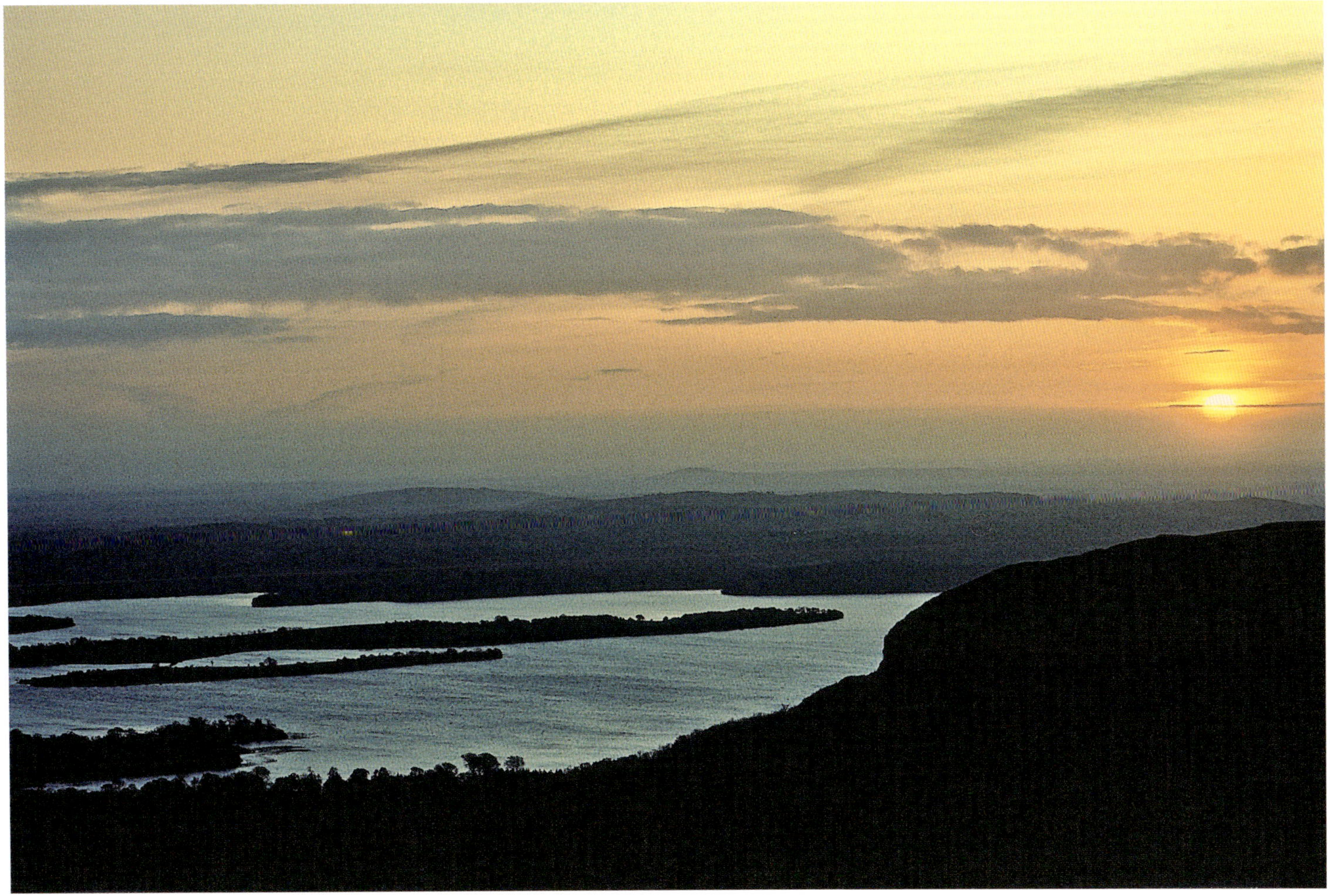

Left page: Dartry Mountains
Right: Lough Arrow

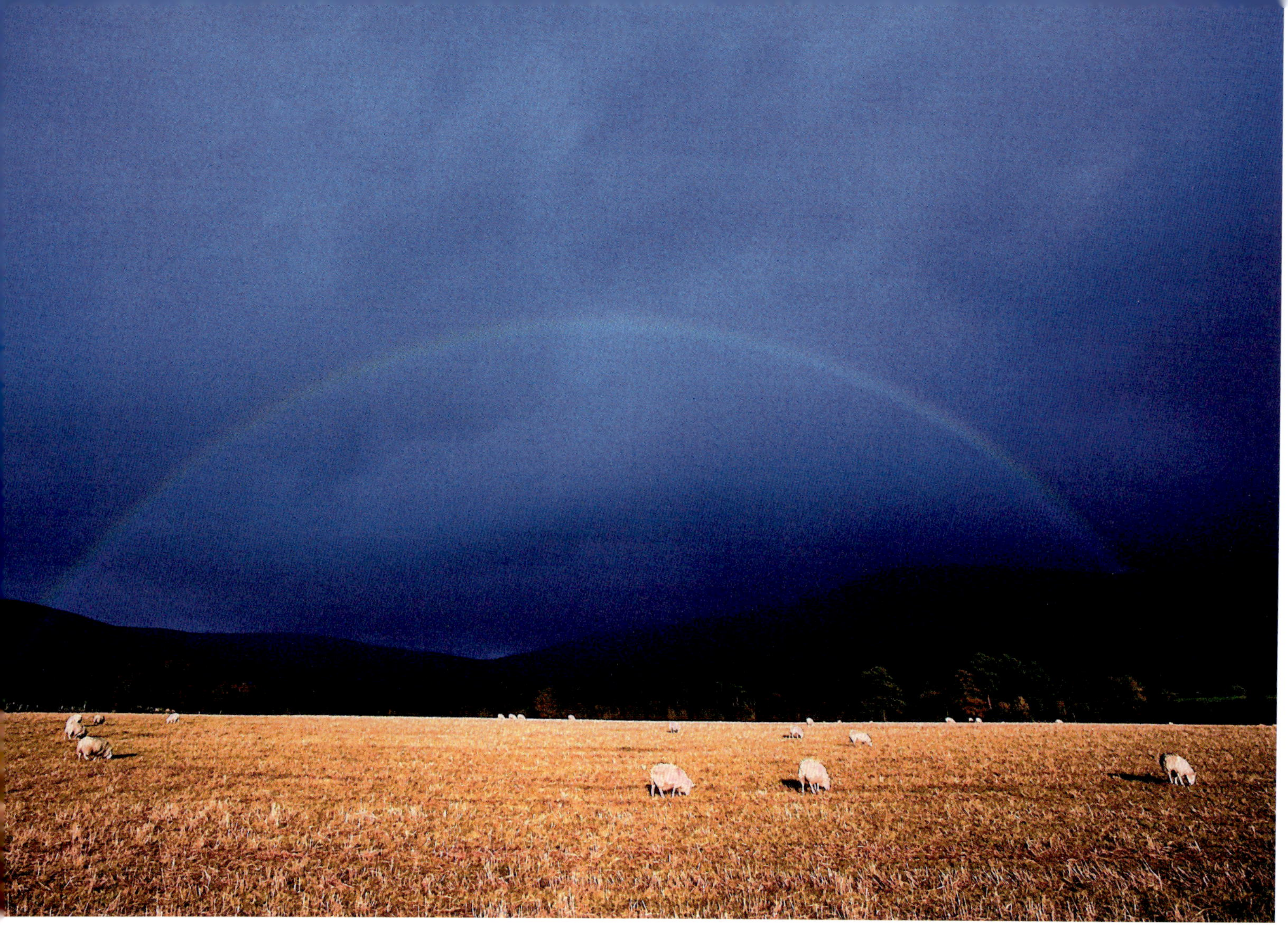

The Crimson Fly

Étaín was the most beautiful woman in Ireland, which was a blessing as well as a curse. Perhaps she was the daughter of the Dagda and Boann, hence a sister to Aengus, but also to Midir, who made her his lover. However, Midir had a wife who did not approve of open relationships. Fuamnach, herself the daughter of a druid, effortlessly turned her rival into a puddle. Étaín fought back and became a worm, then a magical fly, crimson-colored, that flitted around Midir. His feelings for her were unchanged. He flirted with the fly and was lulled to sleep by its soft hum. So Fuamnach unleashed a storm to separate them, and for seven years Étaín floated in the air, unable to land anywhere in Ireland. Midir was beside himself.

A gust of wind finally blew Étaín into Aengus' house, the mound fort in the bend of the river Boyne. He recognized her immediately, took care of her, spoiled her, until Fuamnach found out and unleashed another storm. Now Aengus had had enough; he summoned Midir, who cut Fuamnach's hair. But the crimson fly had already disappeared again into thin air. Over a thousand years, Midir searched for her, while the Milesians settled Ireland and the Tuatha Dé Danann retreated to the Otherworld.

A new wind carried Étaín into the house of an Irish chief celebrating his wedding. For a while, she watched the festivities perched on a rafter, then she fell into the bride's wine glass, and the bride swallowed the fly. Nine months later, the young wife gave birth to a little girl, who was so beautiful that she named her Étaín. Étaín grew up, and it was not long before she was married to the High King of Ireland. They lived together on the Hill of Tara. However, the king's brother also fell in love with his sister-in-law and got so sick with longing that he was ready to die. To save him, Étaín agreed to share his bed. Only the third time, she realized she was not with her brother-in-law but with someone else, and then Midir, her lover of old, revealed himself to her.

Naturally, the High King had no intention of handing back his wife, and the two men decided to settle it in a game of chess. Midir won. But when he went to fetch Étaín, he was met by an army. Now Midir had had enough. Wrapped in a mist, he took Étaín, and the two rose with powerful wings, necks intertwined in the sky as a pair of swans.

Étaín, they say, is a diminutive of the Old Irish word et, which means passion as well as envy.

Left page: Blackstairs Mountains

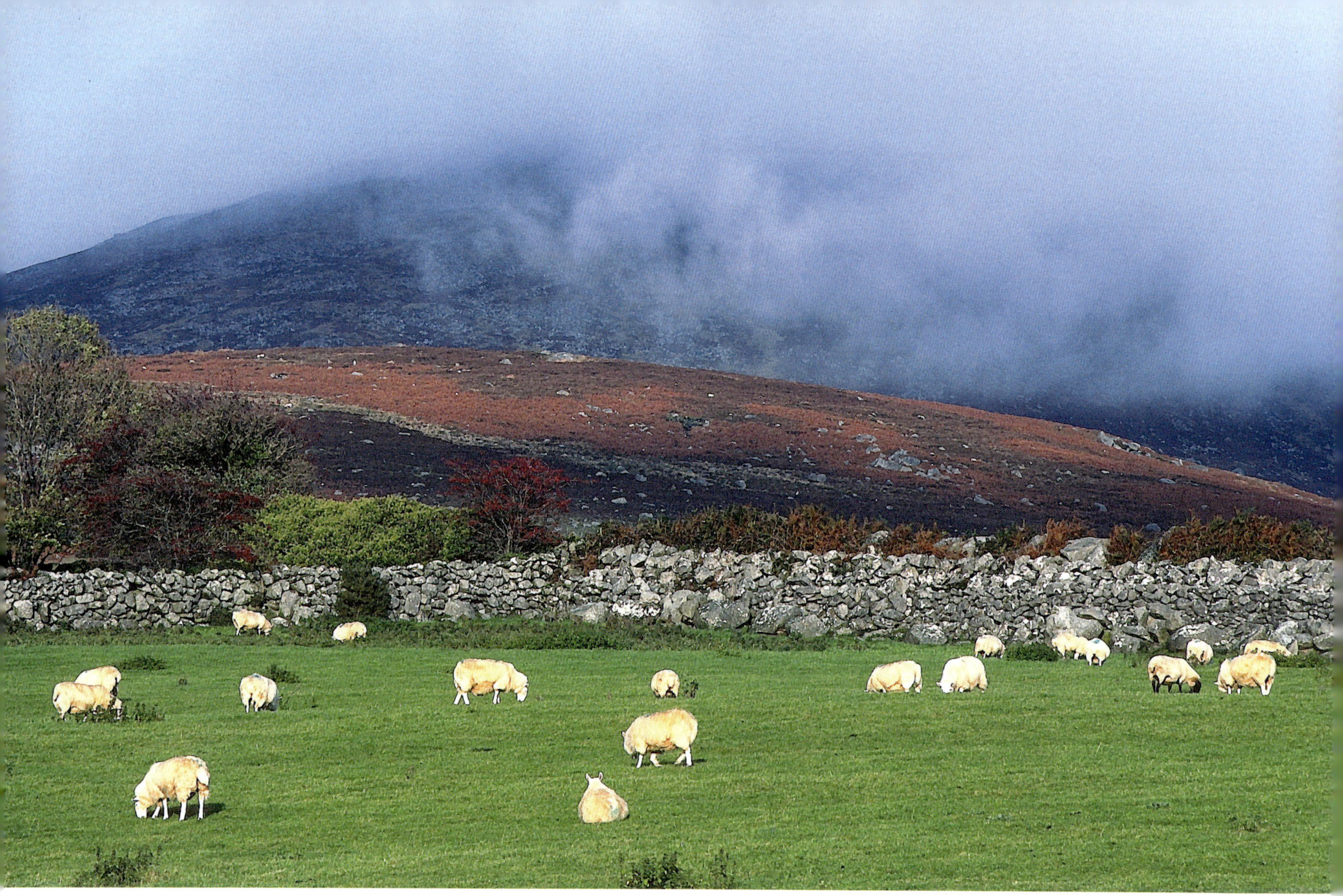

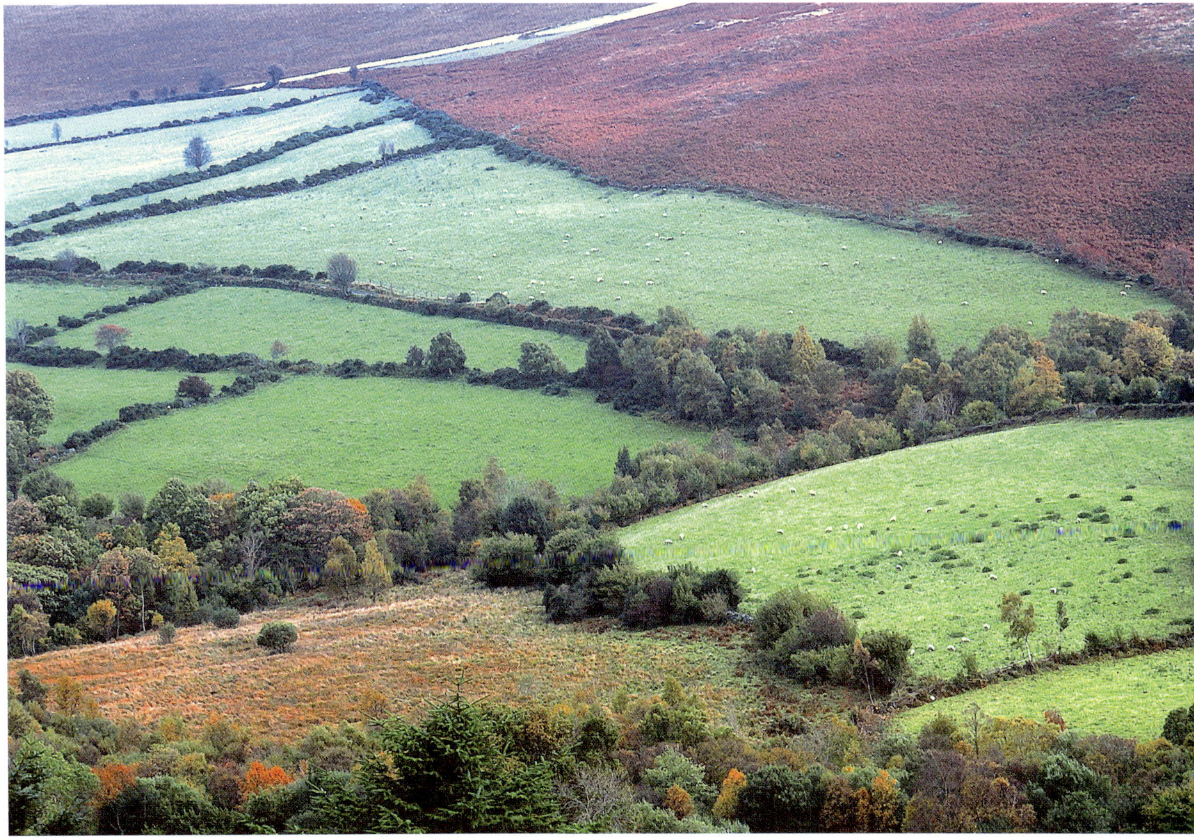

Left page and right: Blackstairs Mountains

The Wave

Early one morning, when Ciabhán was out hunting, he found a boat on the strand with a copper prow. The rising sun made it glow like fire, and he walked around it, touched it. The wind played in his curly hair. He looked ravishing. It was no secret that he was desired by every woman, envied by every man.

"Do you want to leave us?" people asked when they saw him examining the boat.

Ciabhán paused for a moment, then he nodded. The wind grew stronger. They watched him getting into the boat, pushing off into the sea, before they took shelter from the upcoming storm.

Massive waves arched up before Ciabhán, each as high as a mountain, and the salmon leaped in them. The curls of his hair clung to his handsome face. Eventually, he saw a rider on a horse with a golden bridle. For nine waves, the rider stayed underwater; from the tenth, he emerged without a drop on him.

"What will you give to the one who saves you?" the rider asked.

"What can I give him?" Ciabhán asked.

"You can serve him."

Ciabhán nodded and the rider reached out to him. He brought Ciabhán to the island under the water, which is called the Land of Youth or sometimes the Land of Women. There, as it happened, a great feast was just prepared. Harpists and artists gathered, acrobats and aerialists performed the most wonderful feats, but Ciabhán exceeded them all. Clíodhna, who had never loved anyone, watched him and gave him her heart.

Of course, they couldn't stay on the island; it wasn't meant for men like Ciabhán, as handsome as he might be. So, they fled in the boat with the copper prow, returning to the shore where Ciabhán had come from. There they moored in a bay, and the setting sun made the copper prow glow. Ciabhán found a shelter for them. Early the next morning, he went into the forest to hunt.

Not long after he was gone, Manannán mac Lir, the son of the sea, came with forty ships to bring Clíodhna back. Ichnu, the flautist, lulled her to sleep and the sea swept her away. It is not known what became of Ciabhán and the boat with the copper prow, but since that day every tenth wave in this bay near Glandore in County Cork carries Clíodhna's name.

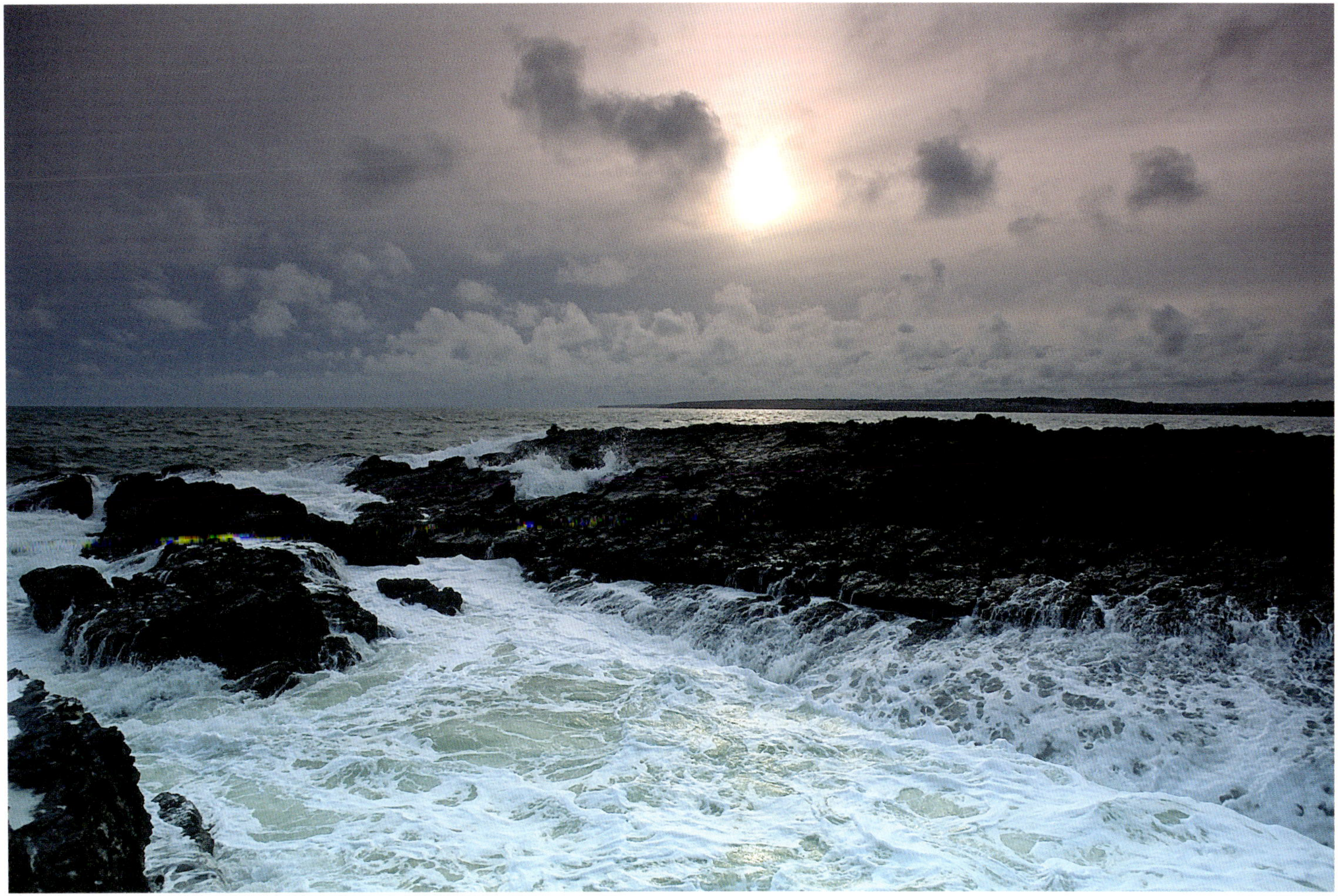

Waterford Harbour

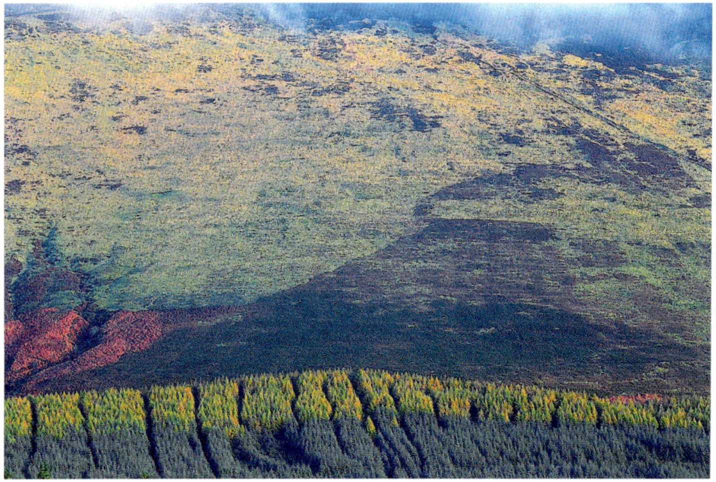

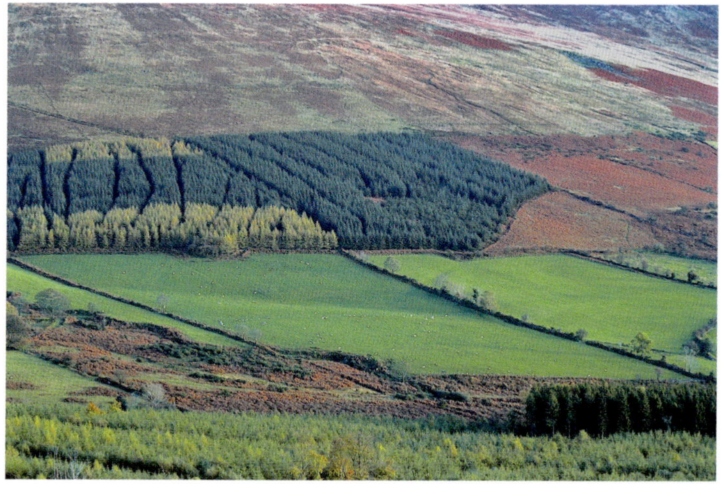

Left and right: Blackstairs Mountains

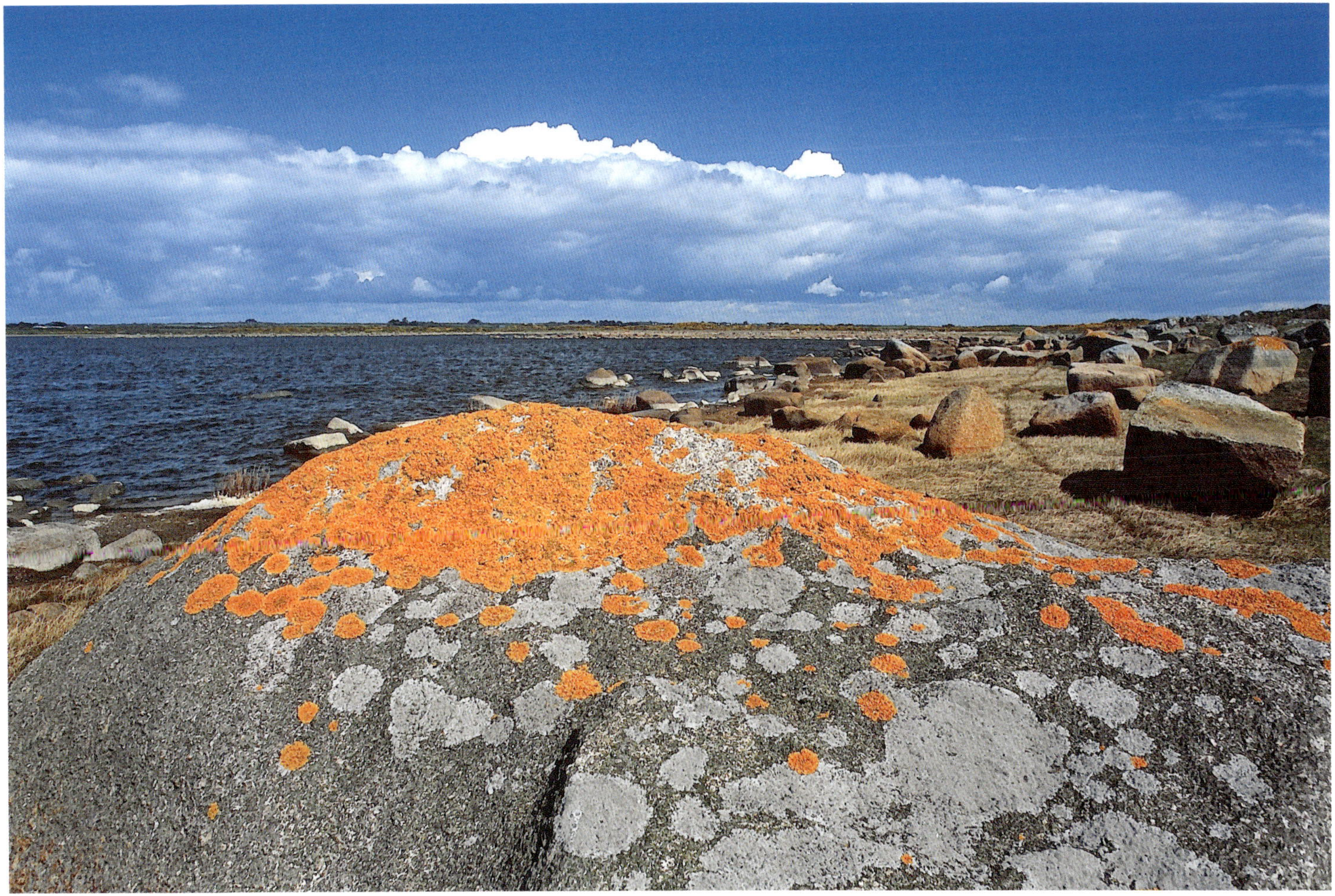

Carnsore Point

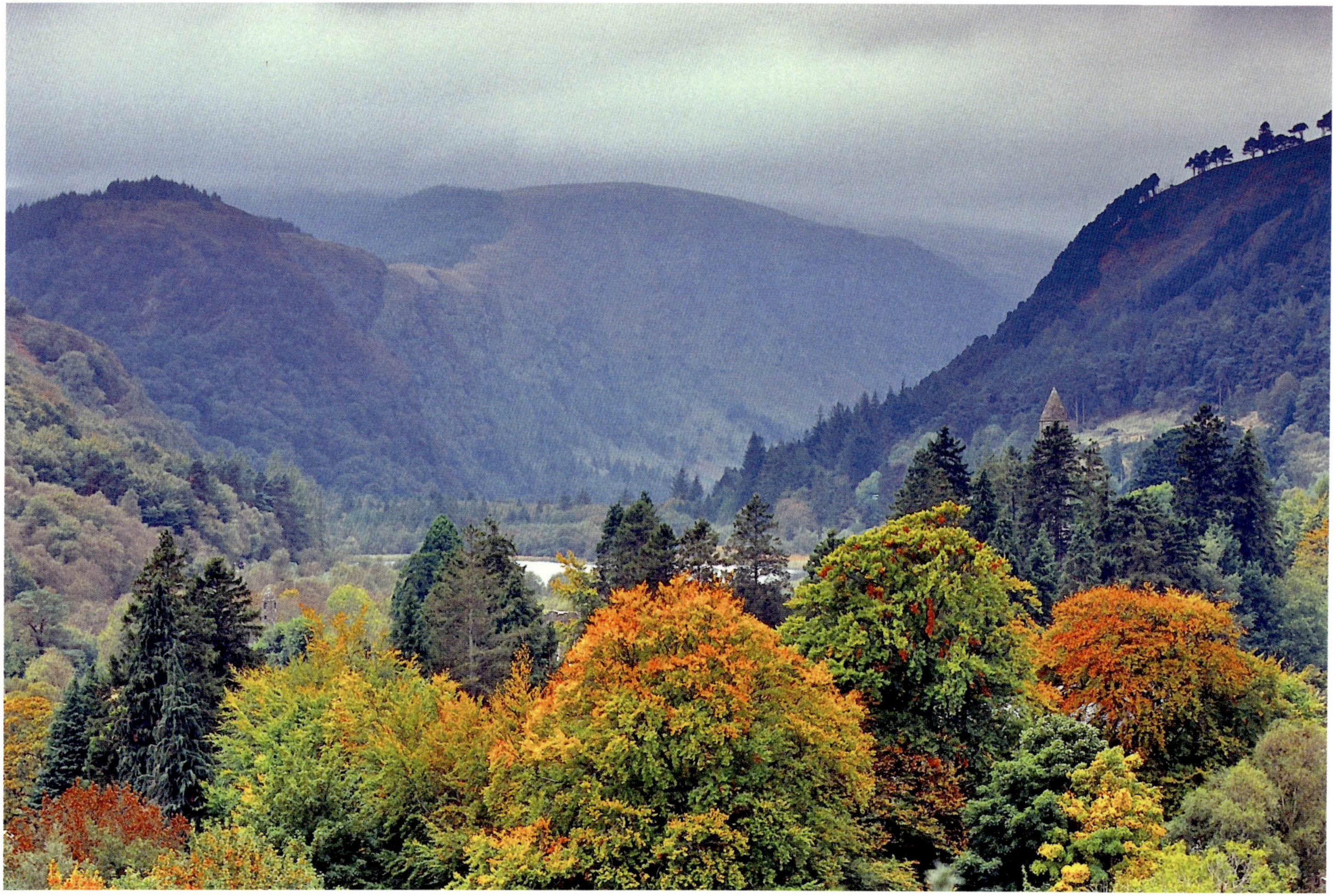

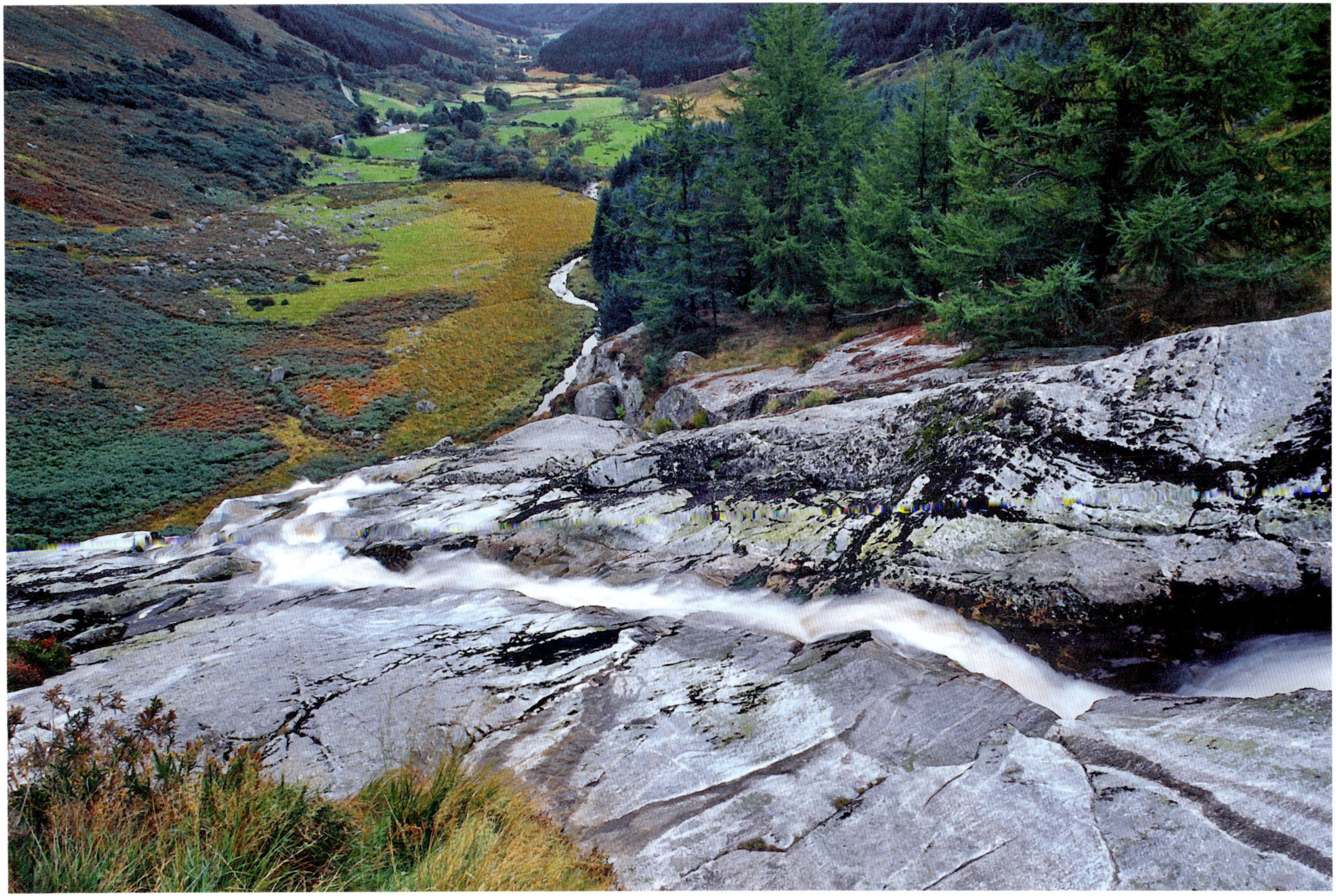

Left page: Glendalough
Right: Glenmacnass

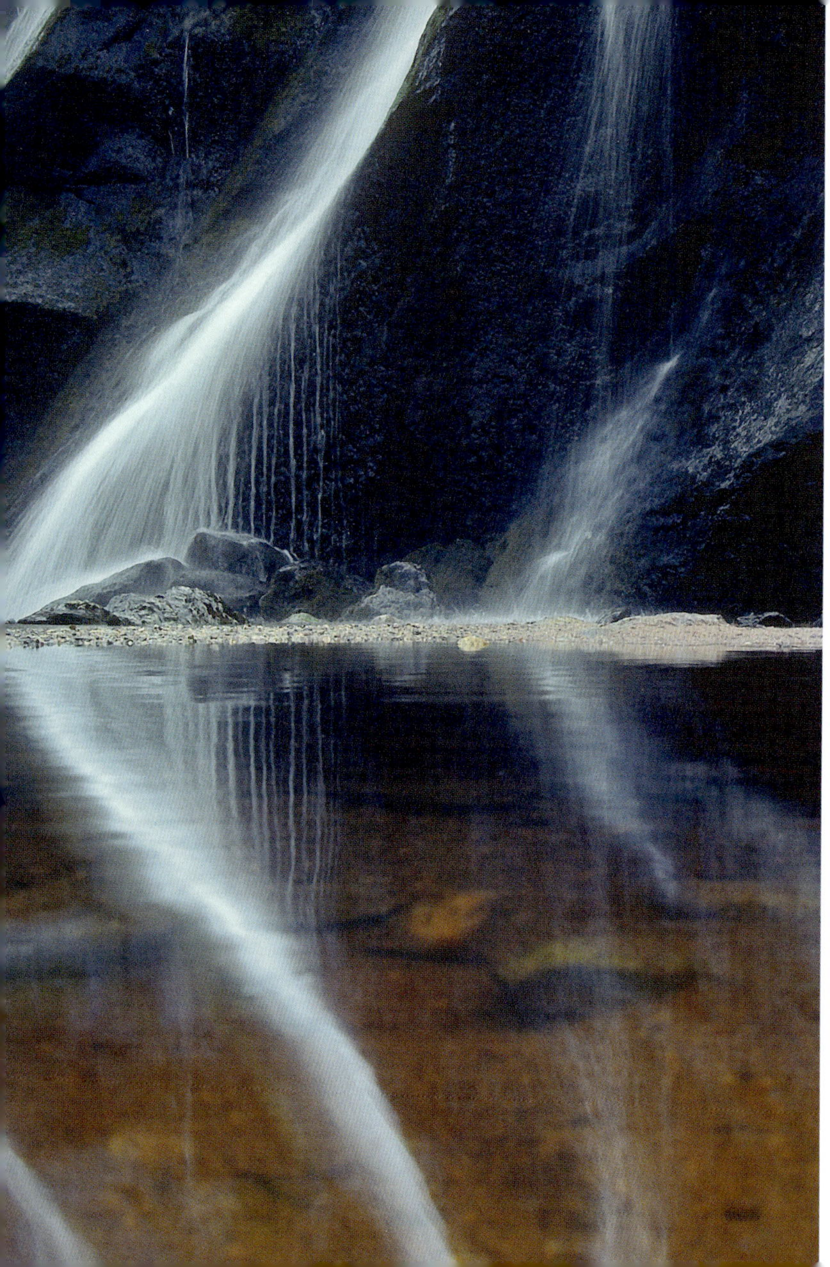

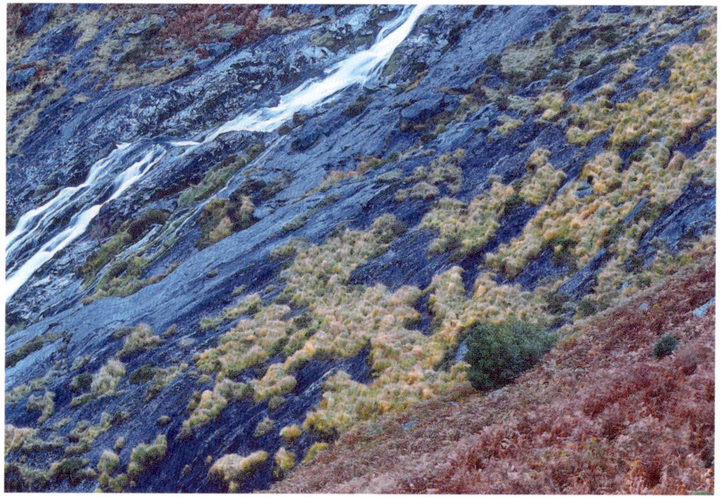

Left: Glendalough
Right: Glenmacnass

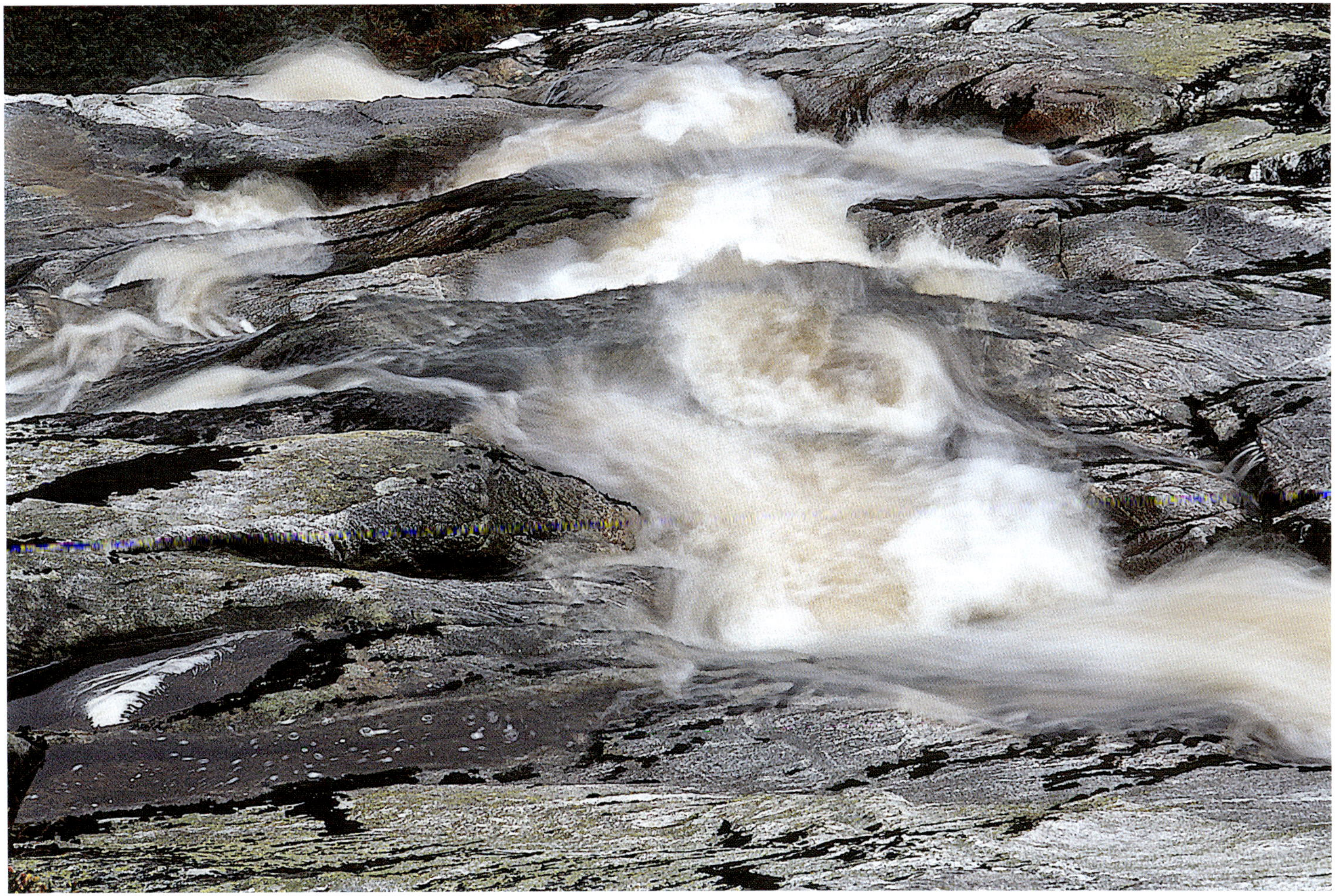

Glenmacnass

The Wailing

Some say it was not Ciabhán's but Clíodhna's hair that was quite special. When she combed it, it made a wailing sound—or maybe she combed it while making a wailing sound. In any case, she was really a Banshee, a woman of the fairy mound. Wearing a green cloak, she sat in a tree, her eyes red from endless weeping, and sometimes she looked quite fearsome. Most of the time, she was small, like a woman shriveled by age, and she always lamented a forthcoming death.

It was the old clans she keened for, the descendants of the Milesians. But she made exceptions for those who were gifted with music and song, as well as the ones who had come later to the island and became more Irish than the Irish themselves. To hear her, clearly, was also an honor, a sign of belonging. And of course, she would also cry for the ones who had to leave Ireland and died far away from home, while the news of their passing did not reach their families until much later.

In some places, there were rumors that she was no fairy at all but just the ghost of a woman murdered, or a mother who had died in childbirth, and there are disagreements as well when it comes to the sound of her wailing. Some heard the voice of a beautiful girl; in other cases, her cries were so piercing they shattered glass. Maybe she was just someone crying about the passing of time, not unlike Cailleach, the Hooded One, who is lamenting the loss of her youth, her old age down south in Kerry and Cork. Cailleach had children or fostered children over several lives until she turned into a hag living in the wilderness with horned beasts, heralding the coming of winter. As a matter of fact, she might be the land itself, barren, until she is loved and accepted, hideous as she is, and turns into her sister, Brigid, the beautiful goddess of summer.

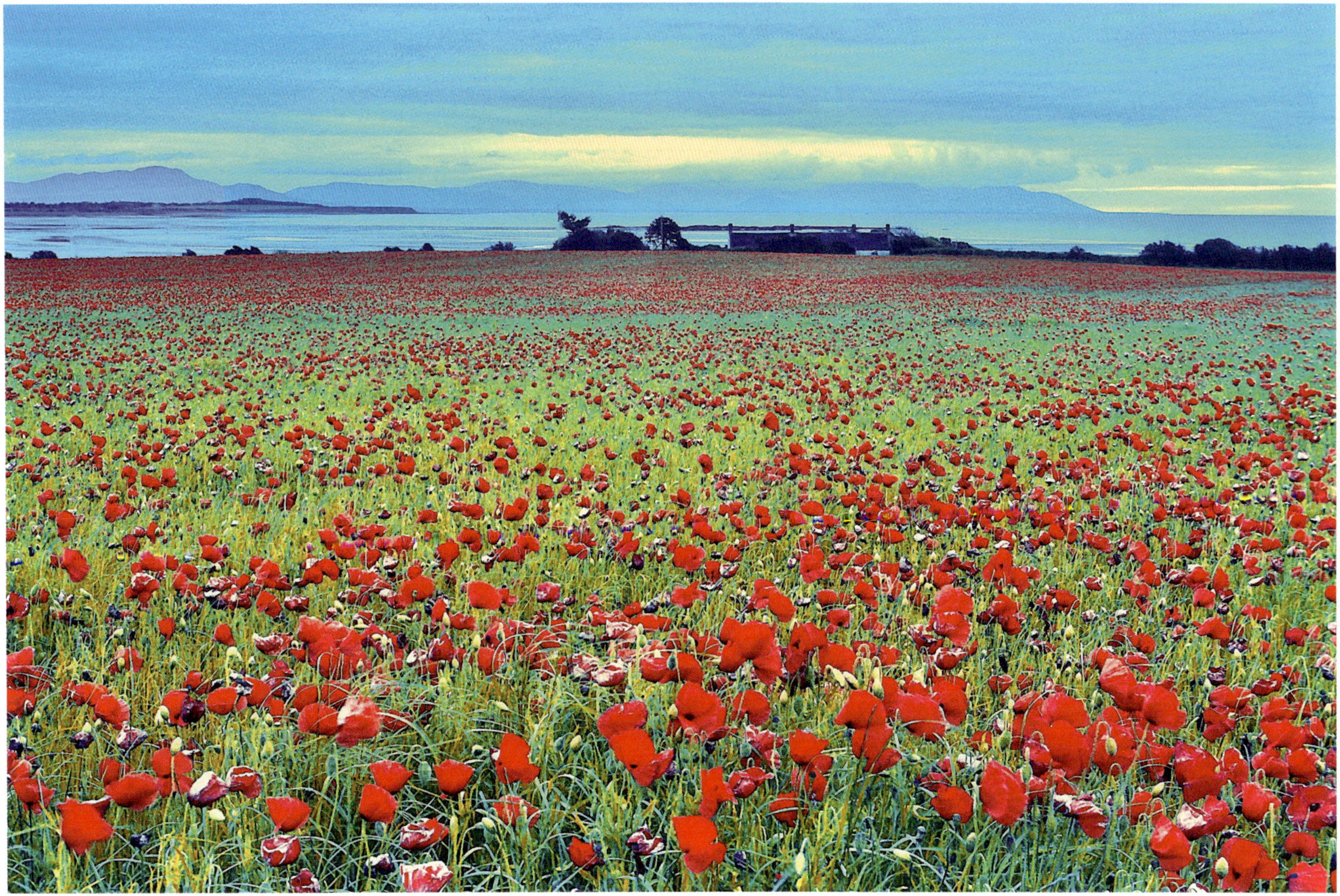

Dundalk Bay, County Louth

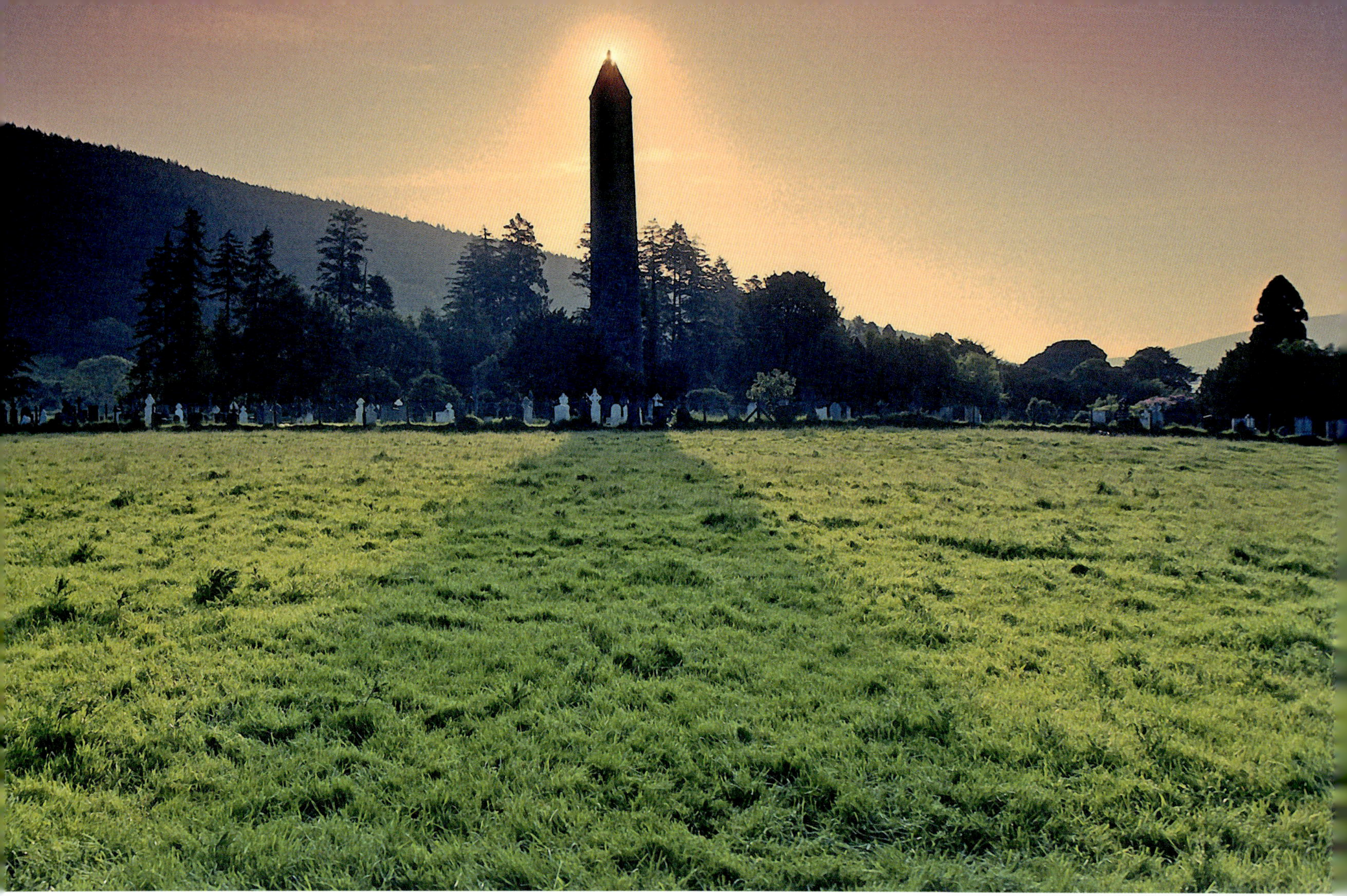

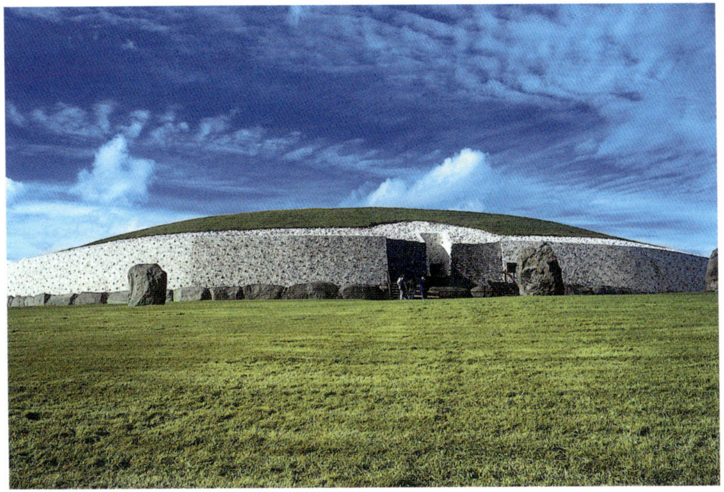

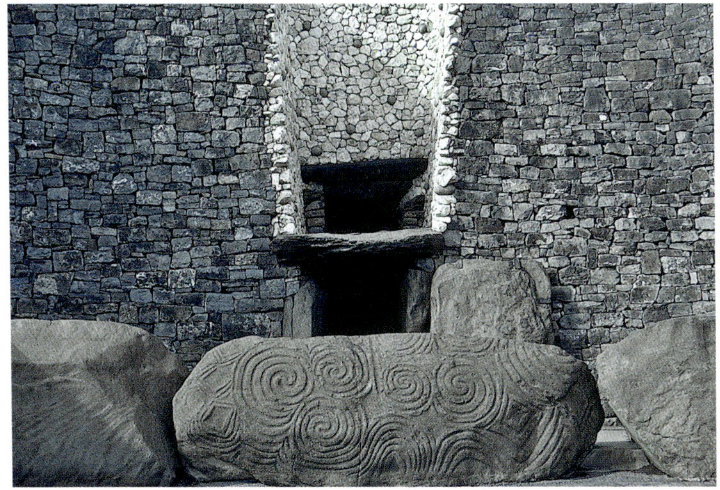

Left page: Glendalough
Left and right: Newgrange, County Meath

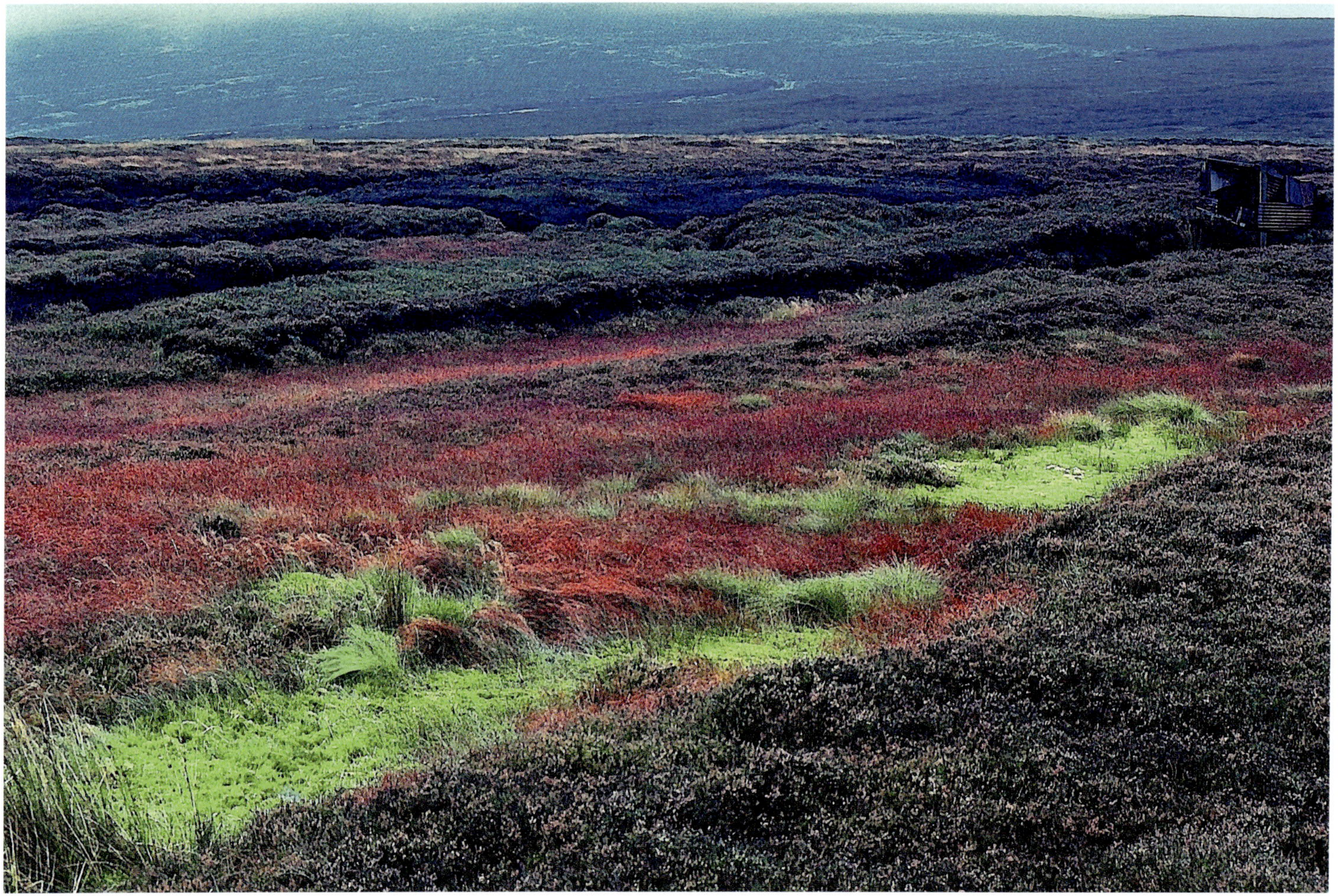

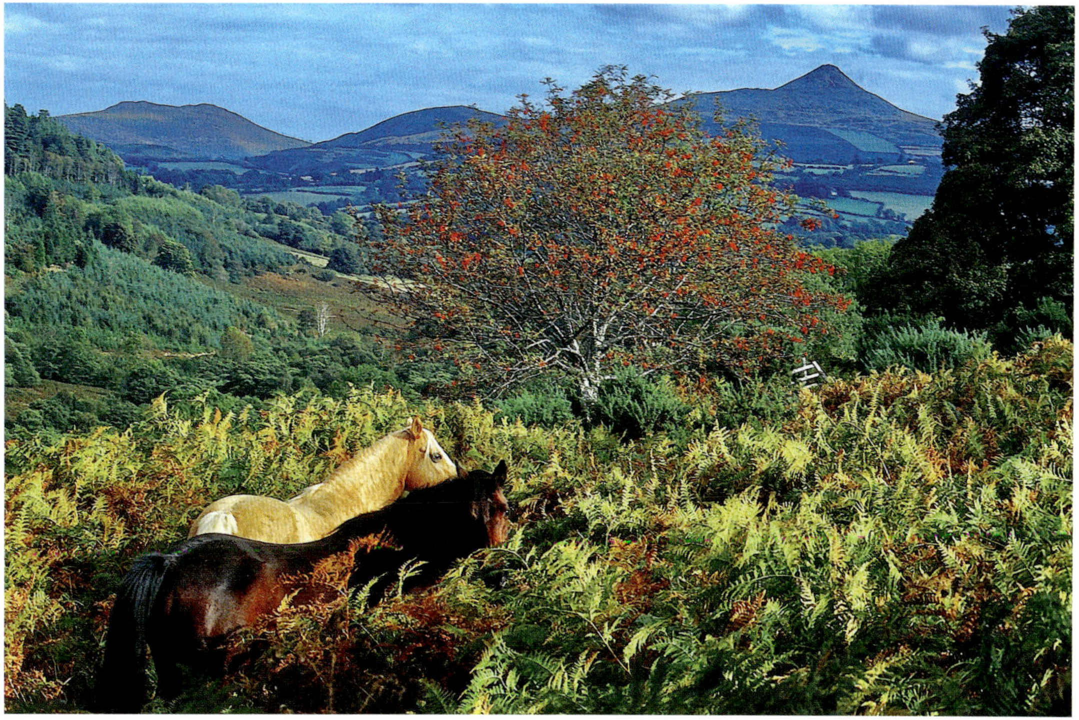

Left page and right: Wicklow Mountains

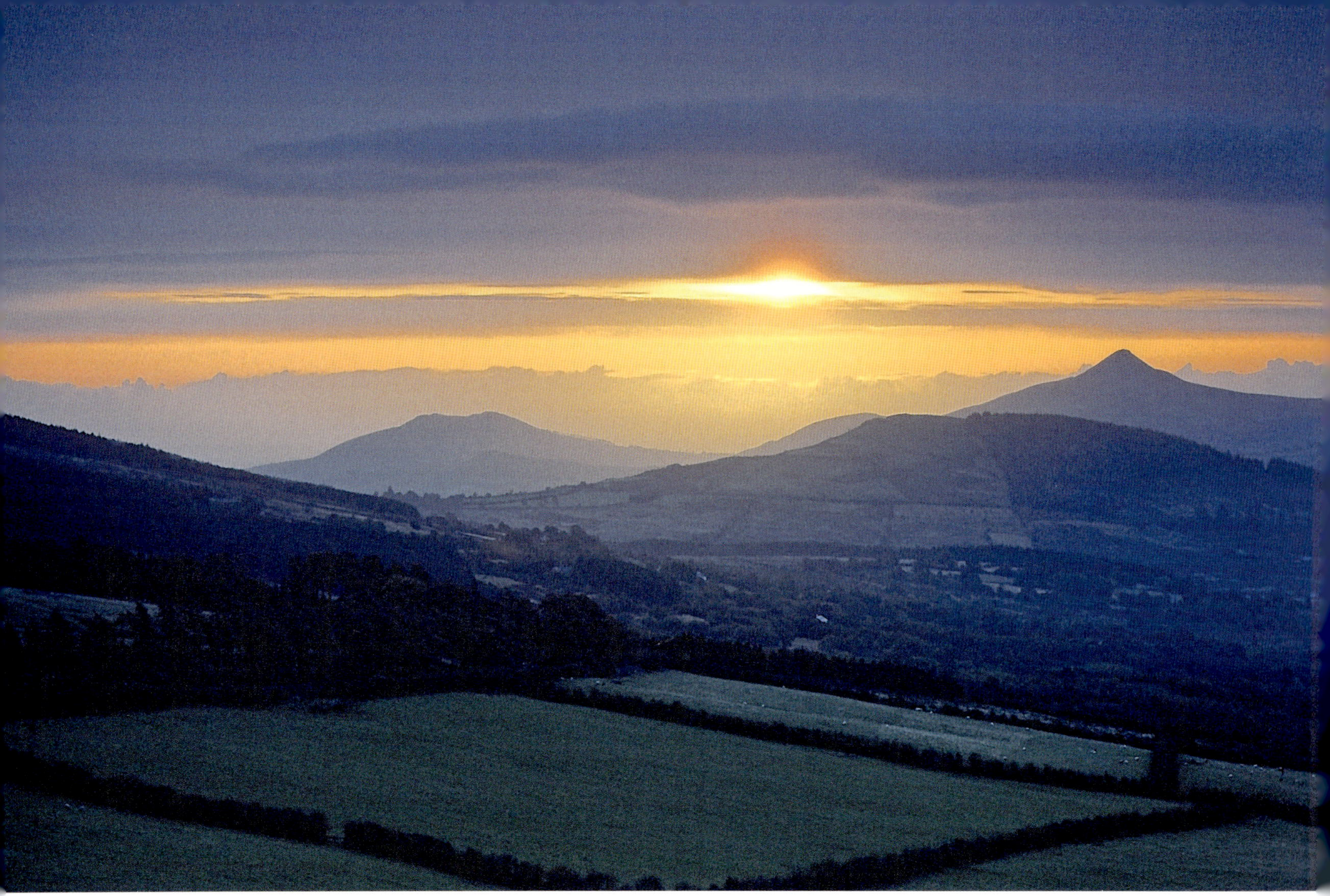

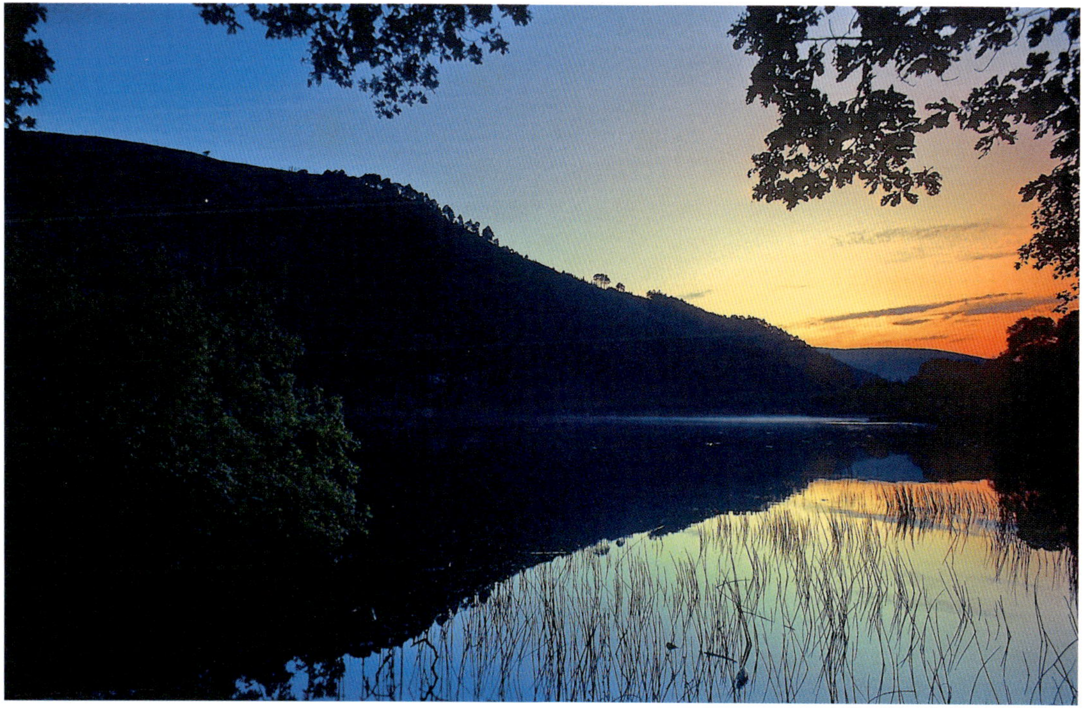

Left page: Wicklow Mountains
Right: Glendalough

The Deutsche Nationalbibliothek lists this publication in the Deutsche Nationalbibliografie; detailed bibliographic data are available on the Internet at http://dnb.dnb.de

ISBN 978-3-7165-1883-0
© 2026 Benteli, imprint of Braun Publishing AG, Salenstein
www.benteli.ch

The work is copyright protected. Any use outside of the close boundaries of the copyright law, which has not been granted permission by the publisher, is unauthorized and liable for prosecution. This especially applies to duplications, translations, microfilming, and any saving or processing in electronic systems.

1st edition 2026

Photographs: Max Schmid
Texts: Gabrielle Alioth
Graphic concept and layout: Michaela Prinz
© Map page 4: AdobeStock–bogdanserban

Product Safety
Publisher: Braun Publishing AG, Arenenbergstr. 2, 8268 Salenstein, Switzerland,
publisher@braun-publishing.ch
EU-Representative: Bookwise GmbH, Zeppelinstr. 67, 81669 Munich, Germany,
info@bookwise.de